How the East Was Won

How the East Was Won

The Impact of Multinational Companies on Eastern Europe and the Former Soviet Union

Charles Paul Lewis

First published 2005 by
PALGRAVE MACMILLAN
Houndmills, Basingstoke, Hampshire RG21 6XS and
175 Fifth Avenue, New York, N. Y. 10010
Companies and representatives throughout the world

PALGRAVE MACMILLAN is the global academic imprint of the Palgrave Macmillan division of St. Martin's Press, LLC and of Palgrave Macmillan Ltd. Macmillan® is a registered trademark in the United States, United Kingdom and other countries. Palgrave is a registered trademark in the European Union and other countries.

ISBN 1–4039–0267–4

This book is printed on paper suitable for recycling and made from fully managed and sustained forest sources.

A catalogue record for this book is available from the British Library.

Library of Congress Cataloging-in-Publication Data
Lewis, Charles Paul, 1964–
    How the East was won : the impact of multinational
    companies on Eastern Europe and the former Soviet Union
    Charles Paul Lewis.
        p. cm.
    Includes bibliographical references.
    ISBN 1–4039–0267–4
        1. International business enterprises–Europe, Eastern. 2. Europe, Eastern–Economic conditions–1989– 3. Europe, Eastern–Politics and government–1989– 4. Post-communism–Europe, Eastern.
5. International business enterprises–Former Soviet republics.
6. Former Soviet republics–Economic conditions. 7. Former Soviet republics–Politics and government. 8. Post-communism–Former Soviet republics. I. Title.

HD2844.7.L48 2004
330.947–dc22   2004054776

10   9   8   7   6   5   4   3   2   1
14   13   12   11   10   09   08   07   06   05

Printed and bound in Great Britain by
Antony Rowe Ltd, Chippenham and Eastbourne

'To my Mother'

Contents

Acknowledgements

My first thanks are to the Economist Intelligence Unit, and in particular Daniel Franklin, Andre Astrow and Laza Kekic, for making the project possible, stretching the rules on sabbaticals almost to breaking point, providing intellectual guidance and allowing me unfettered access to EIU databases. I also appreciate the valuable time taken by the hundreds of company executives, politicians, historians, NGOs, journalists and colleagues whom I interviewed, even though some may not agree with what I have written.

A big thank-you also to Richard Eames and Macmillan editors, for painstaking editing of my text and the countless errors, omissions and convoluted arguments brought to my attention. Many others have made valuable contributions for which I am grateful. They include: Robin Shepherd, whose regional expertise, experience and enthusiasm for the book was a source of both encouragement and lively debate; Hana Lesenarova, for access to her extensive contact list (and some enjoyable dinner parties); Jonathan Stein, for imposing a modicum of intellectual rigour, and for lending me his books; Sadakat Kadri for showing me some of the writer's tricks of the trade; Gavin Gray for helping me through the more technical aspects of economics; and Quentin Reed for insights into corruption. Needless to say, any shortcomings in the text are my responsibility alone.

I have also been very lucky to have the support of so many friends in Eastern Europe and London, specifically Nancy, for help in translating key documents and all manner of other assistance; Glen for logistical support and setting up and interpreting at meetings; Terje for driving me to interviews and to the gym; Nate for contacts and a sofa to sleep on in Warsaw; Tom, Sara, Adriana, and many more, all of whom were there when I needed them but also knew when to keep out of my way. Last, but not least, I would like to thank my mother, Marian, and sister, Rebecca for their encouragement, and particularly my brother Marc for his numerous business stories from the region, contacts and good advice.

Glossary of Key Geographic Terms

East-central Europe: Poland, Czech Republic, Slovakia, Hungary, Slovenia

The Baltic states: Estonia, Latvia, Lithuania

The EU accession states (first wave): The Baltic states and East-central Europe

The EU accession states (second wave): Bulgaria, Romania

Former Yugoslav Republics: Serbia and Montenegro, Croatia, Slovenia, Bosnia & Herzcegovina, Macedonia

The Balkan states: Bulgaria, Romania, Albania and the former Yugoslav Republics (except Slovenia)

Central Asia: Kazakhstan, Uzbekistan, Turkmenistan, Tajikistan, Kyrgyzstan

The Caucasus: Armenia, Azerbaijan, Georgia

The Commonwealth of Independent States (CIS): Russia, Ukraine, Belarus, Moldova, the 3 Caucasus and 5 Central Asian states

Eastern Europe: The three Baltic states, East-central Europe, the Balkan states, and the European states of the former Soviet Union (i.e. the CIS less the three Caucasus and five Central Asian states)

The region: The 27 transition countries that emerged from the collapse of the communist system in Eastern Europe and the former Soviet Union

x

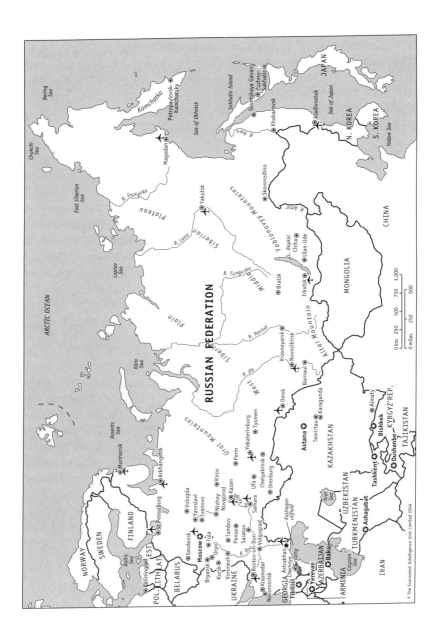

© The Economist Intelligence Unit Limited 2004

Introduction: The Post-Communist Transition: A Corporate View

'You had to bring your own toilet paper to the hotel, and always have a candle and matches with you on trips in the first years after communism...'
Herbert Schmitz, regional president, Procter & Gamble, 1991–2001

Multinational companies have had a bad press in recent years. Accused of political meddling, acquiring state assets at fire-sale prices, exploiting workers, and destroying both the environment and local communities, they have been on the defensive about the benefits that can flow to developing countries from foreign direct investment. Yet masses of ordinary people living and working in Eastern Europe and the former Soviet Union during the decade and a half since communism collapsed might tell a very different story. From Prague to Vladivostok, multinationals have had an extraordinarily positive impact on the region, and have probably done more to help develop these countries than many governments, international institutions, non-profit organisations or charities. They have created opportunities and benefits in countless ways, from providing legitimate careers for young high-fliers, to securing pensioners' savings by rebuilding dysfunctional banking systems. They have laid new telecommunications infrastructure; turned around many communist-era industrial giants (rescuing the surrounding communities in the process); lobbied hard for transparency in government; and underpinned entire economies with their investments and exports. These achievements stand in stark contrast to the behaviour of some local power brokers in the region, who have asset-stripped firms, polluted the environment and brought entire economies to their knees.

Not everyone would regard multinationals so favourably. Many have been criticised for laying off staff, squeezing suppliers, bribing state

1

officials or failing to consult affected groups, as the following chapters will also explore in detail. But on balance, the influence of multinationals has been profoundly positive in most of the countries where they operate in force; and it may be that these companies represent a potential solution to the difficulties of poor country development, rather than being part of the problem. The story of Eastern Europe's economic transition is to a great extent the story of the multinational companies and their managers who in the 1990s braved virtually uncharted waters.

A leap in the dark

In 1990 western corporations stepped into a region that was in a state of great flux and uncertainty. As Herbert Schmitz, a former regional president of Procter & Gamble put it: 'Diversity and turbulence was a feature of the region; diversity of cultures, languages, religions, between rich and poor, war and peace'. Multinationals were navigating power structures that were alien, ever-changing, unpredictable, absurd, corrupt and often dangerous. There were no post-communist precedents in the world to draw upon. Experts were struggling to predict the future development of a region that would soon comprise 27 countries of varying geography, history, populations, political culture, religion, ethnicity and economic progress. Some observers predicted a fascist resurgence, while others were alarmed by the re-election of former communists. A common misreading was to view the central political battle simply as a clash between 'reformers' and 'old communists', while ignoring numerous other political, economic and social undercurrents. Many feared tension between Russia and the West over the entry of the Baltic states into NATO; others pointed to the dangers of nuclear weapons falling into the hands of organised crime gangs.

Some of the gloom proved to be justified. Countries broke up in horrific wars (as in Yugoslavia), though others did so peacefully (Czechoslovakia's velvet divorce). There were civil conflicts, often with an ethnic dimension (Tajikistan, Bosnia, Macedonia and Armenia), attempted coups (Russia) economic crashes (Bulgaria, and many others) and a thriving kidnapping business (Georgia). There were powerful criminal gangs and oligarchs wielding influence in government (Ukraine), and ruling families of former communists that took over governments entirely (Central Asia). It was not even clear whether, or how effectively, the more advanced countries of East-central Europe would reform themselves. The incentive of European Union membership was a distant goal in 1990, and did not translate into specific legal reform until 1997. Slovakia did not fully establish a western-oriented democracy until 1998, having embraced mild authoritarianism for much of the decade.

Pockets of spectacular wealth existed amid poverty, pollution and unpaid wages. There was a seething resentment and avarice that was channelled into getting rich as fast as possible, any way possible. However, amid a mass of disillusion, anxiety and dependency, a dynamic younger generation was poised to leap ahead with entrepreneurial vigour. There were millionaires in their twenties, and even billionaires in their thirties in Russia. Many of the losers in the new system – workers in heavy industry, bureaucrats, divorced mothers, and their hard-drinking ex-husbands – looked back nostalgically to the relative security and freedom from responsibility that communism had provided.

In an attempt to make sense of it all, multinational companies had to unpeel layers of historical, political, economic and national experiences, involving a complex interplay of geography, demography and natural resources. Broadly speaking, multinationals divided the region into three distinct areas: the eight more advanced states in East-central Europe and the Baltics that would be first to join the EU; the seven poorer Balkan countries, some of which were prone to vicious ethnic conflict; and the 12 countries of the Commonwealth of Independent States (the CIS) that emerged from the break up of the Soviet Union in 1991. These countries were typically authoritarian and dependent on natural resources such as oil and gas, precious metals and cotton.

There were exceptions and overlaps. Bulgaria and Romania were defined as 'Balkan' but avoided ethnic conflicts and are currently expected to join the EU in a second wave of eastward enlargement in 2007. Predominantly Catholic Croatia was adamant that it was not part of the Orthodox Balkan world at all, and still has some hope of joining the EU soon after 2007. The Baltic states – Estonia, Latvia and Lithuania – had been part of the Soviet Union, and occasionally fell under Moscow's shadow owing to their large Russian-speaking minorities and dependence on Russian oil and gas. However, they viewed themselves as a Nordic tip of the EU and did not join the CIS.

Much has been written on the political, social and economic transformation of Eastern Europe. This introduction is not intended to break new ground, but merely to highlight some of the underlying themes of the region and provide a relevant chronology of events since 1989 in order to place subsequent chapters in context.

The historical inheritance

Eastern Europe today has been shaped not only by the communist legacy, but also by variations in the levels of development in different countries before the arrival of socialist central planning. In 1989 Czechoslovakia had experienced liberal democracy and had boasted an advanced industrial economy within living memory; Ukraine, by contrast, had no memory of democracy or national independence, and a very skewed form of industrialisation on which to build. In general, communism had taken over pre-industrial societies and economies and had developed them with multiple, contradictory distortions.

Experiences under communism also varied widely. Romania's all-encompassing Ceaucescu regime and its ever-present Securitate secret police made it difficult for Romanians to trust anything but the tightest family unit – and often not even that. The imprisonment of millions of Soviet citizens in Siberia kept ordinary Russians politically impotent – a mood that prevails today. As the late General Alexander Lebed, a candidate in Russia's 1996 presidential election, commented acidly, Russian leaders treat ordinary people like garbage. Citizens in Socialist Yugoslavia, which escaped the Stalinist sphere of influence, had a somewhat easier ride, and had been able to travel to, and even work, in the West. Poles kept alive their Catholic faith, which helped to foster a sense of national loyalty and was instrumental in the Solidarity trade union's bitter fight against Soviet-imposed communism.

Weak state, weaker society

The degree of authoritarianism experienced may have determined not only the speed of economic recovery, but also the difficulties involved in rebuilding civic institutions. The latter point is crucial. As political scientist George Schopflin noted:

> The greatest damage done by communism ... was the destruction of institutions ... Communist systems did what they could to prevent the coming together of individuals in institutionalised groups but could hardly prevent personal loyalties from becoming established as a not altogether satisfactory surrogate for institutions ... new institutions were unable to generate loyalty or enforce discipline.[1]

For foreign investors entering the region after 1989, the most troubling consequences of the corrosion of trust in institutions were the unreliable nature of state bodies and the (at best) patchy implementation of laws. Almost all the newly independent states lacked reliable regulatory or legal protection for investment. Worse, laws were intentionally left vague, full of loopholes and untested in the courts, allowing local businessmen with good political connections to manipulate the system in their favour.

In much of the region, law courts, central banks, trade unions and the media were easily bullied or manipulated by powerful vested interests, and were often little more than fronts for governing cliques. Power was more easily dispersed in East-central Europe than in the CIS or the Balkans but often at a cost. Polish central bank governor Leszek Balcerowicz required bodyguards, such was the hostility to his strict monetary policy, while Slovakia's constitutional court and media struggled to establish their independence right up until 1998.

Crime was rampant, especially in Russia and the Balkans. Western companies were usually not in the firing line, but nor were they immune. Many can recall an ominous visit from a well-dressed businessman with a couple of heavies in tow, claiming that he was owed half a million dollars from some long-forgotten transaction of which there was no record. As one old Russia hand explained: 'you needed to get security, preferably by former KGB men, sorted right from the beginning. At least you can deduct the security costs from your tax bill. You cannot deduct a payment for the thugs to go away.'

Elections and uprisings

Voting patterns were equally unpredictable. The realisation among electorates that they could mix and match their governments, or just 'kick the bums out', appeared to have an intoxicating effect. During the first decade of transition, governments were voted in and out of power, regardless of whether they had performed well or poorly. Political parties of every hue rose and fell – one year a party could be leading a government, the next it might be not only ejected from power, but out of parliament and out of existence altogether.

By the mid-1990s many of the idealistic dissidents, philosophers, playwrights and musicians[2] who came to power during the 1989 revolutions had given way to reconstructed communist parties (now calling themselves social democrats) as voters tired of the post-revolutionary muddle. In Romania, Yugoslavia, and much of the former Soviet Union, many of the old communists never left office.

Western style political competition between left and right did not always apply either. Many countries had ruling coalitions that defied political logic, including extreme nationalists, unreformed communists, trade unionists, religious leaders, opportunists, rabble-rousers, ethnic minorities and a handful of economic liberals. Roughly speaking, countries to the west of the region attempted to emulate the normal left-right divide of western politics. Hungary appeared to produce the most mature political debate, with power alternating between governments of the moderate left and right. Countries to the east, mainly in the former Soviet Union, had governments built around vested interests where party ideology was secondary or irrelevant to the specific interests – usually business or military – that they represented. Some countries seemed stuck between the two; the political divide in Slovakia, for example, was (and is) between moderate left- wing and conservative parties on the one hand, and authoritarian-crony groups on the other.

The transition towards western party politics sometimes required more than elections. Slovakia, Bulgaria, Romania, Serbia and (most recently) Georgia did not make the transition until a 'second revolution' occurred, and mass protests drove out corrupt rulers who had grabbed power soon after communism collapsed. Fighting for democracy not once but twice has helped to underpin the new democratic order, although there is still a risk that some of the gains in Serbia could be reversed. Unfortunately, too few countries in the CIS have reached this critical point yet, and, understandably, many still fear the depths of brutality to which their current leaders might sink in order to stay in power.

Rich and poor

The economies of the region began the 1990s in widely different shape in terms of wage levels, the size of the black market, spending power, national debt, fiscal balances and disparities between rich and poor. One major distinction was between countries with abundant natural resources and those that needed them. Oil, gas, precious metals or cotton alone could drive the economies of the CIS, enabling their governments to thumb their noses at the political conditions typically set by western governments, the IMF, World Bank or private-sector institutions for aid or loans. However, over-reliance on a couple of valuable commodities also stunted the growth of other sectors, which became a problem when the global price of the commodity in question fell. Even

Croatia, blessed with a long coastline, found that it had become over-reliant on a tourist industry that was to suffer badly when the Balkan wars erupted.

The other key economic feature of the region was a ruthless scramble for assets. Some of the most extreme cases could again be found in the CIS, where a ruling family, such as the Aliyevs in Azerbaijan, could control most of the country's wealth. A similar story applied to the dictatorships in Belarus and most of Central Asia. A handful of well-connected oligarchs in Russia and Ukraine became billionaires within half a decade, while much of the rest of the population barely survived on wages of $50 or so a month – if they got paid at all. The asset grab in East-central Europe was not much more subtle, as the manipulation of privatisation programmes gave insiders a once-in-a-lifetime opportunity to convert political power into money (and back into more power). In some cases, people became millionaires more legitimately, following the restitution of pre-communist property to former owners or their descendants. Moreover, the winners (and even some of the losers) in this casino capitalism were determined to flaunt traditional western status symbols such as cars, branded clothes and watches, and not surprisingly were loved by western consumer goods manufacturers.

Ethnicity and nationalism

Ethnic tensions and conflicts also wreaked havoc in the region, with complex, bloody and unpredictable disputes forcing multinationals to assess political risk carefully. Almost every state had some kind of ethnic clash, the worst of which was arguably the break-up of Yugoslavia into five separate countries. Russia's two Chechen wars were no less bloody, and, although they did not fundamentally change the business outlook in Russia, almost certainly helped to determine the outcome of two crucial presidential elections. Conflicts over Abkhazia and Nagorny-Karabakh in the Caucasus kept that region in a permanent state of antagonism. Dictatorship ruled on the other side of the Caspian Sea, while further east, Tajikistan was wrecked by a five-year civil war between communists on the one side and Muslims and secular Tajiks on the other.

Several other lower-key conflicts did not boil over into armed revolt, but bolstered the position of nationalists on either side. The presence of sizeable Hungarian minorities in Serbia, Romania and Slovakia became a source of tension, particularly over language rights, but also as a tool for Hungary to intimidate its neighbours. The same could be said of Russian minorities in Estonia, Latvia or Moldova. Slovaks and Czechs parted ways peacefully – possibly because the two ethnic groups were neatly self-contained in their separate territories – but both countries humiliated their Gypsy (or Roma) populations by secretly sterilising their women and placing their children in special schools for those with mental disabilities.

Geography and demography

Huge variations in geography and demography also played an important part in each country's respective development. A small country of less than one and a half million people, such as Estonia, could easily be transformed by government policy and a relatively small amount of foreign investment. This was not the case in Ukraine, with 50 million people, and certainly not Russia, with nearly 150 million. It was also much harder to implement laws in the outer regions of Russia, where regional governors retained considerable power, making it hardly worth the effort for multinationals to get their goods to far-flung locations. Consumer goods companies usually preferred to focus on the wealthier urban centres. On the other hand, although tiny states were more nimble in transition and easier to handle, they were also less interesting to multinationals looking for economies of scale in their marketing, advertising and logistics.

Location was also key. States in East-central Europe had the overriding goal of EU membership, which helped to focus the minds of politicians and businesses. The EU rapidly became the destination and source of the majority of exports and imports, giving considerable comfort to multinational investors. Those countries further afield had no corresponding geographic role model or home to head for.

Company missions

The picture was further confused by the differing priorities of the multinational corporations that entered these markets. Multinationals generally had one of four motives. Some were looking to sell their products in the region, and so wanted to see rapidly rising local incomes, and preferred large homogenous markets that would provide substantial economies of scale. A second group of investors was looking for a cheap base from which to produce for export, usually to the EU. These companies looked for low-cost, skilled labour and stable, predictable laws (hopefully including tax breaks for foreigners). A third group comprised western companies that were 'buying a market share', by acquiring the dominant company in a given sector, such as a leading bank, the fixed-line telephone monopoly or an energy utility. These investors also wanted political stability, transparent regulations and government protection, and they sought bright, energetic local managers who could in time be left to run the enterprises themselves. Lastly, there were the extractive companies that simply had to go where the oil, gas or gold was buried. They usually needed a clear regulatory environment, or, failing that strong and reliable connections with the authorities, since their upfront investments were often huge and the financial returns would not come through for many years.

Whatever the approach, all companies recognised that Eastern Europe and the former Soviet Union was undergoing what academic Carol Skalnik Leff refers to as a 'triple transition'. Countries had simultaneously to develop a democratic, pluralist political system, an industrial – indeed post-industrial – economy, and a new national consciousness out of the communist ruins. 'We know what these regimes are in transition *from*, from authoritarian communist regimes', she argues. 'We do not know what they are in transition *to*, and it is too soon to be sure that any or all of the efforts under way will turn out to culminate in economic and political regimes that resemble the ones we call capitalist and democratic elsewhere'.[3] Although eight east European countries have now joined the EU, and another two are scheduled to do so in 2007, much of the region still has a long way to go to achieve this goal.

The following chapters discuss the role that multinational companies have played, and continue to play, in that unfolding drama. Chapter One will look at some of the employment opportunities that were opened up for the younger generation. Chapter Two will examine how multinational companies have affected the region's workforce through their relations with trade unions, the pain of mass redundancies, the changes in workplace practices and the huge investment that was made in staff training. Chapter Three will assess the broader influence of foreign investors on the surrounding communities and will show how multinationals have usually lived up to their corporate social responsibilities, and, in the case of company towns, gone far beyond those obligations. This section will also consider the environmental impact of foreign investment which, though positive in many respects, has sometimes been harmful especially in the extractive sector. Chapter Four looks at the role of foreign corporations in the restructuring of the region's industry, most notably the rehabilitation of the telecommunications and banking sectors and the creation of a huge car industry. Chapter Five will show how consumers have seen the transformation of their shops from the drab days of shortages to abundance. The chapter will argue that fears of western brands dominating the market are overplayed; the real impact of western firms has been their improvement of local brands. The transformation has perhaps been most striking in retailing, where the customer is now viewed more like a king, and less like a nuisance.

These changes have had a tremendous effect on the performance of the economies of the region. Chapter Six will attempt to measure the macro-economic effects of multinational companies on the growth rates, exports and financial stability, as the entire region went through a traumatic economic upheaval in the early 1990s. Chapter Seven will consider the role played by multinationals in the development of democracy. Although this has not always been a smooth or successful process, the problems lie not with foreign firms but with local vested interests that hoped to preserve the gains from partial reform and saw foreign corporations as an obstacle to personal enrichment. Multinationals were not always so clean either, sometimes bribing their way to win state contracts for example, but such incidents were far less egregious than the asset-stripping, theft and extortion practised by local vested interests and bureaucrats. The concluding chapter assesses multinational companies' contribution to civil society, and specifically why Eastern Europe's experience of these companies has been so positive, and sets out what the future holds. It also looks at ways in which the power of these firms could be harnessed to help other developing countries out of poverty and along the road to prosperity.

Chronology of Key Events 1989–2004: East Central Europe and the Baltic States, the Balkan States and Commonwealth of Independent States

East-Central Europe and the Baltic States	The Balkan States	Commonwealth of Independent States*
1989– **Eastern Europe's revolutions** Roundtable discussions between Poland's communist government and Solidarity, the previously banned independent trade union movement, take place in March 1989, amid strikes and industrial deadlock. In June, the country holds its first free vote for 35 per cent of the seats in parliament: the communists lose them all. By September, a mainly non-communist government takes power under prime minister Tadeusz Mazowiecki. The government prepares a radical economic reform plan to be launched on 1 January 1990, which will free prices and trade, reduce fiscal imbalances, make the currency convertible and combat inflation. The 'shock therapy' program will be copied elsewhere in the region. Solidarity leader Lech Walesa later becomes president.		

East-Central Europe and the Baltic States	The Balkan States	Commonwealth of Independent States*
Soviet leader Mikhail Gorbachev signals that Soviet troops will not intervene in Eastern Europe if these countries choose their own path to socialism. A breach in Hungary's border to the West prompts a huge exodus of East Germans in the summer of 1989, and the Berlin Wall is brought down in November.	Bulgaria's communist politburo forces president Todor Zhivkov to resign in November, amid massive street demonstrations, and reconstitutes the party as the Bulgarian Socialist party. The United Democratic Front leader Zhelyu Zhelev becomes president in June 1990, and shortly afterwards a 'government of experts' is formed.	
Change is also peaceful in Hungary. In October 1989 reformers quietly take control of the Communist Party, renaming it the Hungarian Socialist Party (HSP), and begin economic liberalisation under prime minister Miklos Nemeth. Despite the change, the HSP is heavily defeated in the first free election in more than 40 years in April 1990 by the newly formed Hungarian Democratic Forum, led by Jozsef Antall. Revolution spreads to Czechoslovakia. A student demonstration in Prague on 17 November 1989 ends in violent clashes with police. Rumours spread (but are later proved to be false) that one of the demonstrators was killed by police, sparking ever bigger street demonstrations and strikes. The	Romania's is the last regime to fall after a public rally in Bucharest in December 1989, nominally in support of the dictator Nicolae Ceaucescu, suddenly turns against him. He is captured trying to escape and is executed. The Securitate secret police fight on until former ministers led by Ion Iliescu establish a provisional government. Iliescu wins a presidential election in May 1990.	

communist government finally gives way to Civic Forum, a new broad-based opposition movement led by political playwright Vaclav Havel, who becomes president on 29 December 1989.

1991
Auto investments in Poland...
Fiat acquires Poland's FSM car plant and agrees to invest some $2 billion to produce small cars. Daewoo, GM and other major car companies follow Fiat into the market.

...and Czechoslovakia; voucher privatisation
Czechoslovakia begins its privatisation programme with the sale of Skoda, its most famous car company to Germany's Volkswagen (VW). This proves to be a somewhat premature signal that foreign investors are welcome. VW also invests in a greenfield plant in soon-to-be-independent Slovakia, and quickly becomes that country's largest exporter. The Czechoslovak government then launches the first wave of its infamous voucher privatisation, which gives

1991–
Yugoslavia breaks up in bloody conflict
After populist leader Slobodan Milosevic comes to power in Yugoslavia in 1989 the country's six constituent states are unable to agree on a common future during a series of roundtable discussions. Slovenia and Croatia declare independence on 25 June 1991. Slovenia wins a brief skirmish with the Yugoslav army, but fighting in Croatia is more intense, involving ethnic Serbs living in the republic. Macedonia's secession is relatively peaceful. However, a bloody civil war rages in Bosnia & Herczegovina, where Bosnian Serb, Croat and Muslim forces battle over territory until 1995. When the fighting ends, Yugoslavia comprises only Serbia and the tiny coastal region of Montenegro.

1991–
A failed coup and the collapse of the Soviet Union
Economic stagnation, social tensions and rising nationalism throughout the Soviet Union, coupled with a policy of greater openness and economic liberalisation, provoke a poorly organised coup by communist hard-liners on 19–21 August 1991 against Soviet president Mikhail Gorbachev. The coup fails but nonetheless marks the end of the road for Gorbachev. He is swept aside by the charismatic, maverick new Russian leader Boris Yeltsin, who declares Russia to be an independent sovereign country, prompting other Soviet states to do the same.

In the Baltics, Lithuania's early attempt to declare independence from the Soviet Union (on 11 March 1990) leads Moscow to impose an economic

East-Central Europe and the Baltic States

vouchers for a nominal fee to all citizens, allowing them to bid for shares in most of the country's state-owned companies. Although innovative, the programme is poorly regulated and ends in failure.

The Balkan States

Albania gets a democracy

A multi-party system is declared in Albania, Europe's poorest state, in March 1991, following demonstrations. The following year the former communists are defeated by Sali Berisha's Democratic Party of Albania (DPA), after which the economy begins to improve.

Commonwealth of Independent States*

blockade. In January 1991 Soviet troops kill 13 Lithuanians who are defending the local TV and radio stations. But following the failed coup in Moscow, Russia recognises an independent Lithuania. Estonia declares independence on 20 August, and Latvia does so in September.

Ukraine's parliament secedes on 24 August 1991 as communist leader Leonid Kravchuk rides a nationalist bandwagon. Belarus follows suit. Moldova also goes its own way, but its Russian minority fears annexation by Romania and establishes a separatist territory of Transdniestr, which it successfully defends in an ensuing civil war.

In the Caucasus, Georgia declares independence months before the August coup. Azerbaijan and Armenia do the same, but the withdrawal of Soviet forces unleashes a bloody war over the Armenian enclave of Nagorny-Karabakh in Azerbaijan. The conflict remains unresolved.

Five new central Asian states emerge, if a little reluctantly, from the Soviet collapse. The hardline communist party in oil-rich Kazakhstan led by Nursultan Nazarbayev supports the continuation of Soviet rule but declares independence after the Moscow coup fails. The same story plays out in neighbouring Uzbekistan, which is led by communist leader turned dictator Islam Karimov. Gas-rich Turkmenistan becomes a dictatorship under Saparmurad Niyazov (later to become the self-proclaimed Turkmenbashi or 'Father of the Turkmens') following a rigged referendum showing 95 per cent voter support. Meanwhile, Tajikistan rapidly descends into a five-year civil war between the communists on the one side and a coalition of Islamists and secular leaders on the other, which claims up to 100 000 lives. Only Kyrgyzstan, which boasts lucrative gold mines, seems keen on independence. Askar Akayev, a physicist and political novice, is the country's new leader and declares independence soon after the failed Moscow coup.

The Soviet Union is officially dissolved on 8 December 1991. All the former Soviet states except the three Baltic republics join the Commonwealth of Independent States (CIS), a loose confederation, later that month.

East-Central Europe and the Baltic States	The Balkan States	Commonwealth of Independent States*

East-Central Europe and the Baltic States

1992–
Klaus becomes prime minister; Czechoslovakia splits up

Vaclav Klaus becomes prime minister of Czechoslovakia in June 1992, heading a centre-right coalition. However, the federal nature of the Czechoslovak constitution is ill-suited to the different needs of Czechs and Slovaks. The two sides are unable to agree on either a loose confederation or a unitary state, and Klaus and his Slovak counterpart Vladimir Meciar agree to split Czechoslovakia into two independent countries. There is no referendum but no violence either, and the two nations part ways on 1 January 1993.

Estonia sets the pace on free-market reform

After Estonia's first free election in September 1992, Mart Laar, a 32-year-old historian, becomes prime minister and sets about creating the most open, liberal market system in the post-communist world. The economy booms. The main banks and much of

Commonwealth of Independent States*

1992
Russia liberalises prices and starts privatisation

A new reformist government takes office in Russia, led by Yegor Gaidar and the gifted, smooth-talking, Anatoly Chubais. The government removes price controls on 2 January 1992, and alert businessmen see opportunities to make money supplying goods, as fragile market mechanisms emerge. But shortages help to create hyper-inflation, wiping out pensioners' savings and plunging ordinary citizens into new hardships. On 19 August 1992 the government introduces rapid voucher privatisation in an attempt to undercut the power of the ubiquitous Soviet bureaucracy.

industry are soon sold, mainly to Scandinavian companies. Elcoteq, a Finnish electronics manufacturer, becomes the country's biggest exporter. Scandinavian banks and companies gradually acquire assets in Lithuania and Latvia as well.

1993–
Hungarian phone privatisation
Hungary begins modernising Matav, its state phone company. In 1993 the government sells a 30 per cent stake in Matav for $875m to a US-German consortium of Ameritech and Deutsche Telekom.

Poland's 'velvet restoration' sees ex-communists voted back into power
Polish voters turn away from the economic and religious conservatism of the Solidarity-led coalition and return reformed communists – the Democratic Left Alliance (SLD) and a peasants' party – back into power in the September 1993 parliamentary election. The following year voters also oust Solidarity's gruff leader Lech Walesa in a presidential election, in favour of the slicker Aleksander

1993
Yeltsin bombards parliament; a new constitution increases his powers
On 21 September 1993 Russian president Boris Yeltsin dissolves parliament, which is still dominated by old-guard communists. They stage a sit-in and call for an armed attack on the state TV station, but the rebels are subdued on 4 October when Yeltsin orders tanks to fire on the parliament building. A new constitution is passed that gives the president far-reaching powers.

East-Central Europe and the Baltic States	The Balkan States	Commonwealth of Independent States*
Kwasniewski, a communist-era sports minister. Political volatility appears to do little harm to the Polish economy, which starts to boom and grows at nearly 7 per cent a year. By mid-decade, foreign direct investment reaches over $5 billion annually, two large banks and Europe's largest copper mine are privatised and tyre maker Michelin and car maker Daewoo acquire major plants.		

1994–
Slovak democracy weakens under Meciar
Slovak prime minister Vladimir Meciar, the authoritarian, nationalist leader of the HZDS party, returns to power after a brief stint in opposition in 1994. He forms a coalition government with a hardline (and easily corrupted) workers' party, and an extreme nationalist party. Meciar cancels the Czech-inspired voucher privatisation and virtually gives away Slovakia's leading companies to his political allies. Democracy under Meciar is gradually, and sometimes violently, whittled away, as the

1994–
Ukrainians vote in a new leader but get a dud
In July 1994 Leonid Kuchma, a former Ukrainian prime minister, defeats incumbent president Kravchuk, but fails to reform the deteriorating economy.

Russia's first Chechen war
On 11 December 1994, Russian troops invade the Russian province of Chechnya, starting the first Chechen war. Three weeks later they enter its capital Grozny, amid the bloodiest fighting in the region.

independence of the media, the constitutional court, the presidency, the electoral commission and the central bank come under attack. The son of the president is kidnapped, probably by secret service agents. The EU snubs Slovakia while inviting its neighbours to start membership talks.

Hungary's Socialists return to power with an austerity programme

The Hungarian Socialist Party returns to power in May 1994 in coalition with the free-market Alliance of Free Democrats. Faced with a possible collapse of the forint, the government introduces an austerity programme in spring 1995. The 'Bokros package' (named after finance minister Lajos Bokros) calls for a gradual, controlled devaluation of the forint, curbing double-digit inflation, reducing public debt and getting the budget under control.

Foreign companies rush into Hungary or expand existing plants. Big investors include GE Lighting, which acquired Tungsram in 1989, car makers Audi, GM and Suzuki, retail giant Tesco, and consumer electronics firm Philips. The country sells three of its

East-Central Europe and the Baltic States

top five banks to foreign investors, which stabilises the financial sector. Hungary tops the region's foreign investment league tables. Despite the government's success in turning around the economy, the electorate votes the more conservative, nationalistic Fidesz party into office in 1998.

1995
The Czech Republic sells its telephone company
The Czech government sells a 27 per cent stake in its decrepit phone monopoly to a Swiss-Dutch consortium for nearly $1.5 billion in July 1995, as global telecom shares begin to boom.

The Balkan States

1995–
War in Bosnia ends
US diplomats facilitate co-operation between Croat and Muslim forces in Bosnia, enabling them to push back Bosnian Serb troops (with air support from US warplanes), and helping to end the war. Parties to the conflict meet at Dayton, Ohio, and agree a settlement that roughly freezes the existing front lines. The Dayton agreement establishes a complex Croat-Muslim Federation in one part of Bosnia and a Serb Republic of roughly the same size in the other. The arrangement proves unworkable politically and economically, although

Commonwealth of Independent States*

1995–
The rise of an oligarchy
The new freedoms in Russia unleash an unparalleled scramble for assets. Organised crime flourishes and Moscow descends into a haze of gang warfare and contract killings. A new generation of young tycoons usurps the old communist factory bosses and acquire immense economic power and political influence. Capital flight reaches panic levels with an estimated $25 billion leaving the country each year. (Foreigners attempting to muscle in risk their lives. In 1996 Paul Tatum, a headstrong American businessman,

further fighting is avoided. The country is in effect run by an International High Commissioner. Investors steer clear.

takes on Moscow's mayor over a sour hotel deal and is assassinated).

With the 1996 Russian presidential election approaching, an unpopular Yeltsin languishes with single-digit opinion poll support and looks set to lose to Gennady Zyuganov, the hardline communist candidate. Russia's leading tycoons, despite their own deadly rivalries, club together to finance and support Yeltsin's re-election campaign. Led by Vladimir Potanin, they hatch the 'loans for shares' scheme, a complex arrangement whereby Russia's new businessmen lend the government $2 billion in return for management rights over some of the country's most lucrative oil, mineral and other assets. Once the election is over the state can either repay the loans or convert them into shares. Repayment is never made and the small circle of tycoons picks up billions of dollars worth of assets on the cheap. An oligarchy is created.

East-Central Europe and the Baltic States

1996–
The Czech economy falters, Klaus falls

Vaclav Klaus is re-elected Czech prime minister in 1996, but his corrupt minority coalition survives only two years. The koruna falls, rendering Klaus's economic policy a mess, and a corruption scandal subsequently brings down his government. President Havel appoints an interim administration led by Josef Tosovsky, the central bank governor, which presses on with bank privatisation and encourages foreign investment. The new direction continues after the June 1998 parliamentary election and the formation of a Social Democratic government led by Milos Zeman (although it relies on the tacit support of Mr Klaus's party to survive). The economy enters a three-year recession, as years of economic neglect under Klaus catch up with the country. Bad loans in the banking sector in the last decade are estimated to be nearly $7.5 billion, equivalent to

The Balkan States

1996–
Romania's incompetent governments

Loose economic policy in Romania pushes inflation out of control, the lei plummets, and the government reintroduces price and currency controls. In November 1996 the Socialist party is defeated by a broad multi-party coalition led by Victor Ciorbea, and Emil Constantinescu defeats the former communist Iliescu for the presidency. Internal bickering paralyses the government. Ciorbea is replaced by another short-lived premier, Radu Vasile, and little progress is made in restructuring and privatising industry and the banks. Industrial unrest breaks out across Romania once again.

Bulgaria's economy collapses...

The Bulgarian economy falls apart, as corruption and the lack of industrial restructuring under the rule of the Bulgarian Socialist Party (BSP) take its toll. Centre-right candidate Petur Stoyanov from the Union of

Commonwealth of Independent States*

1996
Boris Yeltsin wins the presidential election

Yeltsin stages a remarkable comeback with the help of US advisers who explain the basics of political campaigning – smiling, kissing babies and making well-choreographed 'surprise' visits to farms and factories. The new Yeltsin receives favourable coverage from the national TV networks, which are controlled by his business supporters Boris Berezovsky and Vladimir Gusinsky. Yeltsin wins in a second-round run-off after briefly co-opting third-placed candidate General Lebed into the government. Western multinationals and governments breathe a collective sigh of relief.

14 per cent of GDP; 32 per cent of loans are classified as non-performing.

1997–
Poland finally gets a new constitution, and a new government
In April 1997 Poland adopts a new constitution that reduces the power of the presidency. The central bank gains more control over setting interest rates, presaging a fierce battle with the government over monetary and fiscal policy as the economy slows down.

A multiparty coalition under the Solidarity banner, including parties from the free-market, nationalist and religious right, surprises pundits and wins Poland's parliamentary election in September 1997. Solidarity forms a governing coalition with the free-market Freedom Union (which itself was previously part of Solidarity), but both

Democratic Forces party, is elected president in November 1996, but the BSP clings to power in parliament. The currency collapses to one-sixth of its value within six weeks, triggering hyperinflation. Street violence breaks out near the parliament building, followed by waves of mass demonstrations against the BSP government, which finally resigns to avoid a potential civil war.

1997–
... and a reformist government is elected
An interim government is formed in Bulgaria in February 1997. Following an election in April, the centre-right United Democratic Front coalition returns to power with a clear majority under the premiership of Ivan Kostov. The IMF imposes a currency board in July, after which the economy slowly recovers. But western investors show little interest in the privatisation programme.

The failure of pyramid schemes sets off an uprising in Albania
Sali Berisha's DPA-led government in Albania, which has become increasingly authoritarian and corrupt, finally falls in

East-Central Europe and the Baltic States	The Balkan States	Commonwealth of Independent States*
Solidarity and the government coalition eventually crumble owing to bitter infighting.	1997 following the collapse of fraudulent pyramid investment schemes. The founders of the schemes had helped to finance the DPA. Many Albanians lose their life savings, and a mass uprising in the capital, Tirana, spreads across the country, prompting the authorities to declare a state of emergency. An Italian-led force helps restore order. Mr Berisha is succeeded by a socialist, Fatos Nano, who one year later is forced to flee rioters after a political rival is assassinated. **Tudjman's stranglehold in Croatia** Croatian president and independence leader Franjo Tudjman tightens his grip over almost all aspects of the country's political, economic and business life (and even selects the national football squad). The Balkan wars devastate Croatia's tourist industry, its main source of foreign currency, while the lack of economic reform leads to banking crises in 1998.	

1998

Russia's economy crashes

Yeltsin's victory in the 1996 presidential election heralds a period of intoxicating optimism about the Russian market, as shares soar and western bankers and fund managers pour cash into the nascent stock exchange. The optimism is premature. Yeltsin's health deteriorates and he often acts erratically, even appearing drunk in public and on TV. He seems unable to control the machinations of rival oligarchs. The economy is heading for a fall. The stock market declines, falling by 10 per cent on 27 May alone as interest rates are hiked to 150 per cent – a warning of things to come.

Russia's debt-fuelled investment boom fails to generate economic growth as the new owners of major enterprises are more adept at asset stripping than restructuring. The government is unable to finance its $160 billion of hard-currency debt and around $40 billion of rouble debt, despite short-term loans from the IMF and US government. On 24 August the government announces that it is in effect defaulting on its domestic debt,

1998–

EU enlargement talks begin

In April 1998 the EU formally begins accession talks with the five most economically and politically advanced East European countries – Poland, the Czech Republic, Hungary, Estonia and Slovenia. Each country embarks on a marathon legislative and institutional harmonisation programme, involving the incorporation of some 80 000 pages of EU legislation covering almost every aspect of economic, political and commercial life. The process dominates the countries' legislative agendas for the next seven years. Lithuania, Latvia and Slovakia are not invited to start accession talks for another two years, in Slovakia's case because of severe shortcomings in its democracy.

Slovaks unite against Meciar

Almost all Slovak opposition parties, including those representing ethnic Hungarians, successfully unite against the manipulative prime minister Meciar. In September 1998 voters elect a broad-based coalition government led by Mikulas Dzurinda to reverse the country's economic and political

East-Central Europe and the Baltic States	The Balkan States	Commonwealth of Independent States*
decline. Despite infighting, the coalition holds together throughout its four-year term in office, the economy stabilises and the threat of Meciar returning diminishes. The EU is delighted. Multinationals remain cautious, although US Steel takes over the failing Eastern Slovak Steel works, *VSZ*.		freezing repayments of foreign loans and allowing the rouble to depreciate. Investors scramble to get their money out of roubles, and the currency falls by a staggering 75 per cent. Western lenders are given less than 5 cents on the dollar on their loans. The greatest harm is to ordinary Russian citizens and small businesses who put their trust in economic reforms and kept their savings in roubles in Russian banks. Inflation soars again, undermining the main economic achievement of the Yeltsin era. **Oil and gas in the Caspian Sea** The five states bordering the energy-rich Caspian Sea – Russia, Kazakhstan, Turkmenistan, Iran and Azerbaijan – eventually reach an agreement on the Caspian's legal status as a sea, not a lake, thereby giving each state exploratory rights over their respective segments of the seabed.

1999–
NATO expands, arms makers compete for deals

Poland, the Czech Republic and Hungary join NATO in March 1999. Western arms makers, particularly fighter aircraft manufacturers, scramble to supply equipment to the new members. In 2002, American firm Lockheed Martin outbids France's Dassault for a $3.5 billion deal to sell fighter aircraft to Poland, prompting the French company to issue veiled threats about Poland's EU application. The Czech government shelves plans to buy British Aerospace fighter jets, arguing that the proposed purchase is too expensive and unnecessary.

1999
Serbia takes on the KLA; NATO bombs Serbia

The Kosovo Liberation Army (KLA) emerges in Serbia's mainly ethnic Albanian province of Kosovo, with the aim of achieving independence for Kosovo by violent means. Belgrade's troops clamp down. Historic tensions between the two communities flare up, leading to a chronic refugee crisis as ethnic Albanians start streaming into Albania and Macedonia.

After internationally mediated talks culminating at Rambouillet, France, fail to resolve the conflict between Belgrade and the Kosovo Albanians, NATO begins 78 days of airstrikes against Serbia on 24 March 1999. Serbian forces withdraw from Kosovo, and the province subsequently comes under international protection. Kosovo Albanians return, and an estimated 200 000 Serbs flee.

Croatian president Tudjman dies

Domineering Croatian president Franjo Tudjman dies in December 1999, and a subsequent general election brings a broad-based coalition of opposition parties to power. Economic reform is slow, but tourists slowly return to Croatia's coast.

1999
BP's investment disaster

BP loses its 10 per cent stake in Russian oil company Sidanko after the latter is bankrupted by domestic rival TNK. Three years later BP surprises the market by negotiating a merger of its Russian operations with TNK.

Vladimir Putin is appointed Russian prime minister

After sacking four prime ministers in the space of 18 months, President Yeltsin appoints Vladimir Putin as premier on 9 August 1999. Putin is an obscure, icy bureaucrat and former spy from St Petersburg whom Yeltsin regards as his successor (and protector in retirement).

East-Central Europe and the Baltic States

2000–
Poland sells its telecom company; President Kwasniewski wins again
Poland sells a 35 per cent stake in state telephone company TPSA to France Telecom and local group Kulczyk Holdings, for around $3.6 billion. The buyers have an option to acquire a further 16 per cent, but the option is never exercised owing to the collapse in global telecom shares.

Poland's president Aleksander Kwasniewski easily wins a second term in October 2000. Lech Walesa, one of his defeated opponents, leaves politics altogether.

The Balkan States

2000–
Socialists sweep back in Romania
Ion Iliescu wins Romania's presidential election, and the reformed communist Party of Social Democracy (PSDR) gains a majority in parliament in November and December 2000, as voters tire of the endless bickering among ruling mainstream parties. More worryingly, the opposition is now dominated by the ultra-nationalist, racist Greater Romania Party, led by former court poet to Ceaucescu, Vadim Tudor.

Milosevic is overthrown and arrested
In October Slobodan Milosevic loses the Yugoslav presidential election to Vojislav Kostunica, a compromise candidate of the opposition forces. Milosevic initially refuses to accept the result, but is forced to step down following street demonstrations and a well-orchestrated raid of the parliament. He is subsequently arrested and, under western pressure, sent to The Hague in 2001 to be tried for war crimes.

Commonwealth of Independent States*

2000–
Yeltsin resigns, Putin becomes President and asserts his authority
Despite Yeltsin's drunken, out-of-touch appearance, he retains a supreme capacity for political surprise and resigns on Millennium Eve. Putin automatically becomes acting president – a perfect platform from which to contest the presidential election in March 2000. Public support for the youthful, judo-fighting, teetotal Putin soars, particularly after he launches a second brutal war against rebels in Chechnya. Heavyweight rivals in the presidential election melt away. Putin wins in the first round against the hapless communist Zyuganov.

The enigmatic Putin confounds western observers about his policy direction as he juggles the interests of Russia's unruly oligarchs, its still fearsome secret services (from whence he came) and liberal reformers. He appoints the latter to key economic posts, and launches reforms to encourage investment – including from western oil companies. At the same time, however, he arrests and exiles independent media barons Gusinsky and Berezovsky and takes indirect control of their respective TV stations. The moves represent a warning to other moguls thinking of opposing the president. He also adopts an ominous-sounding, if somewhat misleading, maxim: 'dictatorship of law'.

Oil power in Kazakhstan and Azerbaijan

In August Kazakhstan announces the world's biggest oil and gas find in 30 years at the Kashagan field in its section of the Caspian. A nine-member consortium of international oil companies, led by France's TotalFinaElf and Italy's ENI, begins exploration. The oil find also makes several proposed pipeline routes more feasible, including the controversial and endlessly debated Baku-Tbilisi-Ceyhan pipeline project.

Azerbaijan's leader Heydar Aliyev consolidates his family's control of the country and its economy. His playboy son Ilham, who heads the state oil company SOCAR, is groomed to succeed him.

East-Central Europe and the Baltic States	The Balkan States	Commonwealth of Independent States*
		Ukraine's fleeting reforms Ukraine weathers the Russian crash relatively well and President Kuchma appoints his first ever reform-oriented government headed by former central bank chief Viktor Yuschenko. The new government tries to privatise industry and liberalise agriculture but runs up against powerful vested interests and is forced out after only 18 months. The reforms give a brief boost to the sickly economy but Ukrainian oligarchs soon have their men in all key government posts.
2001 **No more Solidarity in Poland** Poland's left-wing SLD party returns to power in September in coalition with the Polish Peasants Party and the Union of Labour. Solidarity fails to win any seats, and the opposition now mainly comprises radical farmers and nationalists.	**2001–** **More war in the Balkans** In March, ethnic Albanian fighters in Macedonia begin an insurgency, demanding greater political representation in relation to the Slavic-speaking majority. The ensuing conflict scuppers plans by the government to attract western investment. The two sides reach a precarious peace deal in August.	**2001** **Ukrainian journalist is murdered** A tape recording that appears to show Ukrainian President Kuchma ordering the murder of an investigative journalist is made public. The journalist is later found dead, having been beheaded. Kuchma holds onto power despite public protests.

Car companies come to the Czech Republic

In December, Toyota and Peugeot-Citroen announce a $1.5 billion joint venture to build small cars in the Czech Republic. The decision confirms the emergence of the region, and specifically the Czech Republic, as a new automotive hub. The economy slowly pulls out of recession.

2002–
Slovenia grudgingly sells shares to foreign firms

Tiny Slovenia, the wealthiest post-communist country, finally gives in to EU pressure to privatise and sell assets to foreign investors, and sells a minority stake in leading bank Nova Ljubljanska Banka to Belgium's KBC. It also sells leading pharmaceutical company Lek to

Bulgarians elect a former King

In June, although approval ratings for Ivan Kostov's government remain high, voters fall for the returning former King, Simeon Saxe-Coburg, who forms the Simeon II National Movement and sweeps to power in the general election on an anti-corruption platform. He continues Kostov's liberal reforms.

Romania begins privatisation

Despite its communist background, the new Romanian government appears determined to reform the economy. In November it sells Sidex, the huge, over-staffed, loss-making steel mill, to LNM Group. The new owner agrees not to make mass redundancies among Sidex's 27 700 workers for five years.

2002–
Crime, corruption and personality cults in Central Asia

The Kazakh government cracks down on an emerging opposition group and threatens journalists, but faces allegations of massive state corruption, including over $1 billion held in Nazarbayev's private Swiss bank account. A US executive with oil

East-Central Europe and the Baltic States

Switzerland's Novartis for over $1 billion. Slovenian company managers support the deals, but state-backed investment funds oppose them.

Slovakia re-elects its reforming government

Following a general election in September, prime minister Dzurinda begins a second consecutive term, but this time as head of an economically radical, centre-right government – making him one of the most successful leaders in the region. Shortly afterwards, both NATO and the EU invite Slovakia to join, and carmaker Peugeot Citroën announces that it will build a $700m car plant in the west of the country. Two years later, Hyundai announces that it will set up a $870m car plant in Slovakia.

Yukos pushes a US rival out of Lithuania

Lithuania's government, which sold a 33 per cent stake in Mazeikiu Nafta, the country's main oil refinery, to US firm Williams International in 1999 to prevent Russia taking more control over the

The Balkan States

Commonwealth of Independent States*

company Mobil pleads guilty to conspiracy and tax evasion in relation to business in Kazakhstan, but western oil companies continue to invest in the country.

Despite car bombings in Tashkent, Uzbekistan's president Islam Karimov consolidates his power. In the 2000 presidential election he faces only one opponent, who publicly declares that he is voting for Karimov. A UN human rights report confirms the use of systematic torture in Uzbek prisons, while the government cracks down on Islamic militants entering the country over the Kyrgyz border. The European Bank for Reconstruction and Development (EBRD) decides to hold its annual conference in Tashkent in 2003, providing the president with more useful propaganda. The dwindling foreign business community complains about continuing punitive exchange controls.

A personality cult is well and truly established in Turkmenistan, where 'Turkmenbashi' Saparmurad Niyazov continues to claim election victories with economy, sees the strategy fail. Williams is unable to guarantee adequate supplies of oil from Russian pipelines, and the US firm eventually sells its stake to Russian oil giant Yukos in September 2002. Oil supplies flow freely again. Lithuanians no longer appear to care too much about Russia's influence, perhaps because their country is about to join NATO.

NATO expands again

In November, seven more countries – Slovakia, Slovenia, Romania, Bulgaria and, most importantly, Estonia, Latvia and Lithuania – are invited to join NATO. Russia had once indicated that NATO membership for the former Soviet Baltic states would be unacceptable, but President Vladimir Putin appears relatively sanguine.

2003– East Europeans vote for EU membership

In referenda held throughout the year, all eight first-wave EU accession countries from the region vote strongly in favour of entering the EU in May 2004.

2003– Serbia and Montenegro replaces Yugoslavia; more chaos in Serbia

Zoran Djindjic, the Serbian prime minister since 2001, quarrels with, and outmanoeuvres, Yugoslav President Kostunica, and attempts some economic

99.99 per cent of the vote, and where his statues and portraits peer down on a weary population from every office and town square in the country. A TV station is entirely devoted to extolling his virtues and teachings. There is no opposition and few western investors – even in the potentially lucrative gas sector.

Even relatively liberal Kyrgyzstan takes an authoritarian turn. Long-serving president Askar Akayev arrests his main opponent Felix Kulov, and troops kill protestors.

More kidnapping in Georgia…

Peter Shaw, a 57-year-old British banker working on an EU aid programme, is kidnapped in Georgia on his last day in the country and is kept blindfolded, chained and isolated in a hole in the forest. He escapes in November after four months in captivity.

East-Central Europe and the Baltic States	The Balkan States	Commonwealth of Independent States*

Foreign investment in Eastern Europe
By end-2003, gross foreign direct investment in Eastern Europe and the former Soviet Union reaches nearly $260 billion. Over $160 billion of this total has gone to just four countries: Poland, the Czech Republic, Hungary and Russia. Poland leads the pack with around $55 billion, although in per-capita terms the Czech Republic is the most popular, with $3931 per head.

reform. A common state of Serbia and Montenegro comes into being in February 2003, following an EU-backed deal in Belgrade in 2002. The EU wants to avoid further Balkan fragmentation, and neither republic can call a referendum on independence for three years. The two republics immediately disagree over a common tariff policy. Djindjic attempts to clamp down on corruption and is assassinated in Belgrade on 12 March 2003. His death prompts the authorities to declare a state of emergency which lasts for 42 days and to arrest thousands of suspected criminals.

2004
More violence in Kosovo
In March violence instigated by ethnic Albanian extremists breaks out in Kosovo; 19 people are killed and hundreds of homes are destroyed. More than 3500 people (mostly Serbs) flee.

2004
...and a Rose revolution
Yet more rigged elections in Georgia result in mass public protests, which spill peacefully into parliament as government ministers and President Eduard Shevardnadze flee. The increasingly corrupt President resigns to avoid civil war. A new presidential election in January and parliamentary

2004
Lithuania's dodgy president
Lithuania's new president, Rolandas Paksas, associates publicly with a spiritual medium from Georgia, thereby casting doubts on his choice of advisors, and is then impeached after it is revealed that Mr. Paksas had links to Russian mafia groups.

election in March produce landslide victories for Mikhail Saakashvili and his party in one of the few genuinely free and fair votes in the CIS.

EU enlargement takes place
Eight East European countries (alongside Cyprus and Malta) formally join the EU on 1 May. Romania and Bulgaria are set to join in 2007.

---

* Former Soviet Union including the Baltic states only until independence

1

Labour of Love: The New Generation

'Amex cards, nice hotels, money: they really know how to trap you'
East European graduate recruited by Microsoft

In the early 1990s, female students at the prestigious Moscow State University were asked in a survey what their favoured profession would be after graduation. The most common answer? A hard-currency prostitute.[1] Although stunning to westerners, this choice doubtless made sense to many students at the time. A young Russian woman could earn more in a night than her friends would in three months, could hang out in swish hotels, and possibly find a wealthy husband to take her to the West. Besides, the alternative was to work in a local firm or government office for a pittance, with no career prospects and no worthwhile skills to learn. In addition, as was the habit in many Russian offices, she would probably be expected to sleep with the male boss anyway. The choice was not much better for a man. He could find a low-paid but cushy state job and live off bribes; set up his own business and fall prey to numerous criminal gangs; or join one of the gangs himself, only to live fast and die young.

In 1990 millions of talented, ambitious students in Eastern Europe emerged from five years of often irrelevant studies (particularly in communist social sciences) and asked themselves what opportunities lay ahead. Where could one get decent training, a job, a career? Would the skills that they had painstakingly acquired be useful abroad? Could money be made honestly? Which role models could be trusted? Freedom was one thing, but what about a career?

For many East Europeans, the arrival of western multinational companies in the region provided the answers. On 7 January 1989, as perestroika was sweeping across Russia, Paul Melling, a UK partner at law firm Baker & McKenzie, arrived in Moscow to set up an office. He began work in a nine-square-metre room with a single desk and a Soviet-era telephone line. Baker & McKenzie became the first western law firm in Russia to hire local staff. It now employs 165 local lawyers. The first recruit was a secretary. She had been a tour guide, and her main qualification was that she spoke English, an unusual skill in Russia at that time. She had no word-processing experience, which was hardly surprising given that there were few word processors in the country. In fact, she couldn't even type. But she soon became head of the translation department for Baker & McKenzie's entire CIS operations.

The first legal professional came a few months later. He was a lawyer in his mid-30s who had worked for the US Chamber of Commerce in Moscow, and had the rare experience of having actually drafted a legal contract. The big question was what to pay him: the average Russian salary for a lawyer with his experience was $1800 a year, but given the shortage of legal talent at the time, Baker & McKenzie was ready to pay him his market worth. 'Is $40 000 all right?' he was asked. 'Christmas and his birthday and everything else had come that day', says Melling.

The firm sent its new hire to the US on a one-year training course to polish up his communication and presentation skills, and to get him thinking like a commercial lawyer trying to solve his client's problems. After six years learning the ropes, he left the firm. 'He's now the senior partner at a Russian firm, whose structure seems remarkably similar to the one Baker & McKenzie set up in the early years', laments Melling.

Thousands of such stories can be told across the region. Multinationals caused a sensation wherever they went in the early days, receiving hundreds, sometimes thousands, of job applications for positions they advertised. Confectionery maker Mars, for example, was hiring so fast in Moscow in 1991, that employees were working three to a desk, and even sharing window sill space. Bright, ambitious men and women were suddenly being given an opening, and were hungry – sometimes literally – to take advantage. One Russian woman was hired in 1991 from a top government post to be a senior partner at a 'Big Five' accountancy firm, and was flown to England for training. As the days wore on she appeared increasingly exhausted in the office. Her managers put it down to the stress of a new job, but the real reason soon emerged. It was still illegal to transfer money out of Russia, and she was broke in London. Too embarrassed to mention this to her new employers, she had walked several miles each day to and from the office, and had hardly eaten for three days.

Multinationals had glamour. They represented 'the West'. The jobs on offer came with thorough training, a higher salary and travel abroad. They were also less risky, since working for a well-known international corporation reduced the chances of being nobbled by Mafia thugs. While many of the 'lost generation' now in their forties and fifties clung to outdated skills in dying factories, their talented sons and daughters could now legally earn ten times as much. In societies where almost everyone had been equally poor, such disparities created tensions not only between generations, but also between dynamic urban centres and poorer rural areas, and between graduates and manual workers. In addition, the new demand for sales, accounting and foreign language skills favoured women, who had predominated in such areas under communism. Over the next decade foreign corporations educated tens of thousands of managers in western business practice. 'Today, they talk and walk like western businessmen and women. All of that has come from the multinationals', says Melling. And for all the new inequalities that it has created, the influx of multinationals did more than anything else to create a meritocracy, in which hard work, ethical behaviour and a desire to learn were amply rewarded.

Talent competition

There was no glass ceiling either. Whether foreign corporations were establishing a small representative office or taking over a gigantic loss-making state enterprise, they expected that these operations would eventually be run by local, western-trained managers. The question was only how quickly the locals could gain the required skills and experience. Marketing and human resource managers were hardest to find, since such jobs had not existed under communism. The posts of managing director and finance director were usually the last to be handed over to locals, partly because of the importance of these positions in the group, and also because it could take as long as 15–20 years for a person to come up to international standards. But the notion that multinationals were coming just for the cheap labour while denying locals promotion to the top jobs was far from the truth. Instead, foreign companies single-handedly created a pool of well-schooled international business executives, groomed to take on huge corporate responsibilities, hold their own within the global corporation, and spread their experience in the post-communist world.

For Peter Skodny, a talented young Slovak computer scientist, the timing could not have been better. He had graduated from the Technical University in Bratislava with a science degree in 1988, a year before the revolutions. 'Science was freedom', he says. 'It was tough to put ideology into science'. His parents had fallen foul of the communist regime in the 1970s, and as a result Skodny and his younger brother had been unable to travel abroad. Skodny planned to escape to the West, but his parents pleaded with him at least to wait until his brother had graduated, as such criminal acts jeopardised the future of the family left behind. So he did his army service, during which time the 1989 revolutions broke out.

When his army service was over and the revolutions had been consolidated, he looked at his options: postgraduate research; a dull programming job in Austria; maybe politics? None looked particularly enticing. Then he saw an advertisement for a job with Andersen Consulting, an American IT and business consultancy (later renamed Accenture). The company was setting up offices in Eastern Europe and was looking for graduates who would become future partners in the firm. He applied – along with 800 others – and took a night train to the interview in Prague, walking in somewhat dishevelled. 'Why didn't you fly up the night before and stay at the hotel?' they asked him. It was the first of many East-West culture clashes, but he got the job. On his first day at the new office, as the desks and cupboards were being moved in, Skodny rolled up his sleeves to help. The Germans there looked on in astonishment. The new Slovak recruits soon became Andersen's first East European employees to be flown to Chicago for training. A stretch-limo was waiting for them at the airport. 'This cannot be for us – there must be some movie star in the airport', he and his Slovak colleagues thought. (He later realised that laying on a limousine was cheaper than hiring several taxis.)

Then came the training, and more culture clashes. 'We were taught under communism not to show your knowledge, so we kept quiet. The Americans typically shout out their answers. But we also realised that they were not as good as we had thought', he recalls, adding that there was a manual for everything. 'If the answer is in the book then it must be correct, even if there were obvious flaws; if it's not in the book it must be wrong', he remembers. For East Europeans, highly adept at technical improvisation, it was a difficult adjustment, but he was impressed by the thoroughness of the coaching and the overall professionalism. After a stint in Prague and Newcastle, England, Skodny returned to Slovakia, keen to pass on his know-how to his compatriots.

He helped train his fellow Slovak employees in everything from computing to marketing, and rapidly built up a corporate client base. By his mid-30s he was heading the Slovak office of 280 staff, handling local and international clients, earning a decent salary and making a good name for himself in both Slovakia and the Andersen global network.

Winner takes all

East European high fliers like Skodny tended to be ten or even 20 years younger than their counterparts in the West. Many multinationals had written off most of the over-30s in Eastern Europe as being too set in their old ways, allowing the younger generation to race to the top. For a Pole, Russian or Hungarian who spoke several languages, had picked up an MBA and worked five years in marketing or sales, the sky was the limit. Salaries soared. In the early 1990s dynamic Poles in their late 20s could earn $50 000 a year, and thanks to a booming market they could, by their early 30s, be heading the local subsidiary of a multinational and making $100 000–$140 000 a year. These were huge sums, bearing in mind that the average annual wage in Poland was around $4000, and that the cost of living in Warsaw was a quarter of that in London or New York.[2] There were also bonuses, travel, perks and training. Job-hopping became rampant as new recruits spent a year or less at the likes of PepsiCo, Procter & Gamble, Philip Morris and other big-name firms before skipping to an even better offer.

Unattractive as ostentatious yuppies can be anywhere in the world, there was something forgivable about the way some very impressive people were getting their due. The general public seemed to reserve its ire not for the new multinational company executives who had genuinely earned their bonuses, but rather for the equally young millionaires who had become staggeringly rich through rigged privatisations, thuggery or the exploitation of legal loopholes, and who flaunted their financial success with the maximum possible vulgarity.

Although there were instances of Russian oil firms poaching both local and western executives from even the best-paying multinational, local companies generally could not compete, and complained that multinationals were swiping all the talent by offering impossibly high salaries. However, the multinationals were also responsible for creating and training that talent. As the 1990s wore on and the supply of foreign-trained executives, accountants and lawyers increased, the job-hopping subsided and young executives looked for other benefits.

Human resource surveys consistently showed that employees in the region put a priority on training – both 'hard skills' such as accounting and finance, and 'soft skills' such as selling, service, conflict management, foreign languages, corporate ethics and teamwork, which were often conspicuously absent in local firms and the country in general.[3]

Perhaps more significantly, western corporations were also looking for talented executives who could run foreign operations. For a lucky few, multinationals have lived up to their name and offered postings to other emerging markets and even to the West. When a young female student with no special contacts or privileges from a small village in Slovakia's Tatra mountains can, by hard graft and raw talent, land a permanent posting in Paris on a western salary with a leading French company, then the multinational system is clearly doing something right. Philips has dozens of Hungarians working abroad, Dutch bank ING has appointed a Pole to manage its online banking business, and US Steel has sent a Slovak from Kosice to head up a division in Pittsburgh. After the August 1998 economic crash in Russia many western firms took a long-term view and held onto their staff: Mars sent dozens of Russian managers to offices in Western Europe (many stayed), while Reebok transferred its Russian management to Sweden until things became more stable back home. Looking further afield, Volkswagen and Thomson Polkolor have a senior Czech and Polish manager respectively in China and Mexico.

Multinationals have also introduced 'post-tax salary equalisation policies', so that managers from any country will have roughly the same purchasing power when they are posted abroad as local staff of the same rank. There is now little difference in spending power between a western expatriate working in the East, and an East European posted to the West. Nevertheless, such western postings are still relatively rare, and often reflect the determination of the individual in question rather than company policy.

With the recent accession of eight East European countries to the European Union, such western postings may also lose some of their glamour. After all, any Hungarian or Lithuanian can now live and study in the West with few problems, and when the last restrictions on labour movement in the 25-member EU are lifted by the start of the next decade, they can apply for a job in their EU city of choice. However, it has taken 15 years for political developments to catch up with the multinationals in this respect, and there are still several East European transition countries that will remain outside the EU for a long while to come, and whose people still crave these opportunities.

Many of those openings will, however, be in Eastern Europe, since multinationals still have a huge need for talented managers as they expand in the region. Rather than send in a western expatriate, corporations tend to post East Europeans, who have a sharper sense of post-communist societies, to other regional markets – as French razor maker Bic did when it sent a Romanian to establish a very successful operation in Ukraine, for example.

A more confident android

This strategy raised the risk of culture clashes. There were fears that Poles might resent being managed by Russians, while the Balkans is loaded with similar dangers. Yet such fears have proved to be largely unfounded, highlighting another major impact that multinational companies have had in the region. While on the Accenture training programme in Chicago, Skodny observed consultants from around the world, including Eastern Europe, and noted a phenomenon simultaneously disconcerting and encouraging. 'We were all the same, copying our bosses, dressing the same way, talking the same way. The same decision processes; the same core values; we were like androids', he says jokingly.

Androids or not, there were few serious culture clashes, because the new recruits were so schooled in the company culture. As Leslie Bergman, Skodny's former boss, reflects: 'These young executives were not nationally distinct between East and West. They were the same as in the UK or France. We never found that you cannot send a Russian to manage a Pole, for example'. He did feel that Russians tended to be self-centred and distrustful of the organisation, and possessed a heightened instinct for individual survival. 'When abroad, they usually outshone everyone else', says Bergman. 'It was just a bit harder, but not impossible, to get them thinking in the Accenture way'. The 'androids' (or 'the suits' as they may be disparagingly referred to in the UK) were part of a culture that transcended national differences and inferiority complexes in a region fraught with them.

By creating this culture, multinationals have given young people from the region a genuine sense of self-confidence. Maria, a new female recruit at Microsoft, sums up the feelings of many young East Europeans:

> I have less of an inferiority complex when I go to a foreign city. You are someone. You can hold your head up. The name of the

company is respected world-wide, and they wouldn't have taken me if I wasn't up to standard. My dress has changed. I'm no longer the sloppy student, but a well-groomed professional. I know that sounds superficial, but it still feels good.

2
Working Life: Unions, Layoffs and Training

'They have been good for us, and good for the country. I have no problems with them'.
Communist activist on US Steel's investment in Kosice, Slovakia

In 1999 Slovak workers marched to the government offices in Bratislava, demanding better wages, more secure jobs and improved working conditions. Their battle cries might have sounded unfamiliar to trade unions in the West; the Slovaks wanted their government to do more to attract big multinational companies to the country.[1] The marchers believed that they had more chance of achieving their goals by working for the subsidiary of a major western corporation than by taking industrial action against local employers. In effect they were saying to the government: bring us jobs – but good ones.

Common feelings between workers and big foreign companies have surfaced in other surprising situations across the region. Chrystia Freeland, a former Financial Times bureau chief in Moscow, describes a meeting she had with Russian miners who were demonstrating outside the parliament building for their unpaid back wages, two days after the devastating economic crash of August 1998. The crash, in which the Russian government defaulted on its debt, also left western bankers holding worthless paper. She reports:

> ... fully expecting a Communist-tinged anti-western harangue, I couldn't have been more mistaken .... 'Tell the western bankers to come down here and join us and together we will demand that the government pay us its debts', said a miner from Vorkuta. 'We'll give them miners' hard hats and share our vodka. They should have asked us before they lent money to the Russian government. We

would have told them that our bastards here in Moscow never pay their debts.[2]

Westerners may find it hard to appreciate the humiliations that workers in much of Eastern Europe and the former Soviet Union have suffered. For them, the arrival of an employer with an international reputation, introducing better health and safety standards, and offering both higher pay (on time) and modern training, must have seemed little short of a miracle.

This chapter will discuss how multinationals were appalled by the working practices that they found on arrival in post-communist Europe, and will argue that far from exploiting relatively cheap labour, western firms in fact did their best to retrain and reward it. Many of the state-owned enterprises acquired by western corporations were so hugely overstaffed that widespread layoffs were inevitable – but there too, multinationals did their best to soften the blow. Some aspects of economic life in the region played to the advantage of the multinationals: trade unions were weak, widely distrusted, and confused about their new role; unemployment was high; and for all the cynicism that already existed towards capitalism, many were ready to embrace it. Still, industrial relations were not perfect, and this chapter will also look at the numerous shortcomings that each side found in the other. Workers complained of managerial arrogance and miserly overtime pay, while employers were often alarmed by high levels of absenteeism, alcoholism, theft and sexual harassment. However, communism had left at least one positive legacy – a technically capable, highly literate labour force that could absorb new technologies and production methods relatively easily, and therefore benefit from the training that the foreign corporations introduced. Such adaptability was crucial in ensuring that the more advanced economies of the region were able to avoid a 'low skills-low wage' trap. In sum, western multinationals and East European workers found much in common – and, for all their differences, generally gained far more than they lost from their new-found relationships.

Nasty, brutish and not so short: working conditions in Eastern Europe

The immediate aftermath of communism's collapse was not kind to much of the region's labour force. Real wages plummeted everywhere, pay packets were sometimes dispensed months or even years in arrears, and in many areas job security evaporated as unemployment reached 20–30 per cent. Workplace conditions were no more encouraging – and were indeed horrendous by western standards. Gunter Thumser, Executive Vice President of German detergent maker Henkel, which now has plants throughout Eastern Europe, recalls his first visits to the local factories that the firm was planning to buy. 'Nothing was protected', he says. 'You needed a mask to enter the powder-filling lines. Staff worked in near darkness, crowding around a single light bulb. It was incredible that people could survive like this.' Henkel immediately installed filters to extract the bad air, covered conveyor belts, placed guards over dangerous turning wheels, and scrubbed the floors.

Hygiene standards were just as bad. Stephen Lee, Vice President for Strategic Planning at US food group Kraft Foods, recalls that several of the factories that the company acquired across Eastern Europe lacked not only showers but even a 'clean area' where workers could take off muddy boots before entering food production rooms. Staff also wore their regular clothes at work. Lee remembers that they were more than happy to receive new uniforms, but then had to be persuaded not to wear them outside the factory. Some plants were infested with insects, while birds flew freely around. As Lee points out, 'The last thing you want is a bird shitting on your chocolate'.

Western managers were staggered by such conditions, but local workers were used to considerably worse. In many cases the situation for those who are still employed in local or state-run factories, with little chance of being acquired by a more humane foreign company, has not improved much since the early 1990s. One of the most damning aspects of working life in such enterprises, particularly in the former Soviet states, was (and still is) the extent to which wages go unpaid – an almost unimaginable state of affairs in the West. Some 80 per cent of workers in the Donbass region of Ukraine reported difficulties with wages, with two-thirds of them not having been paid for more than four months. Late pay was the primary cause of strikes in the region.[3]

The situation has not been helped by the tendency of local bosses to pay their workers not in cash but in kind – almost invariably with the products that they themselves manufacture. Workers in one Russian toy factory were paid in boxes of yellow plastic ducks, and told to sell them if they wanted cash. Teachers in Voronezh in southern Russia were given fences and tombs from a local cemetery in lieu of wages. Workers in Kimovsk, in the Tula region south of Moscow, received not roubles but a thousand tonnes of locally produced manure.[4] Workers on one Russian collective farm who had not received wages for 21 months were provided with a loaf of bread a day, a kilo of sugar and 2–3 kilos of cereal grain a month. As the Russian Federation's human rights commissioner noted in a 1999 report, such practices 'essentially [constitute] forced labour.'[5]

The opportunities to remedy such situations have in general been extremely limited, not least because withholding labour has rarely prompted employers to pay wages. In many regions, people have tended to rely on what economists call 'individual exit strategies', meaning that they grow their own vegetables on tiny plots so as not to starve. Others have adopted real exit strategies by emigrating, but in the face of strict visa regimes in Western Europe have often drifted into grey-market construction jobs in Central Europe, with little protection and no rights. For women the choice can also be harsh, with prostitution often the only practical employment option.

Vlado, who comes from a small town of 15 000 people 100 kilo-metres from Lvov in the west of Ukraine, is one of thousands of young Ukrainians who left the country in search of a job after finishing his army service in 1997. 'There was simply no work, everything around was bankrupt and I had a family to support', he says. A friend was going to chance his luck in Prague, and Vlado went along. They met a man called 'The Client', a Ukrainian who had set himself up with all the necessary legal documents as a supplier of cheap labour to Czech construction firms. The relationship kept the local companies on safe legal ground, but not the workers. 'The Client' would select Ukrainians for the jobs, taking half their wages for himself and leaving around $1 an hour for the workers. 'It was 50–50 whether you got paid', says Vlado. 'Or you would get paid the first month, and the second you'd get nothing. There was nothing that you could do about it'. One day Vlado was working at a building site when the floor collapsed and he fell through to the next level, breaking his leg and narrowly avoiding being killed by falling concrete. He was only given ten days off, without pay. The industry was crawling with mafia and small-time hoodlums, extorting money. The Czech police would have a go too. 'They know you have no papers. When I didn't have money to pay them off – usually around $100 – I had to give them my mobile phone', says Vlado. 'I went home once but the work situation was hopeless, so came back to Prague. It's a nice place, but home is home. My plan is to return with the money I've saved, buy some land in my town, and raise my family.'

Even for those in regular employment, there is a stark difference in the way that workers in local enterprises and big western corporations are treated. Take Skoda, the famously decrepit Czechoslovakian car company that was sold to the German car giant Volkswagen (VW) in 1991. With a national debate raging over whether such a prized company should be sold to a German investor, Jan Vrba, then Minister of Industry and the man responsible for negotiating the deal, was worried that he could not get the Skoda trade unions onside. He decided to ask the Czech union leaders to visit VW's headquarters in Wolfsburg to observe industrial relations at first hand. The tactic worked. 'For [the Czechs] it was paradise', says Mr Vrba, and the Czech unions became the most ardent supporters of the deal. 'We did not care about the colour of the flag', says Richard Falbr, the head of the Czech Moravian Confederation of Trade Unions for most of the 1990s. Indeed, Mr Vrba became concerned that VW was offering the unions too much, and feared (wrongly, as it turned out) that such generosity would raise expectations too far and 'would be a problem for the healthy development of Skoda'. As one Skoda worker recalls: '[The new German boss] asked what wage I was on. When I told him, he replied: "Is that per week or per day?" I replied, "No, per month"' (see chapter 4). Skoda workers are now among the best paid in the country. Although they have threatened industrial action on several occasions, this is widely seen as part of the annual merry-go-round of pay negotiations.

Workers' rights: the decline of trade unions

At first it seems somewhat surprising that less privileged workers than those at Skoda-VW have not become more militant, but there have been relatively few strikes in Eastern Europe over the past 15 years. Those that have occurred have typically involved miners and railway workers in Poland, the Czech Republic, Romania and Bulgaria, and have arisen over layoffs or mining accidents. In other fields, unions have faced considerable difficulty adjusting to the new era. They have been weakened by privatisation and the emergence of millions of dynamic new enterprises – which often regard unions as unhelpful or irrelevant – while many large, moribund enterprises would regard a strike as a good excuse to shut down for a few months, save energy costs and reduce inventories. Governments have also reduced union influence through legislation. Only a few, such as the Social Democrats in the Czech Republic or the reformist centre-right government in

Slovakia – both in the late 1990s – have shown some commitment to dialogue with unions on laws affecting wages and labour conditions, and even then only grudgingly.

Union leaders are also widely distrusted by their own members. Until 1989, union leaders had worked alongside factory managers to fulfil governmental production targets instead of standing up for workers, and many employees greeted the end of communism by tearing up their union cards. Even after a decade and a half of capitalism, old and new union leaders have almost everywhere failed to recapture the trust – or even the interest – of ordinary workers. One poll in Romania in 1997 showed that only banks were less respected than unions (see chapter 4), while a separate poll in the same year by the Soros Foundation put unions at the bottom of the pile.[6] One Russian survey showed that new independent unions were trusted even less than their communist-era predecessors – less, in fact, than every other public institution, but just above 'Westerners advising the Russian government'.[7]

Union leaders argue that the most common criticisms – for example, that they often engage in corrupt deals with management – are unfair, and point out that many workers simply free-ride on union negotiations, receiving any benefits that might be won but refusing to pay the membership fee. What is clear is that union membership has plummeted throughout the region. In the Czech Republic it fell by 10–15 per cent per year during the first decade of reform, and the decline would have been far steeper had older workers not retained their cards as a means of protecting their pensions. Even Solidarity, Eastern Europe's first free trade union, which boasted 9.5 million members during its heyday in 1981, had only 2 million members by 1995 and 1.2 million by the end of the decade.

Yet there can be little doubt that workers rights could be better protected. Most countries in the region retain protective labour laws passed during the communist period, and have ratified hundreds of international labour conventions, but implementation of these measures is weak, and industrial tribunals are usually ineffective. Unions are often on shaky legal ground. In Russia, for example, strong de jure protection has not prevented strikers from being held legally liable for economic damage or loss to a company – and the complexity of Russian labour law and the ease of bribing judges means that caution often prevails over workers' solidarity. When unions do choose to flex their muscle, it can produce hardships for others in society, which elicits plenty of public disapproval.

Falbr, the Czech union leader, believes that one key problem is that union leaders are often uncertain as to what their new role should be at a time when many of their members have embraced the new capitalist system, and multinational employers often provide workers with all their demands – and more – from the outset. Nowhere was the dilemma more apparent than in Poland. The Solidarity trade union had led the revolution against communism and was in government in 1989–93 and 1997–2001, but its grip on the levers of power did little to bring about the workers' paradise that the country's communists had failed to deliver. The Solidarity-led governments pushed for economic reform according to western doctrines of privatisation, industrial restructuring and free trade, and although union leaders argued that the short-term pain would mean long-term gains for all workers, the government's attitude to its proletarian supporters could be uncomradely in the extreme. Even those Solidarity spokesmen who challenged the government's position did so on the basis that a strong union would better persuade workers of the need for deep economic reforms. According to Lech Walesa, the founder of Solidarity and former President of Poland, the government was not there to put workers' interests first. 'We will not catch up to Europe if we build a strong union ... we cannot have a strong union until we have a strong economy', he said.

Solidarity's most useful service to individual trade unionists was to offer them a route into politics, with the obvious effect of depriving the union movement as a whole of a generation of organisers and negotiators. Whenever Poland faced industrial unrest, government ministers typically viewed the problem not in terms of too much capitalism, but too little. The government was sometimes able to exploit nationalism, blame individual opponents or simply co-opt the protests. When 180 000 miners went on strike in 1992 (the largest ever stoppage in Europe), Solidarity moved in to 'lead' the protests, thereby succeeding in neutralising the unrest. In 1998 the Solidarity-led government ruled that a rail strike was illegal, and started prosecuting the strike leaders. In surveys asking workers who best represented them, the most common answer was 'no-one'.[8]

Across East-central Europe, dealings between unions and the new bosses from western corporations involved a similar mix of confrontation, co-operation and confusion. Union leaders sometimes tried to block restructuring out of pure caution, as in 1992 when Polish unions managed to delay the sale of steel mill Huta Warszawa to an Italian firm, despite the difficulty of finding western investors for the steel sector. At other times unions in the region would just bend rules to breaking point, for example by encouraging workers to take several months' sick leave after learning that redundancies were on the cards.

Relations with management tended to be more harmonious in plants where multinationals communicated with trade unions and treated them with respect. The human resources manager at Thomson Polkolor, a French-owned TV manufacturer in Poland, used to spend around three and half hours a week in union meetings, even though only a quarter of the workforce was unionised. Falbr notes that 'the behaviour of multinationals in the early 1990s was positive'. Western firms such as Procter & Gamble and Volkswagen respected the unions that were in place at the time of an acquisition, and negotiated with them fairly, he says. That even-handed approach may also have reflected a tentativeness among multinationals about dealing with the unknown. When Belgian glass maker Glaverbel approached the Czech government about investing in local glass factory Sklo Union, Falbr reports that their first question was: 'what about the unions?'[9]

Unions were often inexperienced in conflict resolution. Willem van der Vegt, a former head of Dutch electronics firm Philips in Hungary, where the company claims to have excellent labour relations, says that many disputes reflected basic misunderstandings and the lack of a process for resolving differences. On one occasion in 1997 unions announced that they planned to go on strike at Philips' Szekesfehervar plant, over the issue of different assessment terms for blue- and white-collar workers regarding pay and performance. Management had to explain that basic conflict resolution steps should be taken before unions embarked on such extreme action. Philips asked them first if the unions were really talking about the right issues; second, if any of conflicts were in fact personal; and third, whether the parties had tried to seek an amicable solution. On reflection, the unions decided that there was no basis for calling a strike.

The prevailing confusion among unions is well illustrated by a story from Poland in the early 1990s, when a foreign firm was told by its unions that they would be holding a strike in support of workers at the famous Gdansk shipyard. When asked what this would involve, union leaders explained that 'they wanted to hang union banners at the entrance to the plant, blow the company siren and share an hour of silent prayer.' However, they wanted to keep working in order that the company could meet its production targets. At the same company, the unions had also agreed to an annual ten per cent pay rise payable on 1 October each year. One year, the management decided to generate some goodwill by increasing wages by 12 per cent and introducing the raise a month earlier. The unions were furious and rejected the offer. They had wanted to present the deal to the workforce as a concession that they had extracted. The management withdrew its proposal, and the wage raise was later re-introduced jointly with the unions.[10]

Redundancies: laying off the layoffs

What made ordinary workers most fearful of the new era, and of the multinationals in particular, was the prospect of mass layoffs. In the case of greenfield investments – where a multinational sets up a plant from scratch rather than acquiring an existing factory – this was irrelevant, since investors were hiring new people. But state-owned enterprises sold to a major western corporation would clearly need major surgery to survive, since they were massively overstaffed as a result of the socialist commitment to full employment. Workers used to taunt their communist bosses, saying that it was illegal for them to be sacked. Most staff had little real work to do, and were unmotivated if they did. The communist emphasis on cradle-to-grave security also meant that big enterprises had many peripheral businesses and community services that were unrelated to the company's core activity. Many western firms that found themselves in control of such huge workforces later wished that they had built their operations from scratch. Redundancies were particularly large in the telecommunications sector. France Telecom delayed layoffs for several years at TPSA, Poland's fixed-line monopoly, before almost 40 000 workers, around half of the total, were made redundant or left voluntarily over a two-year period in the largest downsizing anywhere in Eastern Europe.

However, the feared job losses at the hands of multinational companies were not always immediate, dramatic or even inevitable. Governments sought to delay or control any such shakeout by setting strict limits on future layoffs in privatisation contracts. When LNM acquired Romanian steel firm Sidex, which employed 27700 people, the investor agreed not to make mass redundancies for five years, even though independent steel experts estimated that only a fraction of the staff was needed.

Multinationals often showed considerable sensitivity about the social and economic impact of layoffs on the local area. They were helped in this regard by low wage levels, which meant that labour was less important than raw materials or machinery in the cost structure of many firms. As Christopher Beauman, a senior advisor at the European

Bank for Reconstruction and Development (EBRD) who specialises in the steel sector, points out, laying off thousands of people sometimes made little sense when larger cost savings could be made in other areas. When Norsk Hydro acquired a stake in 1993 in Slovak aluminium maker Slovalco, which is based in an area of high unemployment, the Norwegian investor decided to maintain the bloated payroll and expand the company to absorb the excess labour, thereby minimising the social pain.

In other cases, layoffs were quickly followed by fresh hiring as a business began to grow. When Volkswagen bought Skoda, 'we knew that Skoda was at least 30 per cent overstaffed, and initial layoffs would be necessary', says Mr Vrba, the former Czech industry minister. The company soon expanded and hired around 8000 new employees – slightly more than the number that had been laid off (albeit in different areas of the company).

Sometimes the relative generosity was so unexpected that it was entirely misunderstood. When Procter & Gamble (P&G) bought the overstaffed Novomoskovskbytkhim detergent factory in Tula in Russia, 100 miles south of Moscow, in 1993, the US company also acquired a ballet school, a sewage works and a fire engine for use in the town. After a four-year grace period P&G began its planned restructuring programme, which involved halving the plant's workforce. But P&G did not simply sack these people, as it could have done under Russian law. Mindful of the need to project a positive image in a new market, the company offered general retraining as well as specialist training to staff in those peripheral services so that they could run the operations privately. This stimulated huge interest. One assembly-line worker took a course in professional cooking, while others created a taxi fleet or a cleaning service out of the previous company operations and then supplied their services to the P&G-owned plant. In addition, a voluntary retirement programme offered older workers up to three-and-a-half years' salary for leaving – compared to the legal minimum of two months.

Yet despite the fact that no one was fired, P&G faced a barrage of press criticism that accused the company of buying the plant merely to shut it down and eliminate local competition to P&G's imports. The local press later changed its tune after realising that such claims were untrue, and that the workers in question were receiving an extraordinarily generous offer – getting paid for doing no work for three years, rather than getting no pay for working for three years, as might have been the case in a local Russian firm.[11]

While mass layoffs might have been problematic, firing individual staff could be a legal nightmare. Although Eastern Europe was entering a new world of late-night supermarkets, seasonal industries and commission-based wage structures, communist-era labour laws continued to hold sway and were generally applied by judges who still thought in terms of lifelong 8 am–4 pm shifts. Local courts were usually unsympathetic to employers. After PepsiCo bought Wedel, a confectionery factory in Poland, in 1991, it tried to fire a salesman for cheating the company out of $10 000–20 000. But the law would not allow Wedel to sack him, and the firm had to pay his full salary. To add insult to injury, the salesman sued the company to claim overtime pay.[12] Courts could be heavy-handed in protecting individuals. The Radisson Hotel in Moscow had its bank accounts frozen in the late 1990s while it settled a dispute with two cleaning ladies whom it had fired. The prosecutor's office in Russia might even review the operating licence of a company that lost a civil case. The consequences of hiring the wrong person could be serious, but short-term contracts were often not an option – in Russia these were limited to highly specific activities such as flying to the Mir space station.[13]

Sometimes, the problem was not getting rid of staff but finding them. Despite areas of high unemployment, many western firms could not attract enough skilled labour, because of the region's immobile workforce. Workers from one town would seldom relocate to another for a job; and younger workers in particular often stayed at home supporting parents and grandparents, since relocating meant paying exorbitant market rents for accommodation. Long commutes were also difficult because of the poor state of public transport. Many multinationals therefore had to step in with solutions of their own. In Slovakia Volkswagen uses 35 private buses every day to bring in around 1800 workers to its Devinska Nova Ves factory from up to 100 kilometres away, and subsidises rents in the town for a similar number. The company even shifted some of its operations to central Slovakia, where there were more available workers.

Meet the new boss, same as the old boss? Workers' complaints

Once it became clear that unions in Eastern Europe would not bite (or even bark), and governments would generally stay onside, a second wave of investment in the late 1990s brought in foreign managers who were more confident, even arrogant, and often hardened by their experiences in other emerging markets in Asia or Latin America. 'They came with the attitude that they were the salvation army', Falbr recalls, 'and would not countenance unions at all.' Locally-recruited middle managers, eager to impress their foreign bosses, were often particularly oppressive. Sometimes this reflected poor line management, but on occasion the local manager was merely doing the dirty work expected of him. Alexandr Leiner, President of the Union of Commercial Employees in the Czech Republic has a copy of a letter from the regional director of a German electronics retail chain congratulating a local manager on attempting to eradicate all unions from the stores that were under his control. The zealous manager was rewarded with an extra $600 a month for his efforts. One German company stated categorically to Falbr that no unions would be allowed in its Czech factory. Derecognition was not hard to engineer; some staff were paid an extra $16 a month to leave the union, while others were simply sacked. Leiner also claims that there is indirect discrimination, where colleagues are warned to steer clear of someone because he is a union member, or where union activists are assigned tasks that are impossible to complete. Another German retailer was heavily criticised for not allowing workers sufficient toilet breaks. The manager responded to complaints from union representatives by saying that workers would have to go to the toilet at their desks. According to Leiner, some did; a supermarket checkout woman kept a stock of pampers nappies under the till. Many workers were soon to recall the quip that everything Marx told us about socialism was wrong, while everything he told us about capitalism was right.

The most common complaint about foreign investors is that they expect not just management but also staff to work overtime without pay, even if national labour laws set out a clear scale of overtime pay. Enthusiastic staff in the region could rack up 40 hours of overtime in a month. In 2003 FNV Mondiaal, the Netherlands' largest trade union federation, issued a report into the behaviour of retail chain Ahold, which runs 450 supermarkets and hypermarkets across Poland, the Czech Republic and Slovakia, employing nearly 27 000 workers. The report notes:

> ... a number of cases found at Ahold when [the overtime pay] agreement has not been observed. For example the extra pay for work on weekends, extra 5 days of paid leave for recreation after more than 10 years of work record, etc .... Ahold's collective agreement provides for extra pay for work on weekends. This provision is often not met. After 7 weeks of work with no weekend break one of the workers claimed

access to the collective agreement from the department manager to make sure that the provision of extra pay for weekends is still present in the agreement. The access to the agreement was very difficult (in fact prevented at all), so was the enforcement of the extra pay provision. As a result of this situation, a union organisation has been constituted in order for the workers to be able to enforce the provisions of the collective agreement and approach the employer as a legal partner.

The report also identified problems of what it believes were unrealistic demands for flexible working hours.

Workers, especially those in the stores, very often face unexpected requests for overtime work beyond their contract. These requests are usually presented as a solution to a current exceptional crisis situation. According to the interviewed employees, as well as the unions, the main reason is that the workload in many stores does not comport with the capacity of staff. Stores are understaffed in the long-term (because of saving on wages in order to meet the expected productivity numbers in a particular store) and/or as a result of actual problems (when for example one employee does not come to the afternoon shift because of a sudden health problem, a worker from the morning shift has to stay as a substitution and spend a working day from 7 a.m. to 9 p.m.).

In these cases the FNV report accepts that Ahold's foreign management appeared keen to address the issues. The report also notes that a survey of employees who had left Ahold revealed that their main cause of dissatisfaction was not remuneration, but rather the lack of effective, daily communication from management to employees, insufficient training, and the absence of a proper initial induction for new employees. The high number of departures, according to the report, to Ahold's competitors would seem to indicate that competition brought about by the arrival of western firms, rather than union activism, places the most effective pressure on companies to treat staff better.[14]

Ahold strongly plays down such claims. 'Of course individual isolated problems sometimes occur. Unfortunately generalisation based on individual – often groundless – cases has become more and more frequent', says Lucie Cavina, public affairs officer for Ahold. She adds: 'As for the shift planning, we always proceed according to the labour code, and we respect the salary prescriptions. The shifts are agreed two weeks in advance, and in this agreement breaks between shifts and between the weeks have to be observed.'

Individual complaints, groundless or otherwise, underlie some conflicts. According to Leiner, one employee at western-owned company who had put in 470 hours of overtime over the year asked to be compensated. He was alarmed to be told by his Czech boss: 'You've disappointed us because you have asked for the money', and was duly sacked. (The union eventually won him an out-of-court settlement.) Such problems may reflect the activities of a single maverick manager, or simply the new demands of 24-hour opening and attentive service (see chapter 5). Even UK retailer Tesco, which is commended by Falbr for fair practices and for having a collective agreement in place in the Czech Republic, is sometimes criticised for only offering new staff six-month contracts so that firing them won't be too hard if they don't measure up. (Some workers complain that this policy hardly fits in with Tesco's stated aim of promoting a sense of team spirit and company loyalty, but such a provision is not much different to any western-style probation period.) Such gripes also fail to take into account the appalling work practices that investors such as Tesco inherited and have had to change (see chapter 5) – a tall order in a region where a friendly sales person had been a contradiction in terms for several decades.

Drinker, stalker, skiver, thief: Management's complaints

Because so many jobs in Eastern Europe before 1989 lacked any meaningful incentives, work often became secondary to other daily tasks, such as queuing in shops or government offices. The factory or shop was as much a place for drinking and chatting as for producing or selling goods, and the theft of any merchandise worth stealing was generally considered a perk of the job. The arrival of the first multinationals thus brought both excitement and trepidation. Joining such a firm was a ticket to the modern world, but also a leap in the dark.

Western firms are often highly complimentary about the attitude of their new workforces – particularly that of the younger generation – but overcoming communist-era habits has rarely been easy. When French electronics firm Thomson acquired Polish TV set producer Polkolor in 1991, the firm brought in Stan Urban, an American chartered accountant with Coopers & Lybrand, to turn the plant around. Urban seemed perfect for the job. Apart from his business skills, he was of Polish descent, a fact that eased worries among many of the workers about rapacious western corporations. Urban's father was originally from Lublin, near the Ukrainian border, and had been a pilot in the

British Royal Air Force during the Second World War. His mother had survived two winters in a Siberian prison camp. His parents met in the UK and moved to the US, where Stan was brought up with a strong sense of his Catholic and Polish heritage. He was a scout-master in the Polish boy scouts, and when he was 19 studied in Krakow, in the south of Poland, as part of the country's first student exchange programme. After qualifying as an accountant he became head of the Polish American Credit Union. His credentials were faultless, and made a difference with the selection panel when he applied for the job to run Polkolor. A tough but engaging manager, Urban displays an unusual combination of mastery of 'the bottom line' with a genuine feeling for those people who have lost out in the capitalist transformation. None of his experiences, however, would have prepared him for what he found at Polkolor.

One of the first things he noticed was that output during the night shift was remarkably low. The first step in unravelling the mystery was the discovery that prostitutes were being bussed into the factory at midnight to frolic with the workers in the company's large changing room. The French managers cunningly replaced the room's walls with glass panels (to deter the practice, rather than to watch it), but output remained low. Things only started to improve after Urban found the answer to another puzzle – namely, why there were so many fire extinguishers in the building. Workers were using them to cool their vodka.

The new managers wanted to instil more positive attitudes towards quality standards, but were sensitive about sloganeering, given Poland's rich tradition of ridiculing stock phrases from the authorities. Thus 'Jakosc Bedzie' (Quality will be) was abandoned because it too easily became 'Jakos Bedzie' (It'll get by). Similarly, staff joked that QLP (Quality Leadership Program) really stood in Polish for 'Penises! You'd better work!' In the 12 years until 1991, when Thomson acquired the company, Polkolor had produced 1.6 million TV sets in total, all of the same 1970s styles, quality and technology. By the end of the decade, when Urban left the firm, it was churning out 6.6 million top-range colour sets every year – many of them for export to western markets.

The drive to improve productivity in Eastern Europe was not helped by the existence of a burgeoning grey economy in which staff held down a second job, and sometimes even a third. Factories in rural areas of Romania, Ukraine and Hungary often suffered at harvest time, because many workers were needed on the family farms – the sole guarantor against starvation in hard times. One Austrian shoe manufacturer with a plant in a high unemployment area of Romania says that he could not hold onto staff at harvest time – despite doubling their wages.

Other working practices such as absenteeism, alcoholism and theft gave employers headaches all year round. According to company health experts, about five per cent of a workforce can generally be expected to be absent on health grounds at any one time. Even allowing for the fact that many East European workers genuinely believe that a cold or tiredness is sufficient reason to take a week or more off work, foreign investors that took over local factories in the region throughout the 1990s reported absenteeism rates of up to 20 per cent.[15] In the mid-1990s the average Czech was taking 25 working days off a year due to 'sickness.' Car maker Suzuki started awarding bonuses to employees for full attendance at its plant in Hungary, while consumer goods manufacturers Colgate-Palmolive and Unilever demanded an explanation from floor supervisors for absences, and required sick notes from two different doctors. Unfortunately, a doctor's note was not to be taken at face value either, since for a small payment of around $20 cash-strapped doctors in many countries would happily prescribe a month's rest from work for an employee with flu. Some national health systems even encouraged this practice by placing doctors on a points system based on the number of patients on their books.

For a similar fee Ukrainian hospitals would falsely 'confirm' an illness as cover for alcohol abuse. Eastern Europeans did not even recognise alcoholism as an illness, making the problem more difficult to deal with. Mikhail Gorbachev, the last leader of the Soviet Union, had recognised that excessive vodka consumption in the workplace was causing countless deaths, but he was to become one of the least popular Soviet leaders partly because he attempted to limit its consumption. Western companies opted for zero tolerance in their East European operations, and in general the policy worked as their employees saw good reasons to remain sober.

Workplace theft was less easy to combat. Most foreign investors have a couple of horror stories to relate, particularly from their early days in the region. Staff at one detergent factory in Poland rigged up a pulley system to haul stock over the wall, and then undercut the firm by selling the products in nearby shops. Employees at PepsiCo's Wedel factory in Poland would steal taps, bulbs and lamps, and even on one occasion tried to smuggle a toilet off the premises. Rates of workplace theft in the Czech Republic remained staggeringly high well into the

1990s. One German pharmacy chain reported in 1996 that stock equivalent of 12.5 per cent of turnover was being stolen each year – not by customers, but by sales staff in collaboration with the security team. Yet again, courts were sometimes more sympathetic to the thief than to the foreign firm. One Polish judge, on hearing the appeal of a man sacked for stealing several thousand dollars' worth of company goods, ruled: 'It's obvious from the evidence that the man has stolen, but is that really enough of a reason to fire him when has a family at home to support?.'[16]

Nevertheless, effective management controls could help to limit theft. Willem van der Vegt, a former head of Philips in Hungary, notes that there were a few cases of malpractice, such as employees using the company car as a taxi on weekends, or stealing the company's products on the assumption that this was a perk of the job. But he says that most workers were quick to change their attitude once they were told that, like alcoholism, stealing from their employer was unacceptable.

Sexual discrimination was a trickier workplace issue to handle. It is difficult to assess whether western corporations have improved wages and promotion opportunities for women in comparison to their male colleagues. Women in the region still earn around 25–30 per cent less than men for doing the same job – about the same differential as in Western Europe — but the introduction of performance-based pay has obscured base salaries and made it difficult to know whether the gap is wider or narrower in multinationals. Despite frequently proclaiming that women are excellent workers and managers, multinationals have appointed few East European women to head their offices in the region, and there are few female expatriate managers around to set an example. At the shopfloor level, especially in retailing, many women interviewed by the author say that they see little difference in pay or working conditions between foreign-owned or local employers.

Multinationals can thank communism for the prevalence of skilled women in the workforce, since everyone was expected to have a job in the 'gender equal' communist utopia. Socialist-era enterprises provided childcare facilities, making it easy for women with children to enter the workforce – a more enlightened approach than in many western firms and countries. In practice, the skills women picked up under communism came less from the job itself but rather from learning to juggle a full day's work with running a family in a society of shortages. This required patience and organisational skills, creating a deep pool of latent business talent. Van der Vegt recalls the first-class female logistics manager whom Philips hired at its computer monitor manufacturing plant in Szombathely, Hungary, and many western investors have a higher proportion of women in their workforce than they would in their home country. Women have benefited from their proficiency in fields such as sales, accounting and foreign languages, which were marginalised under communism but were suddenly in high demand after 1989.

But feminism is still widely dismissed by women in the region – partly because of its endorsement by the communist system – making it difficult to tackle the problem of sexual harassment. Multinationals may be increasingly clear in their western offices as to what constitutes sexual intimidation, but the issue is often seen in much less clear-cut terms in Eastern Europe. Women there are far more used than their western counterparts to male colleagues who comment daily on their looks and dress, buy them flowers and request dates. Worse are the prevalence of pornographic pictures in offices and factories, and job advertisements – particularly common in Russia – that ask explicitly for applications from physically attractive secretaries with easy morals. In former Soviet states, the male boss is widely regarded as having 'first rights' over many of the female staff, and it is considered odd if he does not take advantage. A British manager of a multinational company in Central Asia commented: 'I can see the secretaries looking at me expectantly, wondering which one I will ask out.' He avoided mixing work and pleasure, with the result that most of the staff in his office assumed that he was gay.

Lenka Simerska, a project co-ordinator at the Gender Studies Centre in Prague, argues that many western companies often do little to enforce their own internal codes of conduct in the region. This might be because foreign managers remain confused about where to draw the line between local culture and harassment. One story illustrates this problem well. A male employee at a western-owned Hungarian firm was making incessant sexual innuendoes and put-downs to more junior female staff, reducing some to tears. It seemed like a clear-cut case of harassment, and he was eventually sacked. Hearing this, the woman who had faced most of the harassment complained that such drastic action was quite wrong, defending him as 'only being Hungarian'. He was reinstated, and his behaviour continued unchanged.[17]

Social engineering: retraining the workforce

Perhaps the greatest impact that multinationals have had on the region's workforce has been in training. Many multinationals have trained not only their high-fliers (see chapter 1), but every shop-floor worker and salesman too. For all the archaic practices and high levels of absenteeism that multinationals found in factories and offices, there was also potentially a highly energetic and motivated labour force, more so possibly than in Western Europe.

Van der Vegt notes that whereas Philips had feared a communist mentality, Hungarians in fact proved to be relatively unburdened by a West European welfare state ethos. As a result of the greater dynamism, new products that took more than a year to develop in Austria could be developed in a matter of months in East-central Europe, as was also the case in Asia. Their eagerness to learn new skills could be astounding, and their new employer was quick to provide the necessary training.

The onus was entirely on the multinationals to raise the quality of work, since no relevant training facilities and programmes existed in the region in the early 1990s. Burger giant McDonald's sent staff to its Hamburger University in Illinois, while Kraft Foods sent workers and managers from its Baltic operations to Switzerland and Scandinavia for hands-on experience with new technology. IBM and Johnson & Johnson also sent locals to company training centres abroad. Renault trained its mechanics from the former Yugoslavia at a technical centre in Novo Mesto, Slovenia. If staff were not sent abroad, then experts were brought in from western offices. Unilever provided one week's training each year for all 2728 of its factory and administrative workers in Poland, at an annual cost of some $800 000. By the mid-1990s tobacco firm Philip Morris was spending over $1m a year on training staff at its Klaipeda tobacco plant in Lithuania, which it had acquired in 1993.

Improving 'softer' business skills presented the biggest challenge. Philips offered foreign-language tuition to all its East European staff, and those who completed the initial courses went to London for advanced lessons, so that the company opened up promotional paths for secretaries and clerical staff as well as graduates. Most problematic of all were sales and customer care skills. Pizza Hut was so determined in the early years to get its Polish staff to replace glumness with smiles that customers joked about being served by grinning robots. The Polish staff at another restaurant chain could hardly believe that they were being asked to smile at strangers, and told their American manager that in Poland such behaviour was the mark of someone either dim, dangerous or a combination of the two. Western entrepreneurs took a diametrically opposed view. As one restaurateur remarked: 'I don't even want to look at someone who has been trained in a state-run vocational school'. Connex GSM, a British-owned mobile phone operator, was so concerned about Romanian surliness that it sent local engineers to Ireland, Portugal and Scandinavia for up to six weeks' training at a cost of around $30 000 per person. Even lowly sales clerks in the remotest regions were given two weeks of intensive training before being allowed to handle customer service calls. Sofitel, a French hotel chain, was if anything even less impressed by Romanian *politesse*. When its managers advertised for staff for a new hotel in Bucharest, the principal condition was that applicants must have 'no previous experience in Romanian hotels'.[18]

Places that were left untouched by the hand of competition and western-style training, such as state offices, provided a stark contrast, as the author found after arriving in June 2003 in Prague, one of the most westernised and advanced capitals of the region. It did not take long to see that below the surface of modern offices and hotels a communist (or perhaps subversive) mentality remained strong. Sending a one-page fax from the post office, for example, is a lesson in self-serving bureaucracy. The sender must fill out two forms, with the address, phone and fax numbers of both the sender and the recipient. If any of the information is missing, the fax will not be sent. The forms must be signed by the sender, and stamped and counter-signed by the clerk. Then the fax is sent – or so one must trust. The sender is not permitted to take a copy of the confirmation slip. As a favour the clerk may hold it up to the window so that the sender can see the 'Sent OK' confirmation for himself. But there is no chance to check, for example, that it went to the correct number. The sender must also sign a further document to confirm that the fax was sent, which is duly stamped and counter-signed. Finally, all the relevant documents, including a copy of the fax itself, are stapled together and filed in a drawer (irrespective of whether the document sent is confidential). And the 35 koruna cost is at least ten times the actual cost of the fax call. The sender may, however, have a receipt (stamped and signed, of course).

The tidal wave of retraining even reached the more backward, undemocratic former Soviet states in Central Asia. There were few locals with good technical skills who also spoke a western language, and it was left entirely to the investor to pass on western best practices. In early 1997 Cameco, a Canadian gold-mining company, acquired the Kumtor gold mine, which accounts for some 25 per cent of the Kyrgyz Republic's gross domestic product, and launched a comprehensive on-site educational programme for its workers in everything from heavy equipment operations and safety to business ethics and English. ChevronTexaco, which set up a lubricants manufacturing joint venture there the following year, brought over a former plant manager from the US to train the Kyrgyz workers in quality control and manufacturing procedures, while the plant's laboratory specialists were sent to ChevronTexaco's labs in Ghent, Belgium.

Often, however, the biggest problem was not ignorance but government interference. In 1996 Case, a US agricultural equipment supplier, sent 300 modern combine harvesters to Turkmenistan along with 25 western engineers who, as part of a $47m deal, would assemble the harvesters and train local farmers. The plan was simple: start by training 40 farmers, and send the best of them to Ashgabat, the capital, to become trainers themselves, thereby spreading the knowledge more quickly through the farm sector. The problems began when the Ministry of Agriculture, unaware of issues such as class size, sent not 40, but 200 agricultural workers to the first training session. The western trainers went ahead nonetheless, but soon noticed that the numbers in the class were dwindling, until only a couple of dozen students remained in the room. The locals had discovered that the trainers would not pay the students for attending the course – and the government was certainly not going to pay their wages if they were not doing any work. (None of this was mentioned to the trainers.) At the second stage, when those who had done best would be chosen as trainers, the government sent along 24 people who had not even been on the initial course, while the few who had completed the first stage lost interest because of the lack of pay. The multi-million-dollar programme had been intended to upgrade the technical skills of the entire agricultural sector, but in the end the only people who acquired the expertise to run the combine harvesters and train the nation's farmers were the four translators involved.[19]

'The people don't start at zero, they start at minus 25', said a representative of TACIS, an EU aid programme with an office in Ashgabat. 'They have a very good education but today it's mostly useless ... and the people are personally hurt when you question their competence in their speciality'.

Unfortunately, local firms do not always take on the responsibility of training their workers, and western firms in the region spend far more on training staff. For most of the last decade some 80 per cent of people who were enrolled on independent training programmes in Russia, for example, were from multinationals. According to research in the Czech Republic by PricewaterhouseCoopers, foreign firms, or companies with part foreign ownership, spent around twice as much per employee on training in 2001 than domestic-owned firms.[20] That gap was probably much greater in the early 1990s, suggesting that foreign competition has had a positive influence in the wider economy since then.

With the region's education systems falling into disrepair, governments have increasingly looked to western firms to teach both the hard and soft skills required for a modern economy. This policy is probably unwise. Multinationals cannot do everything, and governments can (and should) certainly do more if these countries are not to fall into a 'low-skills trap' by relying too heavily on their cheap, unskilled labour. Supporting retraining programmes, introducing more relevant university courses, promoting free trade, increasing labour mobility and improving road and rail links, would all help to attract higher-value investment. Successive Hungarian governments recognised that rising local wages were making the country less attractive for low-value manufacturing, and began trying to attract more sophisticated investment, such as research and development centres (see chapter 6). But in economies that appear content to rely upon their natural resources – especially Central Asian states with their generous supplies of oil, gas and cotton – the workforces will be unable to benefit fully from the meagre foreign investment that does flow in.

In conclusion, far from punishing local workforces in Eastern Europe over the past 15 years in the name of a capitalist revolution, multinationals have generally been the saviour, not the destroyer, of livelihoods. Where workers and governments have readily embraced the new environment and have tried to ensure a fair balance of interests between company profits and maintaining workers' rights, rather than simply resisting change, multinational companies have improved the life of the labour force immeasurably.

And it's not just the workers who gain. The experience of steel company LNM in Kazakhstan demonstrates how the benefits of foreign investment can extend far beyond the factory gates. As the next chapter will show, the wider communities that have relied on multinationals such as LNM have also flourished.

3
Community Care: Company Towns, Corporate Charity and Environmental Protection

'Before 1995 we were paid with bread and potatoes, now we're paid better than most people in Kazakhstan. The pay is, of course, good, and it's just a move towards capitalism to have some pay linked to production levels. It's business.'
Vladimir Medvedev, 28-year-old metal engineer at the Ispat Karmet steel works

Anti-globalisation protesters wishing to see how a big multinational company can improve the lives of ordinary people might want to take a drive through the barren steppe of central Kazakhstan to a steel town called Temirtau. After miles of bleak, uninhabited, uncultivated landscape, the sight of scores of distant industrial chimneys triumphantly puffing green-grey dust is a strangely welcome sign of life. The chimneys belong to the giant Karmet Steel Works, a truly awe-inspiring example of Stalinist industrialisation. Its blast furnaces, coking plants and rolling mills stretch out over 50 square kilometres, knitted together by 400 km of internal rail track, and employ 22 500 workers.

The billowing chimneys are a welcome sight not just for the traveller but also for the adjoining town of Temirtau, whose 170 000 citizens rely entirely on the plant's continuing success. Both the town and the mill were built during the Second World War to supply the Soviet army with steel, and Temirtau became a permanent home to the descendants of tens of thousands of Russians, Tartars, Germans and other ethnic groups who were forcibly transferred there, or to nearby labour camps. At its peak in the 1960s Karmet was one of the leading industrial producers in the Soviet Union, employing 70 000 workers and running all the town's social services. It was a good place to start a career for an ambitious young communist such as Nursultan

Nazarbayev, the future president of Kazakhstan, who worked there in the 1960s.

But the sight of Temirtau's makeshift, unfinished, rotting apartment blocks and its wide, empty streets reveals a more traumatic recent history. After the collapse of the Soviet Union in 1991, the mill could no longer rely on guaranteed orders of steel from Russia. Karmet was ill-equipped to handle life in a competitive market economy, and output tumbled by 50 per cent, dragging down not only Temirtau, but also Karaganda, its larger sister city 70 kilometres away, whose coal mines once employed 120 000 people out of a population of 600 000. Unable to cope, the steel works and the mines – like so much post-Soviet industry – simply stopped paying workers their wages, sometimes for up to nine months. At first the workers, gripped by a civic and patriotic spirit, wanted to keep the blast furnaces burning and Temirtau supplied with heat and light over the winter, and they worked without pay. 'We must not freeze the cities', proclaimed Grigory Prezent, the head of the Karaganda coal basin, rallying the workers. They responded well, expecting that their back wages would be paid eventually. 'If you don't work, you lose hope', explained one miner. Prezent flew to Almaty, the capital of Kazakhstan, to beg the state-owned power generating companies to pay their coal debts. He failed, and, since they were unable to pay Russia's electricity grid for power supplies, Temirtau and Karaganda were temporarily cut off.

Temirtau soon began to fall apart. Locals recall how people left their freezing apartment blocks to build fires for cooking or simply to keep warm. Pollution was chronic: the air was unpleasant to breathe, and drinking water was foul. Freezing Temirtau never knew a white Christmas. The snow was black, says one long-time resident working at the plant. Roads were potholed, the tram system physically and financially bust, and houses crumbled as tenants abandoned the town in search of work. Emigration soared. Karaganda's population dropped by a third, as anyone with an education got out. By 1995 the steel mill was running at less than a third of its capacity, and persistent interruptions in the supplies of coke, iron ore and electricity threatened its very existence. Unlike many manufacturing industries, steel making is a 24-hour integrated process. If the blast furnace – the heart of any steel works – dies, the plant closes down, and is hugely costly to restart. And in 1995, that is what happened. The blast furnaces flickered and finally went out, the rolling mills stopped, and the giant plant – the lifeblood of two big cities – was on the verge of collapse.

The town spiralled traumatically downward. With little hope of work, young people who were unable to flee the miserable conditions turned to heroin, opium, crack and tayan, a cheap, dangerous, home-made drug, to numb the boredom and sense of hopelessness. Drugs were easy to come by. Temirtau lies on a main trafficking route from South Asia to Europe, and plenty of locals work as drug mules to ferry drugs across the steppes.

According to a 2003 UN report:

> While there are some 1,500 IDUs [intravenous drug users] registered in Temirtau, most believe their number to be closer to 8,000 in a city of only 170,000. An estimated 10 per cent of people under 30 inject opium or heroin. Sveta Zharkova told the UN report: 'Once I tried it [crack] I couldn't stop...After I lost my job at the steel factory there was nothing else to do.' For nine years the mother-of-two used crack as her preferred choice over heroin, and at a cost of slightly more than one US dollar per dose, it was not hard to understand why. [Another,] 24-year-old Ira Rudenko, explained as she coughed phlegm into a jar placed by her bed: 'I continued to use drugs because I no longer cared about myself.'[1]

From drug addiction came Aids. The city was quickly engulfed in a frightening new epidemic as heroin needles were shared and unpro-tected prostitution increased. The number of recorded HIV+ cases in this small town soon headed towards the 1000 mark.

The UN report points out:

> It was in Temirtau that the history of HIV in Kazakhstan began ... In one year alone, 36 people tested positive for the virus – all of them addicts. One year later, of the 437 new cases registered nationwide, 400 were in Temirtau. Today, the city has the highest rate of infec-tion in the whole of Central Asia.[2]

Although the national government belatedly took the HIV crisis seri-ously, it dithered in addressing the economic priority of getting the mill and the mines up and running. The government did not want to relinquish control of an asset that had been a source of personal power for many apparatchiks, and initially limited itself to awarding manage-ment contracts to outside consultants. A consortium of managers led by US Steel was given a go, as was another from Austria's Voest Alpine, but a few flying visits from high-paid western executives were not nearly enough to save the town. The minimum requirement was for a multinational company to come in with a clear strategic business objective, billions of dollars to invest and a management team that was geared up for the challenge. Unfortunately, major western steel firms are a conservative bunch, parochial in outlook and protectionist by instinct. Given that governments in more comfortable East-central Europe were finding it hard to attract major steel investors, getting any of the big players to plough $1 billion or more into a blighted, Aids-ridden dictatorship in Central Asia seemed next to impossible.

LNM's nerves of steel

Enter LNM, a fast-growing steel group owned by Lakshmi N. Mittal, scion of an Indian steel magnate and a famous workaholic. As his CEO in Temirtau, Nawal Choudhary, points out: 'In the steel industry you have to go to where the facilities are located'. Despite the turmoil in the Karaganda region, LNM also saw advantages: tens of thousands of skilled and willing workers, humiliated by their politicians and looking for someone to save them; a production site a mere 400 kilometres from China, the fastest-growing steel market in the world; and huge facilities equipped with the solid Soviet-era machinery (albeit unserviced for decades) already familiar to India's own steel industry. At the end of 1995, a deal was done. LNM agreed to pay $400m for the moribund plant, including debts, invest an initial $850m over the first five years, and not lay off any workers. The plant was renamed Ispat Karmet (Ispat means steel in Hindi). Many experts in the industry were sceptical. Apart from the political and social risks, Karmet's traditional market, Russia, was slapping on protective tariffs, and if the mill was to export to China and Iran as LNM planned, it would have to rely on landlocked Kazakhstan's decrepit rail links. On the other hand, if the deal could be made to work, it would make LNM a serious global steel player, and could possibly trigger wider reforms in Kazakhstan.

When 36 of Mittal's toughest Indian managers rolled into Temirtau they did indeed get more than they bargained for. 'They bought a steel mill and inherited a town', as one steel analyst commented. The more LNM worked on turning around the mill, the more problems emerged. For a start, living conditions were far from satisfactory, partly because the town did not have a reliable electricity supply. In the first year of the acquisition Russia's electricity grid cut the service off 16 times for non-payment, and managers had to stumble to work by torchlight. There was little to do in the town, so the newcomers simply worked around the clock, including weekends, and took few holidays. The Kazakh managers were impressed with such commitment; the Indian managers' wives were not. 'They came over from India, took one look at the living conditions, and some went straight home again', says Uma Jha, the plant's Executive Director. (Other wives stayed and played a part in rebuilding the life of the town.)

Local reaction to LNM's arrival was at first muted, even distrustful, and the mood in the town was unrelentingly sour. The workers had already seen two sets of foreign managers come and go, and had no reason to expect anything different this time. They had no experience of working in a private enterprise, let alone a foreign firm. But attitudes changed quickly when LNM set about its first task – paying off the back wages. Even that was no simple process. There was no reliable banking system in place, and workers and suppliers had been bartering steel for basic necessities such as heating fuel or meat. LNM wanted to sweep away these wasteful and corrupt deals immediately, and inject real money into the local economy. So company executives flew to Almaty and returned with sack loads of local currency to distribute as wages, as local banks didn't have enough cash.

LNM then introduced its own financial discipline into Ispat Karmet, reconciling the books on a daily basis. For the first year, the mill's existence remained on a knife edge. Karaganda Energo, the regional electricity company, would cut supplies for weeks at a time, while increasingly militant miners were no longer prepared to work without pay, thus threatening the life of the blast furnaces. So the next step was to shore up power supplies, which represent at least one third of the costs of any steel mill. In May 1996 Ispat bought the electricity company, which had four turbo-generators with a combined capacity of 435 megawatts, and employed over 700 people. Electricity output subsequently surged from 159 Megavolts in 1996 to 351 megavolts in 2001, providing reliable supplies not only to the plant but to the whole town.

Securing coal supplies was a much bigger undertaking. LNM found that it had no alternative but to take over Karaganda's coal fields as well. Miners, like their steelworking comrades, were apprehensive about the new owners, and again Ispat quickly won them over by paying off all back wages. LNM left the existing mine managers in place, but set them strict financial targets, and then invested $180 million over the next three years in new German equipment. As a result, between 1996–2003 annual coal output rose from 7.3m tonnes to 12.6m, overall productivity doubled (quadrupling at the most efficient coal face), and coal was even exported to LNM's other major East European steel plant in Romania. An enlarged photograph on the wall of Grigory Prezent's office sums up the change: a small group of miners, with blackened, cheery faces, hold a slab of coal with '412 000 tonnes' chalked on it – a record amount of coal extracted by the new equipment of German firm DBT. DBT honoured the miners with a certificate of achievement. The scene was reminiscent of Alexey Stakhanov, the Ukrainian miner who, in a Stalinist propaganda exercise in 1935, mined 102 tonnes of coal in a day (with help from runners), 14 times the average workload, and became a Soviet hero. After the war Stakhanov came to Karaganda, where Prezent, a young miner himself, recalls working alongside his hero.

Nothing to offer but sheet, coil, bars and slabs

Back in Temirtau, life was also slowly recovering. Karmet's workers, who for the last ten years had heard empty promises of investment from the state, were finally seeing it happen. LNM completed construction of new galvanising lines and computerised the blast furnace; widened the product range of hot- and cold-rolled steel, zinc- and alumina-coated sheet metal, tin plate, pipes and slabs; and sold off slag by-products to the cement industry for road construction.

The new efficiencies spread through the plant. Suppliers who used to crowd the lobby of Ispat's newly-built hotel 'like in a bazaar' says Jha, now operated electronically. As with the mines, wages and productivity in the steel works both doubled within seven years. Workers gained high-tech training at a new $1m training centre, and LNM spent a further $1m each year to give every worker an average of 20 hours' tuition. A dozen managers and engineers were even sent to LNM's other mills in the US, Trinidad, Mexico and Indonesia, to gain experience. The machinery repair shops became businesses in their own right, as their local managers built new equipment, quadrupled output, and subsequently supplied other enterprises across the country. Most importantly, Ispat succeeded in re-orienting sales away from destitute former Soviet markets to China and the rest of Asia. Exports to non-Soviet markets rose from 20 per cent of total output to 80 per cent, and the products soon received full international quality certification.

The changes came not a moment too soon. In August 1998 the Russian economy collapsed and the rouble declined in value by around 75 per cent, wiping out that market for the foreseeable future. It is difficult to see how the Karmet steel works would have survived the shock had the mill still been in state hands, and the consequences for the town would have been unimaginable. Yet by 2003 Ispat Karmet was producing over 5m tonnes of steel, double its annual output when LNM took control, and was inching back towards once unsustainable Soviet-era levels of production. The higher output did not translate into more toxic emissions. Although steel production is generally a high-polluting activity, Karmet's dust emissions fell from 32 kg/tonne of steel produced (a level at which breathing is badly affected) to 11.7 kg/tonne, below the maximum advisable level set by the World Bank.

The democratic deficit

Taking over the coal and electricity suppliers meant that Ispat now employed over 56 000 people, far in excess of the numbers it would normally expect in order to run a large steel mill. Though it only wanted to run Karmet, it found by necessity that it had become the largest private employer in the country, with a payroll bigger than that of Kazakhstan's entire oil and gas sector. But LNM's broader involvement did not, and indeed could not, end there. As was the case in so many backward company towns in the former Soviet Union, Temirtau's government was unable to adapt to the free market, leaving Ispat Karmet to fend for itself and in effect replace the communist-era state as the provider of society's every need.

Some such contributions were understandable. Paying for a new building at the Karaganda Metallurgical Institute would increase the stream of graduates to the firm, while other 'social' contributions might be viewed as politically expedient – such as the construction of a lush tennis club where the region's power brokers could discuss their latest rackets. But many of LNM's other functions could and should be handled by local entrepreneurs or government bodies. For example, Ispat runs a textile mill that makes uniforms for the workers (and now exports its goods as well); runs the tram system to get employees to work; funds schools, youth centres and orphanages; and bankrolls the UN campaigns against AIDS and drugs in the city (although LNM did stop short of supplying free condoms to the population, when asked). Overall, Ispat Karmet estimates that it spends around $15m a year on non-steel related activities, which is enough to give plenty of hope to a destitute town.

As Baldyrgan Musin, the mayor of Temirtau, puts it, 'Temirtau is Ispat and Ispat is Temirtau' – a compliment no doubt to the many commitments that LNM has made, but hardly a ringing endorsement of the elected local government. The mayor dismisses concerns about political accountability as premature for such a new country, and also points out that Ispat pays most of its taxes to central, not local, government. LNM's managers should probably not be expected to take on the burdens of democracy-building as well, and Ispat plans eventually to pull back from many of its non-steel activities. In 1995, however, no such group, whether government agency, international institution, private enterprise or charity, was in a position to take on Temirtau's burden with the urgency, know-how and investment that was needed.

Corporate archipelago

Eastern Europe, and particularly the former Soviet Union, is littered with huge industrial concerns like Ispat Karmet that used to provide cradle-to-grave welfare for the local population. Western corporations that acquired such companies found themselves in a tricky position; should they downsize, as they might in the West, and create local upheaval, or take on what would normally be the government's responsibilities? During the 1996–97 economic meltdown in Bulgaria, Kraft Foods not only refrained from laying off staff at its factory in the town of Svorge, but imported bread for the town's inhabitants who had been left destitute by the collapsing currency. Stephen Lee, Vice President for Strategic Planning for Kraft Foods, says that in Svorge 'We are the town'. As a result Kraft probably felt that it had no choice but to step in. Alternatively, multinationals that acquire a collection of other concerns along with the main business can try to offload them, as Procter & Gamble did at its plant in Tula, Russia, spinning off non-core businesses and services to government and new private enterprises, as well as paying for retraining (see chapter 2). The attitudes of western multinationals will vary, depending on many factors. These include: the expectations of the local population; the wealth of the town and its ability to develop independent institutions; the sources of funding of the local municipality; the strength of democratic traditions; government policy; and the long-term future of the industry in question.

Take the case of Volkswagen (VW) in Mlada Boleslav, a wealthy Bohemian town 70 kilometres north-east of Prague. The German company owns the Skoda car plant, which employs 80 per cent of the town's 50 000 inhabitants (see chapter 4) and, by any reckoning, has kept Skoda – and indeed the entire town – alive a result of its investment. VW has spent heavily on environmental clean up, pays the best wages, and, like all major car plants in Eastern Europe, has attracted scores of major international auto suppliers to the area. VW-Skoda is the Czech Republic's biggest exporter, and has restored pride to a much-ridiculed car industry. It sponsors the national ice hockey team and several Czech Olympic athletes, and helps to fund the National Theatre and Philharmonic orchestra in Prague. But many Mlada Boleslav residents see things differently. Ask the town tourist office about the delights of foreign investment, and the staff are arrestingly frank about the German carmaker. 'They provide jobs – and that's it. They do nothing for the town', says one slightly embittered official. 'If you ask me', says her colleague in a half whisper, 'I don't really want the Germans here. No one likes them'. They feel that VW is using the town, its facilities and its population, while putting little back into the local community. The best that VW appears to come up with (according to its own annual report) is to sponsor a clown to visit sick children in hospital.

As Zdenek Barinka, the chief economist in the office of the local mayor, explains, the problem is that like many towns, Mlada Boleslav only receives direct payments from the national government. These amount to a small proportion of what Skoda pays to the treasury. Since the central government cut the town's annual funding in 2000 from around $20m to $13m, the municipality found it too expensive to undertake projects such as road repairs, or to fund local arts, entertainment and sports facilities. At the same time, the giant Skoda plant has a distorting effect on the local economy. Because the company helps to finance car purchases for its employees, the town is congested and parking is tight. And, as Barinka points out, although people are relatively well off, prices are also high. Real estate agencies in the area report that property values are rising by around 20 per cent a year.

However, the problems of Mlada Boleslav are relatively slight compared with those in central Kazakhstan, and it might be hard for VW to convince its own shareholders of the need for greater community involvement. Helping to finance the local theatre in Mlada Boleslav might be a nice thing to do, but is hardly pressing compared to the needs of other, poorer company towns.

US Steel found itself in a different situation in 2000 when it acquired the East Slovak Steel works (VSZ) in Kosice, near the Ukrainian border, and inherited a wide range of social obligations. US Steel chose to continue many of these and has involved itself in many other business, social and charitable projects. It has spent around $6m supporting mainly children, healthcare, sports and educational projects in the town. The firm actively tries to attract other investors to Eastern Slovakia – an area of high unemployment – including those not involved in steel making. Christopher Navetta, the president of US Steel Kosice, says that since acquiring the plant the firm has launched two investment roadshows in the US and seven in Europe. These have resulted in eight new firms setting up in the region, employing around 1000 people. US Steel has also maintained its support for the regional investment development agency, beyond the two-year period to which it agreed.

By most accounts the town appreciates such efforts. US Steel's Christmas street entertainment attracts 10 000 people or more. Its children's day brings around 5000 to the local zoo, many of whom return, thereby keeping the zoo in business. 'It doesn't matter about the nationality of the company. Things are better now than they have ever been. I am optimistic', says Maria, the 72-year-old curator of the local art museum, who has lived in the city for 50 years. 'We need foreign companies to come and show us how to work better', says Kamila, a young hotel receptionist who has lived in the UK. A local Communist Party activist collecting signatures for a petition against the government and capitalism in general could have complained about the fact that US Steel Kosice made a profit of $61m in 2002 and paid no tax. Yet he admits that the company has been a force for good; no one was made redundant at the plant, and wages there have risen by 30 per cent over 3 years.

Gypsy knights

US Steel has also tried to address the more contentious, demanding issue of helping Eastern Slovakia's Roma population (commonly referred to as gypsies) back into the workforce. The Roma community is utterly marginalised, with unemployment as high as 90 per cent in some villages. Distrust among the general population is widespread and mutual, fuelling a vicious cycle of rejection, unemployment and poverty. The social sore cannot be ignored, but US Steel may be out of its depth in trying to solve it. The US firm launched a pilot scheme for Velka Ida, a large village that adjoins the plant, to get its Roma inhabitants integrated into the workforce. One third of the inhabitants are Roma, and live in alarming poverty, with grimy-faced children gambolling around the rubbish tips. Integrating many of these bright-faced, but alienated and unskilled villagers into a modern workforce takes attention, patience and delicacy, and the process cannot be rushed, according to Navetta. 'It's crawl, walk, run', he says.

The arrival in Velka Ida of a western journalist generates a small crowd of villagers scrambling and yelling their complaints. 'When are you going to build us new houses?' shouts one young woman, gesturing towards a tiny one-room hut where a bedraggled mother lives with 11 children. Children of all ages crowd around. 'Why aren't you at school?' they are asked. They giggle as if the question were ridiculous. They ask if we are from Belgium, where, they have heard, life is better. The children playfully shout out their few words of English ('how are you?'), and look at the bags we are carrying, hoping that they contain presents for them. They are asked if life is better with the Americans running the steel mill. There is a momentary pause, and the haranguing stops. 'Yes, they are trying to help us', says a middle-aged man who works for the village municipality. Then the tirade of complaints and demands starts up again.

The new programme allows Frantisek Snir, the non-Roma village leader, to select the Roma, all of whom he knows personally, to get jobs. There is always a surplus of Roma who want to work. 'Work is worth it for Roma with fewer than five children', he says cynically, comparing the wage with the amount they can claim through state welfare. Snir admits that he did not expect the Roma to turn up to their first day's work on time. They all did, and as a result there was not enough room on the bus. Non-Roma in the village are unhappy about the selection, and a few of them get preferential treatment too. Currently, 50 Roma have low-skilled jobs in the mill, such as guarding the perimeter fence, at a good (by local standards) net monthly wage of $200. However, the village leader, not the steel firm, distributes the pay 'to ensure that the Roma spend the money responsibly, says Snir, a 'precaution' that makes the whole process worryingly untransparent.

Besides charitable works and affirmative action, US Steel has helped to create a more transparent business environment in Kosice. Take the example of Peter Sekura, a bio-technology graduate, who was in the Czechoslovak army when the 1989 revolution began. Disgusted by the contamination left by the departing Soviet army – oil soaked a metre deep into the soil – he saw a business opportunity in environmental clean up services, an unheard-of notion at the time. 'It was something new and exciting to set up a joint-stock company', he says. He now employs 42 people, and the steel mill is one of his clients. Before US Steel arrived, winning a clean-up contract from the local cronies who ran the steel works was a highly complicated, almost impossible, task.

Every project had a middleman, who employed subcontractors. No one seemed to work directly for the firm. The middlemen were skilled in finding the right malleable person to bribe inside the organisation. The 'predators', as Sekura calls the middlemen, took 300–400 per cent mark-ups from the company. There was a 'special market for corruption... a bribes market, like a stock market, with well-known players who could extract the most money', he explains (see chapter 7).

The pity was that the town had skilled people who desperately wanted to use their talents in a productive and responsible manner. 'We had the skills; we just needed a reasonable system to work within', says Sekura. The arrival of US Steel quickly cleared out the middlemen, and Sekura was able to pitch his services directly to the firm. Corruption undoubtedly continues in Kosice, but it no longer defines the way people do business.

Charity begins at work

Although company towns tend to place a greater social burden on the foreign investor, the picture of multinationals' communal involvement in less demanding situations in the region is mixed. In general they will extend their global policy on charities to Eastern Europe. Some firms go well beyond normal obligations, others don't care, and many do a little but boast of having done a tremendous amount. Procter & Gamble supports graduate research in economics and backs municipal 'green cities' campaigns in towns where it has a plant. Detergent maker Henkel follows group guidelines, supporting economics programmes at universities, giving internships to top students, donating to local children's charities and supporting young artists across the region. Amylum group, part of sugar producer Tate & Lyle, is proud of its contribution to street lighting in the town of Razgrad in North East Bulgaria, as a result of which the local population 'can now see the potholes', jokes Matthew Trilling, the regional head of Amylum. Tesco has tried to emphasise its local commitment by spending a few thousand euros to support charities chosen by its shoppers in Central Europe – particularly children's groups. However, Zdenek Trebula, the mayor of Kosice (where Tesco has hypermarkets), scornfully notes that the retailer 'heads the group of foreign investors who do little for us' – a characterisation that Tesco wholly rejects.

Not all multinational charity comes straight from the heart; indeed, intimidation and public relations are usually bigger motivations. Multinational investors say that they get approached all the time by local authorities to help fund a school or hospital, build a road or clean a river. LNM was asked, and agreed, to build a $1m orthodox Christian church in Galati, eastern Romania, where it runs the Sidex steel mill. Refusal can in some cases trigger intense scrutiny by the tax office, the health and safety inspectors and many more municipal bodies (see chapter 7). As a result, some firms ride out the investigations, while others pay up with a forced smile and hope that good public relations justify the concession.

Philanthropy can certainly go a long way towards improving a company's image, and attempting to distinguish genuine acts of corporate social responsibility from those motivated by PR considerations is close to impossible. The bigger question is whether companies should be involved at all in good works that are unrelated to their actual operations. Corporations have a primary duty to shareholders, which principally involves increasing the company's value. Many firms argue that if individual shareholders wish to make their own charitable donations, they can do so privately. Some major multinational managers say privately that they are embarrassed by generous social contributions that make them look soft-hearted while contributing little in the way of shareholder value. As The Economist wrote: 'From an ethical point of view, the problem with conscientious (as opposed to fake) CSR is obvious: it is philanthropy at other people's [the shareholders'] expense'.[3] There are, after all, plenty of more relevant ethical issues to attend to: cutting pollution levels; guarding against bribery; adopting international codes of corporate behaviour that go beyond the local law; and, not least, monitoring the behaviour of suppliers or subcontractors on issues such as the use of child labour. If locals then want the investor to contribute more to the community, they must justify their demands within the context of the firm's corporate obligations. The Mlada Boleslav municipality would need to demonstrate that VW-Skoda is not just being merely ungenerous with its charitable contributions but has in fact caused distortions in the local economy which needs correcting, if the town is to receive much more than the company clown.

There is opposition to corporate social responsibility from other quarters too. Some local suppliers, especially in the former Soviet Union, have criticised it as a ploy by western multinationals to exclude local firms from supply tenders on the pretext that they cannot match western quality of governance. For the losers in this process, corporate social responsibility is little more than a notice that 'local firms need not apply', says Simon Bryceson, a former environmental activist and now a specialist advisor to multinationals on social matters. However, such accusations could also be sour grapes on the part of the tender losers. Multinationals may have good reasons to keep an existing international team in place and not bother with opening tenders for suppliers or subcontractors up to local firms. Pharmaceutical groups have an additional fear that newly appointed subcontractors may subsequently steal their products.

For most firms, however, social responsibility comes down to a simple assessment of commercial risk and reward. Are the public relations benefits worth the cost? Firms believe that they usually are. A good public image 'makes recruiting much easier', says Chris Fox, public affairs manager of Tate & Lyle, and can even help to secure exploration licences in the US, admits one oil industry executive. Good PR doesn't always ensure that people will buy more of a company's products, but pressure-group campaigns targeting a well-known brand can hurt sales. Avoiding controversy means that top managers do not waste time having to handle a publicity crisis. Companies in sensitive industries, such as tobacco, tend to emphasise their wider social involvement more emphatically. British American Tobacco, which has a large plant in Russia, is involved in extensive dialogue with 'stakeholders', and holds regular public discussions about what it should be doing for the local community.

Environment matters

Accidents will happen

Perhaps one of the greatest improvements in the quality of life in Eastern Europe since 1989 has been in the environment. Western visitors to Prague in the early 1990s would be shocked to see and smell a pungent green cloud hovering over the beautiful city – a testament to the foul nature of communist environmental neglect. The combination of popular revulsion against this legacy, the desire to meet EU environmental standards, and the arrival of multinational companies with less harmful production processes has been a breath of fresh air to many in the region. The odours are still there further east and south, however, with an ever-present stink of leaded petrol in most Balkan and Soviet cities, and the continuing pollution of rivers by state-owned industrial giants. 'The legacy of environmental contamination left behind by Communism is staggering: 65 per cent of Poland's rivers are too polluted even for industrial use; 80 per cent of Prague's annual output of

40 000 tonnes of hazardous waste is untraceable; 73 per cent of the forests in the former Czechoslovakia have been severely affected by acid rain', according to Lynda J. Oswald, an environmental and business expert.[4] Pollution is generally not the fault of multinational companies, according to Jan Haverkamp of Greenpeace in the Czech Republic. 'The situation is better in [firms] with foreign capital ... the problem is in the monopolies that are state-run', he says.

The higher standards of environmental care among western manufacturers are partly the result of pressure-group campaigns in the West over the last few decades. East European governments have been quick to demand the same standards from foreign investors, placing stringent requirements on them to clear up communist-era environmental damage in the firms that they acquired through privatisation. When Kraft Foods acquired its factory in Svorge, Bulgaria, the company was alarmed to find that waste water from the plant was sent straight into the local river. Having seemingly closed their eyes to this practice before, the local authorities immediately asked Kraft to introduce high treatment standards for the non-toxic effluent discharges that came from its coffee, chocolate and salty snack production. Kraft says that the stretch of river after the factory is now cleaner than the upstream section. Henkel, a German detergent producer, carried out a similar environmental clean-up of part of the Tisza river in Hungary in 1992. The local authorities, which were concerned about pollution in a river used for swimming, subsequently found that the water downstream from the Henkel plant was cleaner than that upstream. Many other western companies tell similar stories.

When Shell bought Chemapol Litvinov, a Czech chemical company, it had to close down two-thirds of its operations, largely for environmental reasons. VW had a tough job cleaning up Skoda after 1991 and spent nearly $300m on environmental investment – far beyond its legal obligations – mainly to improve the plant's dreadful emissions record. US Steel also spent heavily, investing an estimated $750m in new dumps, dedusting technology and emissions reduction, in preparation for Slovakia's EU accession. Swedish furniture maker Ikea says that it will not work with any logging firm that operates in areas defined as young forests by Global Forest Watch, an environmental group. Ikea has turned down numerous wood suppliers in Russia for that reason, according to Kjellowe Rahlskoj, the firm's global forestry manager.

The relationship between multinationals and environmental groups is not always harmonious. A particularly acrimonious dispute broke out in 2001 between the authorities in the western Czech town of Plzen and Nemak, a Mexico-based car parts producer in which Ford has a 20 per cent stake. Nemak was looking to build a plant to make aluminium cylinder heads – a process involving aluminium recycling, which results in heavy dioxin emissions. Protestors in Plzen told Nemak to take their dirty business elsewhere, and the Czech investment agency offered the company a less problematic industrial area in Most, north of Prague. But Nemak wanted more pleasant surroundings for its workers, and threatened to leave the country altogether (though it eventually went to Most). In general, however, when multinationals fall short of environmental standards, it is often because local managers do not properly implement codes of conduct set out by head office.

Extracting the Mickey

If the environmental impact of multinationals in the manufacturing sector has been broadly positive, the same cannot always be said for those in extractive industries such as gold mining and oil, especially in the remoter parts of the region. Petr Hlobil, international oil and climate co-ordinator for Bankwatch, a non-governmental organisation (NGO) that monitors projects financed by international financial institutions, especially the European Bank for Reconstruction and Development (EBRD), claims that almost all multinational investments in the extractive industries are contentious in some respect.

Perhaps understandably, extractive companies simply want to get to the goods lying below ground, and get out as quickly and with as few risks as possible. Their main requirements are political stability and minimum outside interference. However, although large projects may have economic benefits for an entire country or region, the local community generally bears the environmental (and other) costs. As the World Bank concluded in a review of its own lending policies: 'Often the accelerated selling off of key mineral and hydrocarbon assets, mostly to foreign investors, resulted in contracts that locked in weak environmental and social standards for ten years or more'.[5] In corrupt, authoritarian states where so much of the world's precious resources lie, the financial benefits are usually enjoyed by a fabulously rich ruling elite, and the local communities that bear the brunt of the projects seldom get either compensation or the benefits (referred to by economists as positive spillovers) from the investment.

One of the biggest negative spillovers occurred on 20 May 1998 near the Kumtor gold mine in Kyrgyzstan, one of the largest mines in the former Soviet Union, which was being developed by a joint venture between Canadian mining company Cameco and the Kyrgyz government. A truck carrying packs of cyanide (used to extract gold) slid out of control, and more than a tonne of its contents spilt into the Barskaun river. The town authorities say that 2577 people, most of them from the nearby town, were poisoned and 850 hospitalised, of whom at least four died, according to the Kyrgyz health ministry. Pressure groups say that the true figure is probably higher still, once misdiagnoses are taken into account, although the consequences for the environment, at least in the short term, appeared to be contained.[6]

What worried environmental groups was not only the accident itself but the inadequacy of the emergency response plans, given the inherently dangerous nature of cyanide. Local people, for example, were only informed of the spill by the authorities five hours after it occurred, and were still using contaminated water. The situation would have been worse had a soldier standing on the bridge not witnessed the crash and raised the alarm.

The Kumtor spill was not an exception. On 30 January 2000, a dam broke at a gold mine in the northern Romanian town of Baia Mare, allowing 50–100 tonnes of cyanide and other heavy metals to flood into the Sasar, Lapus, Somes, Tisza and Danube rivers. The spill left a toxic trail all the way to the Black Sea, killing fish in Hungary and Yugoslavia, and caused interruptions to the water supplies of at least 24 municipalities in the area. Mine operator Aurul, a 50:50 joint venture between Australian firm Esmerelda Exploration and the Romanian state mining company, had been warned by environmental groups that monitoring and safeguards at the dam were insufficient. The use of cyanide in gold mining, already controversial, was particularly worrying so close to a large river system. The irony is that Esmerelda, which had waited seven years to obtain all the necessary environmental permits from the Romanian authorities before it could begin operations, was brought in specifically to help clean up existing contaminated ponds, enabling the town to expand. The firm had arrived with state-of-the-art technology to extract residual gold, which was to be used as payment for their clean-up work. Tom Popper of the Regional Environmental Centre in Budapest refers to it as 'one of Europe's worst environmental disasters'.[7]

Esmerelda had planned to build up the dam over time, but was caught out by a combination of heavy rains and melting snows that raised the contaminated water level over the edge. Although the company blamed freak weather conditions ('the worst in 50 years', according to the company), such a scenario was predictable. Even though Romanian law did not require extensive anti-flood and other safeguards, or any special emergency planning, these should have been in place, and subsequently were. As with Kumtor, what infuriated local people was the failure to plan for the unexpected. The lesson was clear: cutting corners in situations where environmental controls are less stringent is a recipe for disaster.

Yet the impact of the spill was not as bad as indicated by contemporary press reports, and some suspected that the Hungarian media may have been exaggerating the damage because of political and ethnic axes to grind with Romania. Heavy rains subsequently diluted the spill and washed it into the Black Sea, and although many fish were killed, aquatic micro-organisms recovered within a few days. The attitude of Esmerelda may have been unforgivable, but it is also worth bearing in mind that the spill was a drop in the river compared to the decades of communist pollution in the area. As one UN report points out:

> The county has high levels of chronic ('persistently recurring') soil, water and air contamination that comes from many pollutants. These were released over decades of past industrial activities that used environmentally unsound technologies .... Some Baia Mare residents live within 50 metres of highly toxic, chronically leaking, waste sites. The World Health Organisation identifies Baia Mare as a health risk hotspot, with the population's exposure to lead being among the highest ever recorded. Lead in the blood of some adults averages almost 2.5 times above safety levels. In some children, it averages nearly six times above safety levels. High lead levels in humans are now thought to be associated with impaired learning ability, mental retardation, problems with kidney and neurological functions, hearing loss, blood disorder, hypertension and death. Baia Mare residents have complained about dust from industrial processes for some time.[8]

Pipe dreams from Baku to Ceyhan

Lesser-known mining companies are not the only foreign investors accused of cutting corners on environmental protection while hoping that the worst won't happen. Huge oil and gas multinationals such as BP or Royal Dutch/Shell appear to take their social responsibilities seriously, but have been somewhat late in accepting the need for more planning and better local consultation over potential disaster scenarios – especially in the remoter areas of the former Soviet Union where accountability is weakest. Perhaps the most controversial project is the proposed Baku-Tbilisi-Ceyhan (BTC) pipeline, a $2.9 billion investment led by BP and part-financed by the World Bank and the EBRD. The pipeline will bring Caspian and Central Asian oil and gas to Western Europe via Azerbaijan, Georgia and a marine terminal near Ceyhan in southern Turkey. The idea for the pipeline evolved in the early 1990s but was subject to numerous delays, and construction did not begin until 2003. The project is expected to be completed in 2005.

The delays and difficulties in the project reflect not only commercial but also huge geo-strategic calculations. The pipeline will unleash vast supplies of new oil onto world markets and will circumvent not only Iran but also Russia, thereby potentially diminishing the latter's influence in its own 'back yard'. For these reasons, the project has strong US support, and it is also backed by the UK, partly because BP is leading the consortium. The biggest supporters of all have been the governments of Azerbaijan and Georgia, through which the pipeline is routed, which stand to earn billions of dollars in transit fees. Azerbaijan has a strong authoritarian government, as did Georgia until 2004. Such powerful backing has raised questions as to whether the concerns of the relatively powerless local communities along the route will be properly taken into account.

The project should involve a thorough and open consultation process, a fair and transparent compensation mechanism for those whose land is expropriated, and a full assessment of possible environmental risks. 'The level of consultation was unprecedented', says Tobi Adone, a BP spokesman. 'We didn't have to do it, but we want to work to the highest standards'. Local and international NGOs see things differently. Two originally proposed routes for the pipeline went close to the Armenian border, and were not considered to be an environmental threat. But these were rejected by the BTC consortium because of the perceived risk of terrorism from over the Armenian border – arguments dismissed as absurd by NGOs. The third (and most probable) route crosses two major waterways, two landslide hazard areas and the Borjomi-Khargauli national park, a 6000 hectare nature preserve in central Georgia. The principal environmental concern was that the proposed pipeline would go through areas of high seismic activity and would be vulnerable to landslides. These could result in leakages, and pollute a renowned mineral spring and local water supplies in Borjomi. The technically less advanced Baku-Supsa oil pipeline in Georgia, which was built in 1997–99, has experienced leakages.

Moreover, NGOs were worried that it would take far longer than the stated ten minutes to close the valve on any such leak in the BTC pipeline, given the difficulty of transporting response teams to the snowy mountains where the BTC pipeline would be buried. According to one calculation by Georgian scientists, delays could result in 20 000 gallons of oil invading the surrounding environment. Many groups, including the Dutch Commission for Environmental Impact Assessment and the Georgian science academy, expressed concern. The Worldwide Fund for Nature (WWF) concluded that 'BP/BTC has not carried out sufficient research and analysis of the impacts to justify putting a pipeline through this area'.

Although Georgians had the chance to put such questions to BTC officials at specially organised meetings in Borjomi and Tbilisi, these meetings revealed not only the inadequacy of the answers but also major shortcomings in the entire consultation process. Local journalist Ursula Kazarian says that when she asked about these risks, she reports that she was told that her 'background information regarding the amount of spilled oil was incorrect, although the correct amount was not immediately retrievable as the report was elsewhere.' After chasing up the BTC official during the coffee break, she reports: 'Finally it came out: the official Oil Spill Response Plan was still 'under development' and would not be available to the public until November.... How could anyone make an informed decision regarding something as serious as constructing and burying a 1770 km pipeline without a complete and detailed Response Plan?'.[9]

BP says that it is now implementing failsafe measure to avoid a major spill. The company points out that the pipes are half an inch thick, the thickest BP pipes anywhere in the world, and are less vulnerable than other pipes it uses to seismic shifts. The company says that it adopted eight specific conditions set out by the Georgian government to minimise environmental risks. Most notably, the BTC consortium has doubled the numbers of sensors and safety valves on the pipeline section that goes through the Borjomi region, and claims that the pipeline would close down within one minute should there be any leak or disruption. The consortium has also organised local horseback patrols to monitor any attempt at sabotage. Yet within weeks of this apparent shift towards greater safety, BP was facing new, equally worrying allegations that it had incorrectly applied coating for the pipes and that cracks had been found in the joints of pipes yet to be laid. According to UK press reports, 15 000 such joints had already been laid, and the cost of digging them up and recoating them could be around $500m.

The potential danger of the BTC pipeline and other natural resource projects is that foreign corporations fail to consult openly with stakeholders and cut corners on safety risks, believing that accidents probably will not happen. This danger is magnified by the fact that major western energy firms are often forced to deal with unpleasant authoritarian regimes. Bankwatch and other NGOs claim that the BTC consultation procedure – a lending criterion of the EBRD – had numerous failings that had all the hallmarks of the low-key 'agenda control' typical of authoritarian political systems. Key documents were not translated, information leaflets were poorly distributed, there was too little publicity of meetings, and the attendees, often government-connected NGOs, were preselected. Meetings were too short for a proper discussion, with much of the time taken up by non-simultaneous translation. Genuine participants complained of receiving inadequate answers to their questions (or none at all). Were these the sort of organisational errors to be expected in a country unused to public consultation, or were they part of a deliberate carve-up? Nothing is clear. Locals suspect that the public hearing involved just a tiny fraction of those interested in attending, and that those present had been warned to show nothing but fierce support.[10]

Those independent, local NGOs or individuals who do dissent are indeed taking personal risks by speaking out:

> [Azerbaijan prime minister] Aliyev threatened to punish anyone opposed to the Baku-Tbilisi-Ceyhan project or questioning the disbursement of money from State Oil Fund. In Georgia, high level officials openly stated during various meetings – including a public hearing in the Georgian Parliament – that citizens who raise concerns about safety, environmental and land compensation issues in front of International Financial Institutions represent 'traitors to the state'.[11]

Organised crime is another reason for locals to be afraid. When the names of those obtaining compensation for land expropriation were published, criminal gangs were quick onto the scene:

> ...criminal groups extort 20 per cent of the compensation fee from landowners... [who] are afraid to give evidence and to speak out due to the prevailing insecurity. ...one landowner was robbed of $7000 by this criminal group. The people of the Borjomi and Akhaltsikhe regions have accused local government representatives and criminal groups alike of robbery and vandalism.[12]

BP has urged the Georgian and Azerbaijani authorities to ensure that their oil transit revenues are made transparent, with the IMF monitoring the flow of funds. Whether such measures will be sufficient to ensure that ordinary people see the benefits of the BTC pipeline is doubtful, given the countless methods by which these governments can fleece their people, and the fact that the project will create only a few hundred long-term jobs. The BTC consortium members have made some effort to mitigate this, financing a three-year, $16m project to help local communities along the pipeline route in Georgia and Azerbaijan. The project, to be run by local NGOs, is aimed at restoring plant and animal life disrupted by the pipeline's construction. Otherwise BP claims to have little influence over where the Georgian or Azerbaijan government's oil revenue goes. But many suspect that the money will not flow to those who most need help. Petr Hlobil recalls a meeting with a refugee from the Nagorny-Karabakh conflict, which neatly sums up the situation. 'She was sitting on top of the Baku-Supsa pipeline, resting after collecting firewood. Although millions of dollars of revenues were flowing right underneath her, as a refugee she had no chance of getting a job, and received food from the state for only 50 days a year.' Hlobil wants to ensure that the BTC project does not lead to the same state of affairs.

Big fish in Sakhalin

Non-governmental groups are equally critical of Shell, which heads a consortium including Japanese firms Mitsui and Mitsubishi that is developing a huge oil and gas project on Russia's far eastern island of Sakhalin, barely 40 miles north of Japan. The Shell consortium, Sakhalin Energy Investment Company ('Sakhalin-II'), follows the Sakhalin I project led by US oil company Exxon, which began work in 1996. Sakhalin II is investing $10 billion, the largest ever foreign investment in Russia, to develop two major oil and gas deposits, and build two oil and gas platforms, a liquefied natural gas plant and terminal, and two 800-kilometre oil and gas pipelines stretching the length of the island. The project began producing oil in mid-1999, and is expected to continue doing so for decades.

Sakhalin Environmental Watch, a local pressure group, argues that the project poses several major environmental risks. The pipelines will cross more than a thousand rivers and streams, home to the salmon stock that forms a crucial part of the local economy, so any pipeline damage could jeopardise local livelihoods. In addition, the territory is in a sensitive seismic area where earthquakes could reach nine on the Richter scale.

Shell claims that its underground pipelines are safe enough. 'Sakhalin Energy has studied the route of its onshore pipelines extensively, and has selected a route that avoids active faults wherever possible. This has already reduced the number of active faults crossed by our pipelines to 24. ...The pipeline is designed to withstand earthquakes predicted to occur once every 1000 years', says Rachele Sheard, Head of Issues & Stakeholder Management for Sakhalin Energy.

Sheard adds that the project is expected to generate some $45 billion of tax revenue for the Russian treasury over its lifetime. However, Russian oil analysts expect that the figure will be lower because of cost overruns. Others question how much of the money will end up in Sakhalin, let alone in ordinary people's pockets. Shell says that it is contributing $100m to the 'Sakhalin development fund', which promotes various social and environmental projects, and that the project will create 3000 jobs during the construction phase. But critics say that many workers will be brought in from outside and will live in self-contained, self-sufficient encampments giving little help to the local economy. Shell also claims that major improvements have been made to the island's public infrastructure system, including upgrading municipal roads and bridges, the Nogliki Airport, the railway system and Kholmsk Fishing Port. But opponents claim that basic infrastructure only gets a facelift when the consortium itself needs better bridges or roads in the north of the island. 'It took six months to negotiate $0.5m worth of repairs to a bridge that had been damaged by the transport of oil', says an indignant Hlobil. Despite the island's natural wealth, an estimated half of the 600 000 population are living below the poverty line, many in unheated apartments. Shell promises to gasify the island, but this will be of little help to locals if they are charged international prices when the gas does finally come on line.

The project may also threaten the feeding habitat near the northern shore of Sakhalin of the last hundred or so western pacific grey whales left in existence, particularly the females. 'In 1999, scientists for the first time reported "skinny whales", or whales that were showing visible signs of malnutrition. By 2000, 27 skinny whales ... had been identified', reports Sakhalin Environmental Watch. Vassily Spiridanov, a marine programme co-ordinator for the WWF, notes that the condition of the whales was caused by disease and not the Shell-led project, but says that the building of new underwater pipelines could seriously undermine their chances of recovery. Scientists at Russia's Marine Mammal Council say that moving the platforms just 12 km further out to sea would offer the whales sufficient protection against sonar disruption. NGOs accuse Shell of ignoring its contractual obligations to discuss seriously such alternative plans. 'There is plenty of local anger in the area', notes Hlobil, who claims that Shell 'behaves like a big fish and does not believe that it must consult with anyone'.

Again, Shell denies this. 'The location of the offshore platforms and pipelines reflects the need to balance safety, technical feasibility and to minimize the impact on the marine environment .... The mitigation measures designed by the company to protect marine mammals are based on seven years of research and work with Russian and international bodies', says Sheard.

However, the WWF accuses the consortium of concluding its research too late to affect its plans – and therefore too late to encourage a meaningful discussion about preserving the lives of the whales. EBRD President Jean Lemierre also expressed reservations in April 2004. 'We are not yet satisfied with the answers we have received and the present situation, and we have said so to the sponsors of the project, with whom we are working', he says.[13]

How much responsibility should a major corporation have to those people affected by a huge project under an authoritarian regime, given that the consultation process may well be a sham? Can the multinational hide behind national sovereignty and blame the problem on an undemocratic government? Or must it either urge the government to be more transparent in its own dealings, or take on some of the burden of compensation and redistribution itself, to ensure that help is actually delivered? Oil firms may point out that they have to go to where the oil is, not where they would like to operate, and often have to sign confidentiality clauses regarding how the money that flows from the projects is spent. But UNDP officials say that such agreements also work in the interests of the oil companies, since it may be easier to turn a blind eye to financial malpractice than confront it. Looking out for those who lose out is still a work in progress. For multinationals, going part of the way is not far enough.

4

The Rebirth of Industry: Finance, Phones and Cars

'A money-losing, run-down plant and a foreigner wants to buy it? We should be so lucky if we find a fool in the West who wants to buy it and try to make it profitable. Everyone will benefit from that, except perhaps the Western investor'.

Vaclav Klaus[1]

When the communist system in Czechoslovakia collapsed in 1989, the economy ministry was quick to invite advisors to help sort out the country's industry. Ivor McElveen, an Irishman with extensive experience in the UN, the World Bank and the EU, arrived in 1990 to help set up CzechInvest, a quasi-independent bureau with the job of attracting investment from foreign companies. He took a trip to the colossal Skoda engineering works in Plzen, near the German border. The state-owned company was pumping out locomotive engines designed specifically for the Russian market – except that there was no market anymore. McElveen asked why the company was still producing these engines if no one was buying them. Because no one told us to stop, they replied. 'So I told them, 'Stop!', and they did', he says.

Such timely intervention looked set to save the company; German industrial giant Siemens was ready to come to the rescue and sign joint-venture deals with parts of the rambling conglomerate. Unfortunately, the investor was unable to disentangle Skoda's messy ownership structure, and the deal was called off. The Czech company moved in and out of state management, while attempting its own complicated restructuring plan under controversial local manager Lubomir Soudek.[2]

The story illustrates how precariously adrift so much communist-era industry had become in 1990. Unlike Skoda Plzen, however, many sectors of the economy were indeed saved by the intervention of large western corporations, as this chapter will show. Multinationals brought about huge changes in East-central Europe in the automotive, banking, brewing, chemicals, electricity, electronics, petrochemicals, pharmaceuticals, pulp and paper, retailing, steel, telecommunications and tobacco sectors. Although in some cases, the main contribution of the foreign investor was a lot of cash to the treasury during privatisation, local industry usually gained from the introduction of management know-how and marketing and the cultivation of export markets, and whole swathes of communist-era industry were restructured.

Western firms had a less dramatic impact in Russia, where there was far less privatisation, and where continuing high political risks deterred investors from establishing new plants. The oil and gas sector has been a relatively recent exception to this trend. In 2003, BP ploughed $4.25 billion into a merger of its Russian oil operations with those of local company TNK (see chapter 7), and a Shell-led consortium plans to pour around $10 billion into an oil and gas development project on Sakhalin Island in Russia's far east (see chapter 3). But the main players in the sector remained under the control of either the state – in the cases of gas company Gazprom and pipeline monopoly Transneft – or local oligarchs. Western multinationals have been kept out of the big oil privatisations, and spent much of the 1990s trying to obtain production-sharing agreements from the government before investing. Russian companies, meanwhile, stole a march on their potential foreign competitors by hiring top international managers, and introducing the latest technology to reduce extraction costs.

Western energy companies have played a larger role in Central Asia and the Caucasus, specifically in Kazakhstan and Azerbaijan. Kazakhstan has attracted almost all the western oil majors to search for and develop onshore and offshore fields, and to build pipelines to markets in Russia and the West. The most notable project is the one led by Italian oil firm ENI to develop the Kashagan field in the Caspian Sea, believed to be the world's largest oil find in 30 years. In Azerbaijan, several western consortia have formed joint ventures with SOCAR, the state oil company, which is run by Ilham Aliyev, the former President's son and successor. Turkmenistan, which draws almost all of its wealth from natural gas fields, has agreements with a variety of western gas companies. The Kyrgyz Republic has placed its main gold mine, Kumtor – one of the world's top ten – in the hands of Canada's Cameco.

Of all the sectors that multinational companies have created or rehabilitated in Eastern Europe since 1989, the three that have had the widest impact on the rest of the economy and society are banking, tele-communications and car manufacturing. These sectors between them account for the majority of all non-oil sector investment in the region, and are the main subjects of this chapter.

An efficient banking system is the lifeblood of any modern economy, channelling savings to where they are most needed and where the returns are highest. When banks fail to work the entire economy is hobbled, forcing firms to seek finance from their suppliers (usually by not paying them) or out of their own profits (if there are any), and in the more backward regions, to rely on barter trade. The western banks that arrived in Eastern Europe during the 1990s have lent money on the basis of business plans and not the needs of the government, have introduced a slew of new products to underbanked markets, have lowered lending rates, and in most cases have strengthened banking oversight. New technology, better management and huge investment have also transformed the region's telephone companies, and, with them, the lives of ordinary people and businesses alike. This chapter also focuses on the development of the car industry (often referred to as the 'industry of industries' because of the broad range of other sectors that are involved in production). The automotive sector has attracted more foreign investment than any other manufacturing industry in the region, creating a major industrial hub in East-central Europe in the process, and reviving a longstanding, but decaying, car making tradition.

Banking: a new account

John Vax, formerly managing director for Central and Eastern Europe at Commerzbank Securities, is fond of putting the region's banking problems into perspective. In the US, he explains, a bank will normally operate with non-performing loans (NPLs) accounting for around 0.5 per cent of its total loan portfolio. Regulators take a closer look when that share goes over one per cent. If it gets close to five per cent, the bank may come under administration, and above that level, insolvency beckons.

Leading Czech bank Ceska Sporitelna, by contrast, had an NPL ratio of 45 per cent before it was sold to a foreign bank in 1999. Komercni Banka, its main rival, had a 38 per cent NPL ratio, and the sector as a whole had bad debts of around 32 per cent. The 'Czech way' of running a banking system was dysfunctional and costly. The bailout bill amounted to more than $10 billion over the course of the 1990s, with the state assuming $7 billion of bad debts, equivalent to some 14 per cent of the country's 2002 GDP.

The mess in the Czech Republic was bad, but similar problems existed elsewhere. The 1990s witnessed financial meltdown from the Baltics to the Balkans, shaking public confidence and devastating East European economies. Slovakia's banking sector had an NPL ratio of 40 per cent as late as 1998, when its three main state banks began to be overhauled. Romanian banks collapsed twice, in 1996 and again in 1999, with leading trade bank Bancorex having an estimated 80 per cent NPL ratio. Bulgaria's banks also folded in 1996, taking the government with them and almost triggering a civil uprising.

In 1995 Latvia's number one bank Baltija went under, the bank's president was jailed, and the government spent the equivalent of seven per cent of GDP on compensating depositors, before itself falling. In Lithuania, a market research survey published that year by *Baltic Surveys* revealed that only six per cent of citizens trusted their banks. As one investment-savvy Lithuanian journalist said: 'I keep most of my money in a sock'.

High-profile financial scandals and frauds littered the region, even within the central banks that were supposed to be regulating the system.[3] Although in most cases depositors were protected, they didn't always get all their money back. Many had to wait a year to gain access to their savings, receiving no interest in the meantime, as insurance investigators sifted through the accounts. Ordinary people were stung in other ways. The cost of recapitalising deposit insurance systems was high, and taxpayers ultimately were hit with the bail-out bill. Czechs in effect lost half a decade of economic growth owing to the cost of cleaning up their banks' balance sheets. Depositors in Russia may not have lost all their rouble savings in 1998, but their dollar value was decimated owing to the collapse of the local currency.

The road less travelled

Problems in the banking sector were inherent from the outset of transition. As the EBRD put it:

> The transformation of socialist banking systems was bound to be difficult. While cement companies could still produce and sell cement, the services of socialist banks were of little use in a market economy. These institutions were primarily bookkeepers for the planned allocation of resources, providing monetary accounts for resource flows.[4]

The newly created banks had little money to finance their modernisation and limited access to international capital markets, and there were few other sources of domestic capital to draw upon. Stock markets did not function, while governments, particularly in Poland and Hungary, had budgets to balance and foreign debts to service in the early 1990s.

From this starting point, policymakers in Eastern Europe took one of three paths: they kept the banks in local hands, sold them quickly to better-equipped foreign banks to run, or dithered between the two options and watched as the banks lost money. Most governments in the CIS adopted the first strategy. Communist-era savings monopoly Sberbank, which still accounts for nearly 90 per cent of household deposits in Russia, remains in the grip of the state, while newer Russian banks became integrated into financial industrial groups, the business empires run by a few local tycoons. These groups could, at least until 1998, generally rely on political support to prosper. Citibank is the only western bank to have made substantial inroads into the Russian market.

Hungary took the opposite path, investing some $1 billion into its troubled banks, mainly to cancel their bad debts, and then selling strategic stakes to wealthy and respected foreign banks. This policy was not driven by free-market ideology alone. 'The only reason we privatised the banks was because they were about to blow up', says Peter Mihalyi, number two in Hungary's privatisation agency at the time.[5] Hungary's government was also desperate for cash, and banking privatisation was a good way to plug the budget and current-account deficits, and stabilise the currency. As a result there were some rushed sales, including that of Budapest Bank to GE Capital in late 1995. Two major banks remained under local control. OTP, the largest savings bank, was kept under Hungarian management but is now owned by a disparate group of local and international portfolio investors following successive share offerings. Postabank, which had one of the largest branch networks in the country, stayed in state hands while the authorities bailed it out. But the rest were sold to foreign banks – in general a smart move. Competition in the sector soon intensified, with lending margins narrowing or even disappearing. Bad loans were minimised (see Table 4.1).

Few other countries followed Hungary's example, and instead they struggled ideologically and financially with their banking system for the entire decade. Privatisation in Poland, the Czech Republic, Slovakia, Bulgaria, Romania and elsewhere was sluggish and fraught with political conflict. Banking policy in Poland seesawed with each

Table 4.1   **Getting better all the time**

	Hungary's banking sector: loan portfolio quality (per cent)			
	1993	*1994*	*1995*	*1996*
Performing	70.7	78.7	83.9	89.4
Special watch	6.8	7.8	7.1	5.7
Substandard	2.9	2.1	1.6	1.0
Doubtful	6.1	3.4	2.5	1.2
Bad	13.5	8.1	4.9	2.7
Total	100.0	100.0	100.0	100.0

Source: State Banking Supervision.

successive government. The early reformers liberalised the sector and by 1992 had created 82 banks, the top 13 of which were spun off from the central bank. But privatisation was delayed by subsequent socialist governments, which attempted to consolidate several banks into 'national champions' to compete with large EU-based financial houses. Although that plan was abandoned as being unrealistic, the attempt by both the government and particularly the central bank to restructure and regulate the top banks was surprisingly successful, halving the value of bad loans during the mid-1990s. Before foreign competition had arrived in force in Poland, the banks had improved their services and even expanded into the virgin retail lending market. Although this did not make Polish banks as efficiently run as leading banks in the West, it did mean that foreign investors eventually paid higher prices for the banks than they otherwise would have done.

The Czech Republic also claimed to be turning its state-owned banks into competitive institutions, but unlike in Poland, the system lacked effective oversight, and all but one of the banks ran up chronic losses. Fifty banks were created in the first years of transition under a naïvely developed central bank licensing system, but most had collapsed by mid-decade. The four big state banks posed bigger problems. One of them, IPB, was sold to two chancers with good political connections but no knowledge of finance – 'utterly incompetent', according to Patria Finance's Zdenek Bakala, a financial adviser on several bank and other privatisation deals. IPB and other banks were linked to major industrial enterprises by a network of cross-shareholdings and soft loans that helped bring the entire economy to a standstill (see chapter 7).

If the problem of how to reform the banking sector had been just one of lack of investment finance, then delaying banking privatisation across the region might have been understandable. Unfortunately, the difficulties went far deeper, and attempts by policymakers to create efficient new institutions were 'like wrestling with a blancmange', as one banking analyst put it. The first problem was that bankers did not (and could not be expected to) have any useful credit assessment experience. Collateral – usually old buildings – was typically worth far less than banks estimated, and securing loans against cash-flow was a virtually unknown concept. 'They learnt from textbooks', says Pavel Mertlik, the former Czech finance minister, who was responsible for the sale of the country's four largest banks.

The second problem was rampant corruption, as political parties, politicians and local entrepreneurs took advantage of often deliberately ill-drafted legislation to enrich themselves. Those lower in the banking hierarchy could feed off the system too. Typically, lending officers took backhanders of 10–20 per cent of the value of any loan granted to their uncreditworthy clients. The region is brim full of stories about white-socked 'biznizmen' getting a loan for a bar or restaurant despite having no experience and the sketchiest of business plans. In addition, few countries had an effective bankruptcy mechanism that could be triggered by creditors. This served as a huge disincentive for borrowers to service their debt, leaving banks little alternative but to roll the loans over.

What made the problem even worse was the tendency of many governments to use state-owned banks to feed uncompetitive, near-bankrupt industry, in order to prevent unemployment rising further. Governments worried that private investors, especially foreigners, who bought these banks might let unviable communist-era businesses fold. Some politicians therefore played the nationalist card and called for these banks to remain in local hands in order to protect their own shady deals, while others genuinely believed that local bank managers were up to the job. Bank chiefs were often political appointees, and parties squabbled to get their respective men into position. There were still plenty of backroom political deals in Poland, despite a genuine attempt to upgrade the country's banks. Many observers wondered how Kredyt Bank – which was stuffed with managers from the political nomenklatura – could win tenders to buy much larger banks, outbidding high-grade foreign competitors.

Even Hungary was not immune to political cronyism. The decision by the 1994–98 Socialist government to sell many banks to foreign investors appeared increasingly fortunate in the light of subsequent revelations that Postabank, the last big bank still in state hands, had operated a 'VIP list' of political clients who received preferential interest rates on loans and deposits. The bank's lending record was so bad that in 1998 it made a loss of $616m, representing one-third of its total assets. On returning to power in 2002, the centre-left Hungarian government bailed the bank out and replaced its management, and Austria's Erste Bank took it over in September 2003. Even when banks were privatised, they were often sold very cheaply (as with the sale of Slovakia's IRB to a local steel magnate in 1996) on the understanding that the new owners would co-operate with the government.

The mix of ignorance, corruption and political interference meant that many banking systems in Eastern Europe had little chance of survival if they remained in local hands. The result of political indecision was that company bosses 'tunnelled' the new loans into private accounts, industry remained weak, and the banks (and eventually the companies that they were expected to save) became insolvent.

What foreign investors did for us

As the Hungarians had realised early on, the solution inevitably had to come from abroad. By the turn of the millennium, everything had changed, and almost the entire banking sector in East-central Europe, the Balkans and the Baltics was being run by foreign institutions. In some cases, western banks had scrambled to buy assets. But often, as the true awfulness of balance sheets came to light, they were not quite as eager as governments had hoped. Poland began selling its banks to foreigners only after the IMF agreed to help bail out and restructure the troubled ones; Slovakia only began its selloffs in 1998; the top Czech banks were not all under foreign control until 2002, after successive governments had wasted the best part of 12 years deciding how to deal with them; and Bulgaria struggled to attract well-resourced international banks.

All but one of Poland's banks are now in western hands, while Baltic banks are run by safe Scandinavians. Bulgaria completed its 'foreign' privatisation by 2003, and Romania was on its way to doing so too, with just one major bank, BCR, still searching for a strategic foreign parent. Around 90 per cent of Croatia's banking assets are controlled by western groups, while Serbia plans to sell more banks in 2004. Even Albania sold its largest bank, Savings Bank, to Raiffeisen Zentralbank for $126m at the start of 2004.

Three quarters of the new EU accession countries' banks are owned by foreign investors, mainly West European banks. As a result, the region's financial sector has become immeasurably safer and more efficient. The share of non-performing and bad loans has fallen towards EU levels; provisioning has become more disciplined; and the introduction of new banking products for individual and corporate borrowers now depends more on commercial viability than good connections. Pavel Mertlik, the former Czech finance minister responsible for rehabilitating his country's sick financial system, admits that 'it could not be done without foreign investment in banking ... and their practical know-how.'[6]

Foreign investors certainly appeared to offer a great deal. They were well enough capitalised to weather most financial storms. They were less susceptible to government meddling, reporting to a commercially focused parent who, along with the local central bank regulators, demanded a responsibly run unit. Western banks brought in a plethora of new services, drove down borrowing costs, provided better-trained lending officers (some of whom left to join other local groups, thus spreading their knowledge[7]), and strengthened their new subsidiaries' balance sheets. Their sturdier reputations attracted more savings, which could then be channelled back into the most productive parts of the economy, helping to drive GDP growth – as a well-run banking system should.

Until the mid-1990s, a dominant state-owned or recently privatised bank could survive by taking deposits and investing them in low-risk government bonds. Nowadays, greater competition for those deposits and the higher returns to be had from expanding into new financial areas have put pressure on all banks, foreign and locally-owned, to improve service, cut costs and implement new technology.

This is particularly true in high-growth retail banking. In the early 1990s, a bank's prime function everywhere in the region appeared to be making simple money transfers (and doing so very slowly). 'Surly staff, in between coffee and cigarette breaks, would deign to allow customers the privilege of accessing their own money', as one saver in Poland described the process. One decade on, East European shoppers commonly pay for their groceries or theatre tickets with debit and credit cards (they never passed through the cheque book stage) or get their cash from new ATMs. Young families can move out of the parental home thanks to new mortgage deals, or get a dream car a few years early through a leasing arrangement. Their bank will insure them, buy stock for them and even arrange a pension.

In Hungary, leading retail bank OTP, which has weathered the competition well, has inevitably seen its dominant position whittled away. Austria's Erste Bank expanded rapidly in the retail market on the strength of its home loan business and the acquisition of Postabank. GE Capital, KBC and HVB are also increasing their retail banking presence in Hungary through local subsidiaries. The provision of retail services is booming in the Czech Republic, Slovakia, Poland, the Baltic states (where credit card ownership has trebled in just three years), and even the less developed Balkans. Retail banking market is certainly worth fighting for; as bankers like to point out, clients are more likely to get divorced than to change their bank accounts.

If foreign entrants have taken retail banking by storm, the picture has been more complex on the corporate lending side. The problem in the past has not been too little lending but too much, and the task of the big western lenders was to dampen the market, not fuel it. One US banker involved in the takeover of a failing Czech bank describes his first meeting with the credit committee to discuss the bad loans situation. 'None of the staff wanted to confront borrowers face to face and tell them that their credit lines were closed. In fact they wanted to lend more. Their attitude was: "who cares, it's not our money"', says the US manager. 'There was a depressing inertia. No one seemed bothered to review loans, many of which seemed to be politically motivated', he recalls.

Once a more effective credit points system was introduced, a healthy caution set in, and the situation swung the other way. 'We have plenty of cash, we just can't find a decent company to lend to', says one frustrated loan officer at the same Czech bank. This is partly because some local entrepreneurs continue to keep their books closed for fear of a tax inspection. Where there are viable projects, corporate borrowers have enjoyed lower interest rates. According to the EBRD, small and medium-sized companies in Eastern Europe typically used to pay a premium of 3–5 percentage points over the rate charged to larger corporations in the mid-1990s. With the arrival of foreign competition, that premium soon fell to around 2 per cent, about the same as in the EU. In Poland and Hungary, where competition between multinational banks is especially intense, the premiums are even lower – possibly too low, say some analysts.

As foreign-owned banks became more cautious about lending to companies, and inflation rates fell, savers became more confident about entrusting their money. Bank Austria Creditanstalt calculates that private-sector bank deposits as a proportion of GDP among the eight new members of the EU had risen to around 40 per cent on EU entry, compared to an average of 70 per cent in the existing EU member states. The re-invigorated banks are flush with money, with the value of deposits often more than 40 per cent higher than that of the loan portfolio.

How it stacks up

Jack Stack, an engaging, self-effacing former Chase Manhattan banker, has 22 years of retail banking experience in the US, but before 2000 had never been to Eastern Europe. Then the Czech government sold Ceska Sporitelna (CS), one of the 'Big Four' banks, to Austria's Erste Bank, which regarded East-central Europe as the perfect area for foreign expansion. (The government bluffed the Austrians into thinking that there was a rival bidder, and raised $500m from the sale.) Andreas Treichl, the respected chairman of Erste Bank, had known Stack for a long time, and called on his friend from the US to come and help turn the new acquisition around.

Zdenek Bakala, a financial advisor to the government on the privatisation, recalls: 'CS was a cesspool ... Documents were missing ... the loan book was all smoke and mirrors'. The bank fed the corporate favourites of the Klaus government, who spirited money into private accounts, and paid their dues to the governing party. Managers had little banking experience and set absurd lending targets for staff, who pushed loans on any old company. '"Don't you want a credit from Ceska Sporitelna?" they would ask anyone', says former finance minister Pavel Mertlik. Inevitably, the loans were never repaid. Around 45 per cent of the loan book went bad, all of it to corporates, with possibly half of the bad loans involving friends (and kickbacks). For Stack, it was the sort of challenge he was waiting for.

He was optimistic. CS had 15 000 employees and was clearly overstaffed, but most of them were ambitious and wanted to work for a good bank. They seemed disheartened that an institution with a 175-year history was on its last legs. They knew that change was necessary, and didn't mind where it came from. 'Just tell us what to do', said some of the managers. Despite 40 years of communism and 10 years of corruption, Stack felt that the level of service was no worse than at any West European bank in the late 1970s or early 1980s. The challenge was to get through 20 years of modernisation in two years – or at least get it 80 per cent right, and deal with loose ends over time.

The key was staff training. 'They worked hard, but not smart. ... The systems were all Rube Goldberg or Heath Robinson', he says, referring to the humorous cartoonists' absurd contraptions. Suggestions in meetings were misinterpreted as orders. Staff feared failure and being punished as a result, and there was a lot of back-covering going on, says

Stack. He needed an early success to show them that the new way was worth the hard work. So every three months all 684 branches called up hundreds of customers to gauge their views, and the customer satisfaction scores for each branch were posted up in the bank. 'All hell broke out', says Stack, and there was an immediate, dramatic improvement.

When bank staff saw the reactions of customers to the changes, the reforms gathered steam. In the second year, every staff member was trained how to answer the phone and interact with customers. Soon compensation was tied to the survey results. The bank set up a telephone centre in the southern Moravian town of Prostejov, and staff spent a couple of weeks in the US observing best practice. When they returned they were able to replicate a good two-thirds of the skills, so that the Prostejov centre became a full telephone banking facility. Credit risk management training was far more intense; staff had previously taken a one-week crash course, but now studied for six months, focusing on how to manage bad loans. Every loan proposal was taken through a hierarchy of approvals. 'We looked into every nook and cranny' for ways to improve service, says Stack.

He got the quick results he was hoping for. Within three years the bank had invested $200m in information technology, and the number of retail customers had increased by 35 per cent. Revenues grew by 25 per cent annually, with the stock of mortgage loans growing by 50 per cent a year. In 1999 the bank had made a loss of $50m; in 2003 it was in profit to the tune of $230m.

Too good to be true?

Not everyone in Eastern Europe is convinced of the benefits of foreign banks. Many instead give the credit for the improvements in the region's banking systems to the policy-makers who opened up the market to competition, whether local or foreign, and point to the improvement in Poland's state-owned banks during the mid-1990s, or Hungary's OTP. Critics argue that the region did not even get the best international banks. The global players (with the exception of a fairly reticent Citibank) have stayed out. Instead, the market has been dominated mainly by medium-sized institutions from Austria, Belgium, Italy and Scandinavia, which are not noted for their dynamic financial sectors. Critics also ask whether such banks are keeping the East European market stable, or vice versa. Erste Bank has fewer branches in Austria than it has over its Eastern borders. Belgium's KBC, one of the biggest banking investors in the region, services 50 per cent more clients there than in Belgium.

Other mid-sized banks have made hasty exits when times became tough. ABN Amro and Societe Generale left Hungary in the late 1990s when the competition intensified, and Germany's Bayerische Landesbank left Croatia in inauspicious circumstances in 2002. The German bank's local subsidiary, Rijecka banka, went bankrupt after rogue trader Eduard Nodilo – not unlike Britain's Nick Leeson at Barings – ran up nearly $100m of foreign-exchange losses and wiped out three-quarters of the bank's capital before the parent company or the local regulator realised. The Germans simply gave the bank back to the government, swallowing a $70m loss in the process. Croatians were angry at the apparent ease with which Bayerische Landesbank could lose interest in the country when trouble struck – especially trouble that it probably should have seen coming.

Another foreign institution not in for the long haul was Japanese investment house Nomura, which was mistakenly viewed by many as a hands-on strategic investor in Czech bank IPB after it bought a minority stake in 1997. But Nomura primarily wanted to get its hands on IPB's lucrative investment fund, which controlled two undervalued breweries, and IPB was left to go bankrupt under its own mismanagement.

Is parental oversight, therefore, really as effective as it is cracked up to be? Piotr Bednarski, a banking supervisor at Poland's famously strict central bank, sees risks involved with the entry of foreign banks into Eastern Europe. These include huge parent banks taking too little interest in their tiny, seemingly unimportant, subsidiaries, and shifting decisions on risk away from local boards and back to headquarters. This latter step is often taken as a cost-cutting measure, but potentially leaves the subsidiary with nothing to do but boost sales. Risk analysts say that risk should be managed in the location where it is generated. There is also the question of the safety of the parent bank itself. 'How much is their guarantee really worth if they face a crisis?' asks Bednarski. Foreign ownership is good, he says, but only if the foreign banks are the right size and have the right reputation. Bednarski retains a soft spot for the few reasonably well run locally-managed banks, such as OTP (which has even expanded abroad with acquisitions in Slovakia Bulgaria and Romania). If they survive, could they offer better guarantees of the financial stability that the region craves?

Poland's response to these perceived risks has been to take a 'belt and braces' approach to bank regulation. As well as selling stakes to strategic investors, the Social Democratic government also floated bank shares on the Warsaw stock exchange in order to bring the new foreign owners under additional regulatory control. Other countries are less watchful.

Another criticism of western-owned banks is that they have shown little zeal in corporate lending, especially to small and medium-sized enterprises (SMEs), the bedrock of any healthy economy. According to an EBRD survey of 515 banks in the region, the ratio of corporate loans to GDP is 20 percentage points below market economy benchmarks.[8] New firms find it hard to get hold of start-up capital, and SMEs in particular struggle to obtain long-term finance. True, banks in Eastern Europe have had a bad experience with medium-sized companies, but with bad loans now a mere one per cent of some East European loan portfolios, the trends highlighted by the EBRD suggest more than just caution. Western banks clearly see more profit in servicing the local units of their multinational clients, lending to government and throwing money at the underbanked retail market than in lending to small local entrepreneurs.

There may be some validity in these criticisms, though many are speculative. It was not impossible for local institutions, given an adequate shareholding structure and proper regulation, to survive, even in the face of international competition. With their incumbent advantages of local knowledge and an existing branch network, and with the foresight to hire western expertise, they might have thrived. That so few have done so is ultimately an indictment of misguided government policy. In this respect, western banks, though not always the biggest, the best-managed or the even safest, served one crucial purpose: their presence eroded the networks of crony politicians, businessmen, fixers and state enterprises whose soft loans and insider deals had brought large chunks of the region's financial system crashing down. If only for that reason, Eastern Europe is enormously better off with the multinational banks.

The telecommunications revolution

The creation of a modern telephone system has been one of the most significant contributions that western multinationals have made to improve the quality of life in Eastern Europe since 1989. In many cases this took much longer than it should have done, largely because of delays caused by political wrangling. As the EU enlarges eastwards, many western-owned telecom companies in the region are still in the doghouse for failing to give competitors proper access to the fixed-line network, raising prices or providing relatively poor service.

However, such complaints are a far cry from the early 1990s, when the question was often not 'What's your telephone number?' but rather 'Do you have a telephone?'

In the early 1990s, the vast majority of people in the region did not have a telephone. To arrange a meeting one would be forced to trek around town looking for a public phone that worked, usually trying five or six before getting a dial tone. This made it nearly impossible to arrange a specific time to call a person, let alone do business. That was just the beginning of the problems. Lines often cut out in mid-conversation, crackled so badly that it was impossible to make out what the other person was saying, or simply fell out of order for weeks at a time. Worse, the telephone exchange operators were widely believed to be making private calls on the accounts of unwitting customers, who had no itemised bills with which to check. The situation was intolerable for small businesses. One hapless entrepreneur in Prague recalls how he had no alternative but to share a line with his alcoholic neighbour, who continually interrupted incoming business calls with drunken abuse.

It was virtually impossible to get a private line without paying a huge bribe to a moonlighting telecom technician. The going rate in the Czech Republic in 1995 was up to $2000, equivalent to half a year's wages for most people. When Telsource, a joint venture of Dutch operator KPN and Swisscom, acquired a 27 per cent stake and management control of SPT (later renamed Cesky Telecom) in 1995 – almost six years after the revolution – there were still three quarters of a million people on the waiting list for a telephone. One man had been waiting 20 years. When Telsource technicians finally arrived at his apartment to install the line, they were told that he had already died.

This state of affairs grew out of communist-era neglect and isolation. Before 1989, telecommunications in Eastern Europe was largely the preserve of the defence and space industries and was therefore deemed top secret. No account was taken of domestic needs. Sophisticated Soviet satellite systems, for example, were generally located far away from switching centres, making it difficult to integrate them into a domestic telephone network – even if policymakers had wanted to. Fibre optics and digital switching technology had barely been heard of. The gap with the West grew ever larger. By the mid-1980s, people in the US were making around 200 times more international calls than Soviet citizens were.[9] Even inter-city calls had to go through an operator, with many regional phones in the Soviet Union connected through Strowger exchanges – a late 19th century electromechanical marvel that had barely been upgraded since.

To be fair, the Soviet-era system also suffered from restrictions imposed in the West by COCOM (Co-ordinating Committee for Multinational Export Controls), which blocked the sale of high-tech equipment to the cold war enemy. The region was allowed only to import outdated devices, mainly via limited joint-venture and licensing agreements with western companies. Hungary, for example, was able to develop some telephone exchanges in co-operation with Ericsson, while Poland and Slovenia had limited deals with Alcatel.

A welcome call

When communism disintegrated and COCOM restrictions were lifted, Eastern Europe was technically so far behind that local suppliers were in no position to develop an up-to-date telephone system on their own, and at the very least needed to attract western firms into fully-fledged joint ventures. Some countries, notably Hungary, welcomed western components makers, who helped to restructure the country's telecom industry quickly; others, such as Russia, continued to protect domestic manufacturers, whose equipment, with the possible exception of satellite technology, was already obsolete.

The onset of the global telecommunications revolution in the 1990s confused the policy options in Eastern Europe. Those countries ready to grab the opportunities could leapfrog an entire generation of technology and move into the 21st century world of mobile telephony and internet services. But they faced colossal tasks: to incorporate sprawling state telephone exchanges into a joint-stock company; find billions of dollars of investment capital; overhaul existing technology; increase penetration rates (that is, the number of lines per 100 people) and eliminate waiting lists for lines; restructure the telephone companies into well-organised competitive market players; offer competing cellular and, later, GSM mobile licences; and, finally, introduce competition for fixed-line services over the 'last mile' to customers – a condition of EU membership. The obvious and quickest way to achieve these aims was to sell a strategic stake and management control in the fixed-line monopoly to more adroit and deep-pocketed foreign telecom companies.

Different countries came to this conclusion at different speeds. As with the banking sector, some governments wanted to keep their treasured systems in state hands, while others argued that local management could do the job well enough itself. As with bank privatisation, Estonia and Hungary were quickest off the mark. In 1992

Estonia sold a 49 per cent stake in fixed-line monopoly Eesti Telefon to BalTel, a joint venture of Finland's Sonera and Swedish operator Telia. Eesti Telefon built up telephone and internet services (including free internet access) that soon rivalled and surpassed those available in many EU member states. By 2003, 3.4 per cent of Estonians had broadband internet access, almost the same proportion as in the EU-15.[10]

Even before 1989, Hungary's last communist government had developed a 'ten-year plan' to digitalise the network. In 1993 the country sold a 30 per cent stake in Matav, the newly incorporated fixed-line telephone monopoly, to MagyarCom, a German–US consortium of Deutsche Telekom and Ameritech (they gained majority control two years later). The consortium also obtained management control for 25 years. In addition, Hungary had issued analogue mobile phone licences as early as 1990, and awarded two GSM licences (one to Matav) in 1994 – shortly after mobile operations began in Western Europe.

The Czechs were next to move, and in 1995 the government sold a 27 per cent stake in what is now Cesky Telecom to Telsource. The rest of Eastern Europe was slower to bring in foreign investors. Romania sold a 35 per cent stake in Romtelecom to Greece's OTE in 1998 (the stake was later raised to 54 per cent), Poland waited until 1999 before selling a similar stake in TPSA to a France Telecom-led venture, and Slovakia sold its phone company to Deutsche Telekom in 2000 (see Table 4.2).

Table 4.2   Telephone density

	Fixed-line penetration		Mobile penetration	Fixed-line investor (year of entry)
	1990	*2002*	*2002*	
Bulgaria	25%	37%	32%	Advent (2004)
Croatia	18%	42%	51%	Deutsche Telekom (1999)
Czech Republic	10%	36%	84%	Swisscom/KPN (1995)
Estonia	23% [1]	38%	63%	TeliaSonera (1991)
Hungary	9%	31%	68%	Deutsche Telekom (1993)
Latvia	26% [2]	30%	37%	Sonera, Cable & Wireless (1994)
Lithuania	21%	27%	47%	TeliaSonera (1998)
Poland	9%	31%	36%	France Telecom (2000)
Romania	10%	19%	23%	OTE (1998)
Slovakia	13%	39%	56%	Deutsche Telekom (2000)
Slovenia	26% [1]	41%	87%	Domestic-owned

Note: 1. Figures for 1993; 2. Figures for 1994
Source: Pyramid Research.

The changing tone

The new owners were under immediate pressure to perform. Although most governments had allowed incumbent operators to retain their fixed-line monopolies until around the turn of the century, giving the new owners time to invest and restructure the companies, the privatisation agreements also set strict targets for improving service and line penetration. Ordinary users soon saw the benefits. When the German-US consortium MagyarCom took over MATAV, the company had one of the lowest line penetration rates in the region – only 14 lines per 100 people (better, admittedly, than nine lines per 100 people in 1990). By 2002 the penetration rate had risen to 31 per cent, and the queue for new lines had long been eliminated. By 1998 Eesti Telefon had digitalised half its network and reached a penetration rate of 35 per cent, while Cesky Telecom had eliminated its waiting list for phone lines after only three years of operation.

Providing new phone lines on demand wasn't the only task. In most cases the privatisation contracts also set the new owners rigorous targets, with a sliding scale of fines attached if targets were missed. They included everything from increasing the number of available public payphones, to shortening the time to get a dial tone, an international connection or an operator response. Romtelecom, owned by Greece's OTE, boasts of having reduced the number of line faults (usually caused by ageing copper wiring) from 70 in every 100 lines to 20, in five years of service. Meanwhile, annual customer complaints – usually over billing or the lack of a dial tone – dropped from 130 per 100 lines to 40.

Most of these targets were achieved through the rapid digitalisation of the networks. In some respect it was sad to see the old systems being ripped up. Technicians in the communist era had developed impressive ways to improvise, keeping mechanisms operating well past their normal life. Sentimentality got the better of Siemens when the company found a 50-year-old switching system still in place in the Czech Republic. It was removed, and placed in the company's telephone museum in Munich, Germany.

The investment required was huge. Telsource, for example, spent around $5 billion in the first seven years after it bought Cesky Telecom, building a completely new digital network. In most cases that technology had to be imported. But sometimes there were also profitable spillovers into the domestic economy. The first democratic Hungarian government, for example, had based its open sourcing policy on the condition that big players such as Siemens and Ericsson would locate their production in Hungary itself. As a result these firms made Hungary a research and development centre, building up close relations with the Technical University in Budapest.

In Russia the job of upgrading a network that covered nine time zones and was run by 86 regional telephone monopolies, most of which were part-owned by the huge Svyazinvest holding company, appeared too big for either the government or a multinational company. In the mid-1990s Russia entertained a spectacular plan to bring in foreign investors to digitalise exchanges in the country's top 50 cities, laying 50 000 kilometres of fibre optic cable and 20 million new lines. The estimated cost of the 10-year project was $40 billion, far beyond the means of any investor (and certainly of the Russian government), and the project was abandoned. Russia's telephone development has instead been driven by the mobile phone 'frontiersmen', the partly foreign-owned firms that have raced across the country installing their own networks.

High-wire act

Many East European governments defended their delay in selling even part of the state telephone monopoly to a western multinational on the grounds that they were protecting national assets. However, the smart governments sold a minority stake to a strategic investor early on, and then saw the value of the remaining state shares rise rapidly as the foreign partner upgraded the network and telecoms enjoyed a worldwide boom. Many of these governments were subsequently able to sell further chunks of the fixed-line operator at high prices before the rise of mobile telephony and the worldwide crash in telecoms shares closed the door to such deals. Those investors who ploughed billions of dollars into East European fixed-line operators in the 1990s were later left holding much less valuable assets. Hungary received $3.2 billion in total from the sale of Matav shares – a huge amount in per-line terms compared with US telecoms valuations. Serbia sold a combined 49 per cent stake in Telekom Srbije to OTE and Telecom Italia for $920m in 1997, and six years later bought 29 per cent back from the Italian operator for the much lower sum of just over $200m. Journalists dubbed the Polish government's sale of a 35 per cent stake in TPSA to France Telecom in 2000 as 'the sale of the century' because of the high price paid. France Telecom had also acquired an option to buy an additional ten per cent, but the company let it expire in 2001 because the exercise price was almost three times higher than the market price at the time. And investment guru George Soros described his shareholding in a group that paid $1.9 billion for a 25 per cent stake in Russian telecom holding Svyazinvest as 'the worst investment of my life'. Most of that money was not even invested in the telephone company, but went straight into the Russian treasury.

Bessel Kok, a vice-chairman of Cesky Telecom, says that the $1.3 billion that Telsource paid in 1995 for a 27 per cent stake in the operator was 'totally, outrageously high ... even at the time'. Mr Kok, a Vaclav Havel-lookalike with a wry, dry sense of humour, is philosophical about the deal. At the time of the sale, he recalls, there was euphoria among telecom investors, who were forecasting rapid fixed-line growth and 75–80 per cent penetration rates. However, the fixed-line penetration rate in the Czech Republic currently stands at a much lower 38 per cent, and the popularity of mobile phones means that it is unlikely to rise much further. Mr Kok, the inventor of the bank swift code system in the early 1970s, and a former chess grandmaster who has pitted his wits against the likes of Karpov and Kasparov, realises in hindsight how bad Telsource's move into fixed-line telephony was. 'We were caught in the mobile revolution,' he says. 'There was no way we could get any serious return on that investment ... We would have to be crawling on our knees to find customers.' For the Czech government, it was their best privatisation ever, he says.

The only saving grace was that Cesky Telecom was also given a 51 per cent stake soon afterwards in leading mobile operator Eurotel, the profits from which offset some of the losses on the fixed-line purchase. Whereas in Western Europe a mobile phone is regarded as an added convenience, in Eastern Europe it is a direct alternative to a fixed line, says Jim Hubley, CEO of Romtelecom, Romania's dominant fixed-line operator. Between 2000–02 mobiles overtook fixed lines everywhere in Eastern Europe. By 2003 there were 5.5 million mobiles in use in Romania, a penetration rate of 24 per cent, compared to the 20 per cent rate for fixed lines (see table 4.2). Given the low level of economic development and subsidised domestic tariffs, there is little room for the fixed-line market to grow. Telecom companies say that local call rates need to be higher so that they better reflect the cost of providing the service, but governments, particularly in Romania, want to avoid a political backlash and have prevented such a move.

No perfect connection

On the other hand, dominant foreign-owned operators, particularly in Poland and Hungary, have hardly rushed to open up their networks to alternative operators once their monopolies end, as required by the EU and usually by the privatisation contracts as well. This has led to complaints from regulators and the competition. Playing the regulatory game (by stalling on liberalisation) is one way to improve returns, admits Jeffrey Hedberg, formerly head of international operations at Deutsche Telekom, which owns fixed-line companies in Hungary, Slovakia, Croatia, and (through Matav) in Macedonia. Alternative fixed-line providers are thus finding it hard to compete, and claim that the telecom regulators who are supposed to be facilitating competition are acting too slowly.

The leading telecoms company in each country has sometimes come in for scathing criticism from the press. TPSA, for example, has been attacked for closing down service centres and replacing them with a 'blue-line' telephone service contact to sort out customers' needs.[11] Across the region, customers continue to complain about poorly trained staff and billing mistakes. There are still plenty of stories of bill collectors hounding honest customers because the telephone company has mislaid the paperwork. Countries that sold their telephone companies relatively late have an uneasy sense that the real benefit coming from the investor has been not so much from the technical and managerial upgrade, but simply the amount of money paid to the treasury for the share stakes. And the investors themselves also question whether owning several fixed-line providers across the region has provided any economies of scale besides possible savings on procurement.

Creating a well-resourced, competitive, integrated telecom company out of an inefficient, dilapidated phone system was in itself quite an achievement. Although East European telecoms companies often had thousands of engineers, they had no marketing or sales people, and management tended to be weak and disruptive. Hedberg, formerly of Deutsche Telekom, highlights the difficulties involved in centralising decision-making while regional fiefdoms remained powerful and distrustful; or in keeping downsized departments motivated while introducing yet more tough financial controls. Telsource made an early mistake by implementing a complex matrix management structure at a time when Czech staff expected clear lines of operational responsibility, and a clear sense of who their boss was. Staff did not want to change their old ways. Bessel Kok discovered that his own office was bugged when he first arrived. When he attempted to introduce an open-plan office and remove all the heavy padded doors, there was outraged protest.

Foreign investors tend to point to improvements in line productivity, that is, the number of fixed lines per employee. Matav raised line productivity by around 70 per cent within three years, while Rom-telecom improved from 181 lines per employee in 1998 to 300 per employee in 2003. However, 'higher line productivity' may not reflect an increase in the number of lines laid, and is sometimes a euphemism for large-scale redundancies. Staff numbers at Romtelecom fell from a staggering 52 000 when OTE arrived in 1998 to a still-high 23 000 in 2003. By 2002 Cesky Telecom had gradually laid off some 16 000 staff, more than half the total that Telsource inherited in 1995, while Poland's TPSA undertook the biggest layoff programme in Eastern Europe, reducing staff numbers by 40 000 in two years. In this respect, the arrival of multinationals was a harsh experience for many people, but there was little alternative. Telecoms operators were so overstaffed that even the trade unions understood that the situation was unviable.

Some state-owned telecom companies claimed that they could have realised much of the restructuring and line growth without the help of multinationals. Slovenia, the wealthiest post-communist country, raised fixed-line penetration rates from 23 per cent in 1993 to 41 per cent in 2002 without a strategic investor. Before Deutsche Telekom bought 51 per cent of the Slovak network in 2000, the local operator had already invested some $1 billion to increase fixed-line penetration to 32 per cent and digitalise three-fifths of the lines. But the Slovaks admitted that they could not afford to maintain the necessary level of investment on their own. And Bulgaria, which started the 1990s with one of the highest penetration rates in the region, found that delays in attracting a deep-pocketed investor allowed the rest of the region to catch up and move ahead.

The entry of foreign telecom companies to Eastern Europe has not eliminated restrictive practices, bad management or billing errors. And although governments often did very well out of privatisation, tens of thousands of telecom employees subsequently lost their jobs. Yet it is hard to imagine that local companies could have carried off the trans-formation as effectively on their own. The early acquisitions, in which foreign investors took over largely unimproved communist-era phone systems, had a hugely positive effect overall – not least by ending the daily humiliation faced by the mass of people unable to make a simple telephone call.

The speed of that change hinged mainly on the attitude of govern-ments in the region. The best thing they could do for business was to give up their traditional role as provider of all telecommunication ser-vices, bring in well-resourced foreign players, open the market to com-petition and adopt a sensible regulatory policy – including tough regulation of the foreign operator. The alternative, as those communities in remoter areas have found, was to be left out of the global telecommunications revolution.

The automotive drive

Eastern Europe's automotive industry suffered from one important drawback under communism: state planners believed that the motor car was a bourgeois luxury that should be discouraged. Private car ownership was associated with personal wealth, social aspiration and too much freedom (although this did not stop senior party members enjoying the use of limousines). Mass production in the auto industry was instead directed towards military vehicles, but few of the technical innovations flowed into civilian production, as they might have done in the West. As with telecommunications, these were deemed to be state secrets. Deprived of official backing, money, and access to new technology and design ideas, the industry languished.

It had not always done so. The Czechoslovak car industry was born as long ago as 1905, when motorbike makers Vaclav Laurin and Vaclav Klement switched to making cars. In 1925 their company was acquired by the Skoda engineering works, and Skoda Auto became one of the most successful automobile makers in Europe. Despite the communist takeover in 1948, Skoda produced high-quality motors, such as the convertible Felicia, up until the mid-1960s. However, the rigid economic system started to take its toll, and by the end of the 1980s Skoda had become a joke in much of Western Europe. The brand did retain considerable appeal in Eastern Europe, but largely because the alternatives (such as the Trabant and the Wartburg) were even worse.

While Czech engineers and technicians were still capable of knocking out a viable motor under communism, Poland, Romania and the Soviet Union had a much weaker technical base for carmaking. These countries imported technology from the West through joint ventures and licensing agreements that brought Renault to Romania, Ford to Russia and Fiat to Poland. Russia's car industry, however, remains dominated by AvtoVaz, which produces half a million squat, but surprisingly reliable, Ladas each year. The only other major carmaking base in the region was Yugoslavia's Zastava plant, which was relatively advanced technically, but deteriorated owing to a lack of money from the 1980s onwards, and was nearly finished off by NATO warplanes in 1999.

The transformation of parts of the region's car industry after 1989 was extraordinary. In the space of a decade foreign automotive manufacturers revitalised a dying sector, underpinned the region's export-led economic performance, employed hundreds of thousands of people directly and indirectly, and rehabilitated a well-recognised but floundering brand name. None of this was inevitable, essential, or, for many western investors, even profitable. Car companies did not always get an easy ride in the region, and were taking as much of a gamble on this region as any other investment in the world.

Although Eastern Europe was an obvious place for leading global car-makers to cut costs while remaining close to the EU market, the massive oversupply in the global car industry meant that many firms should have been retrenching rather than looking for low-cost areas in which to produce. Nor did the cost calculations always add up, since lower wages came with lower productivity. There were also political and operational risks to consider. Plenty of car investments struggled or failed – from Ford's venture in Russia to Rover's half-hearted effort in Bulgaria.

Of the dozens of foreign car companies that came to the region after 1989, only Volkswagen (VW), Fiat and South Korea's Daewoo made a serious financial commitment. By the end of the 1990s the latter two had run into difficulties. Fiat had acquired the FSM car plant in the southwestern region of Tychy in 1992 for around $2 billion, a deal that grew out of a longstanding licensing agreement to produce Unos, Cinquecentos and other small cars in Poland. But the Italian parent's finances were tottering, and its output in Poland declined rapidly. Daewoo also showed an early boldness, acquiring the rival FSO factory in Poland, and setting up in Uzbekistan, Ukraine and Romania too. However, the bankruptcy of its parent company in 2001 left Daewoo's East European strategy in tatters. Another threat came from the EU, which accused Daewoo of dodging import taxes by importing finished cars into Slovenia, disassembling them and shipping the parts to Poland for re-export to the EU.

There have been three other sizeable car investments in the region to date, all of which have landed in the Czech and Slovak Republics. The first, announced in 2002, was a joint venture between Toyota and Peugeot-Citroën, to invest $1.5 billion to build a new small car plant in Bohemia. A few months later Peugeot announced plans to build its own $700m plant in western Slovakia, and in 2004 Hyundai said that it too would build a similar-sized plant in northern Slovakia. As a result Slovakia will soon become the largest producer of cars in Europe on a per-capita basis. The country attracted these investments through a combination of low taxes, a relatively cheap workforce and its proximity to the rest of the EU. Some argue that Slovakia, and indeed whole swathes of East-central Europe's economy, has now become too reliant on the automotive industry, but the creation of a powerful automotive cluster means that the possibility of a sudden upheaval with investors leaving to lower-cost locations in the near future is less likely than if these investments were isolated, or spread across the region as a whole. There wasn't always a cluster of like-minded carmakers. For more than a decade it was only Volkswagen that took the risk and laid the groundwork for others.

Power to the people's car

The success of the automotive sector in Eastern Europe over the last decade and a half is essentially the story of Volkswagen. Its 1991 purchase of Skoda in Mlada Boleslav, north-east of Prague, was the first big privatisation deal in the region. The Skoda plant would rapidly become the largest car maker in Eastern Europe. By the end of the decade, another VW plant in Slovakia would become the region's second biggest, while its Audi subsidiary was producing a million engines a year in Hungary for global distribution. VW also had smaller operations in Poland, Bosnia and Ukraine.

More significantly from the local perspective, VW wasn't simply looking for a cheap assembly site to churn out existing western models, as other manufacturers were, but saw Skoda as a brand in its own right, with its own corporate history and culture. Rather than putting the distressed trademark out of its misery, VW decided to regenerate a name that still resonated throughout Eastern Europe, and turned it into a globally respected brand of which the Czech Republic could be truly proud.

The VW deal was a product of the unique circumstances of post-revolution transition. In 1987 Skoda decided to develop a new car, with up-to-date technology, but it soon became obvious that no amount of Communist Party exhortations would ever make this happen. While western manufacturers had shifted to Japanese-inspired 'lean production' in the 1980s, Skoda was struggling with 1960s processes. 'The state laid down rules for everything. There was a rule book for everything. There was no creativity, let alone money for modernisation', says Vladimir Hamacek, an engineer who has worked for Skoda for 25 years. In order to source affordable, compatible components such as anti-lock braking systems, diesel engines or automatic gearboxes, the company needed to be part of a bigger global network, or to pour huge amounts of money, which the government did not have, into technological investment. Put simply, 'we needed a new car and were not able to produce it', says Jan Vrba, Czechoslovakia's Trade and Industry minister from 1990–92.

So Skoda managers began whispering about a possible joint venture with a western company, to bring know-how, finance and better designs. They considered BMW, some Japanese firms, Renault and VW. Then came the revolution and the collapse of communism, and talks began in earnest with the latter two firms. Renault appeared only to want to run an assembly plant in Czechoslovakia. But VW had a broader vision. Czech negotiators recall that the VW delegation didn't spend time 'schmoozing' with the ministers, but rather sent their best engineers to talk about hundreds of specific technical shortcomings in the Skoda cars. They were 'open, straightforward and transparent', says Vrba.

The agreement to sell Skoda to VW was seminal in many respects. As the first big transaction in the region its political significance was huge. If the Czechs could nail this one so early in their economic transition, it would send a powerful signal to the world that the country was serious about becoming an open western economy. Indeed, the country traded on the success of the deal for many years, even as subsequent Czech privatisations became uncomfortably murky.

The nature of the negotiations was also unique. No one in Eastern Europe had ever done such a deal. There wasn't even a privatisation law in place, so legal principles were developed as the negotiations went along. This was possible because all the key decision-makers – the Czechoslovak trade minister, finance minister and federal prime minister, as well as industry experts and financial advisers – crowded together into smoke-filled rooms with their VW counterparts, hammering out details until four o'clock each morning. It proved to be a very effective, if unorthodox, way to sell a company. The talks went at lightning speed, since every issue could be decided without anyone having to report back to their superiors. There was no corruption or lobbying involved either, as everything was discussed in the presence of everyone else. At that time the ministers were quite idealistic about rebuilding the economy, says Zdenek Bakala, who worked for Credit Suisse First Boston as a financial adviser on the deal. 'Simply, it was the best privatisation. Few could match it', he declares.

However, there were differences of opinion on the Czech side. The unions had been won over to the deal (see chapter 2), but many politicians were whipping up anti-German feeling, and the public was calling for Renault to come in instead, unaware of its weaker offer.

Vaclav Klaus, the ambitious finance minister who was well aware of the populist mood, argued for putting Skoda through the voucher privatisation scheme (see chapter 7) and letting the new investment funds decide what happened to the shares. 'The politician took over from the economist', says Vrba. But Klaus, the man who was to dominate Czech politics for the next decade, was not powerful at that time and was easily overruled.

The final agreement ran to a thousand pages. Because of the lack of legal precedent, everything had to be spelled out in the contract. The terms included minimum future production volumes, investment levels, the introduction new car models, and permissible redundancies. VW agreed to pay D-Marks 620 million for 30 per cent of Skoda's shares, and would increase its stake to 70 per cent four years later for an additional D-Marks 1.4 billion.

Lightning attack

VW's arrival at the plant was explosive. The German company wanted to implement its changes quickly in order to win over doubters among the factory's employees and the general public. Josef Stafl, a human resources chief who had been at Skoda over 40 years, recalls: 'Suddenly there were hundreds of German and international managers all over the place. There were new computers and telephones (not so easy to come by in the country at the time), plush office furniture, newly painted walls and a staff restaurant with better food. There were completely new departments that the local workforce had never even heard of and didn't know what they did.' Even more disconcertingly, the German managers worked late into the night, setting a completely new pace. They led by example because it was hard to communicate. None of the VW executives spoke Czech, and only one Czech in the technical department could speak German (and a very technical version of it at that). There was a lot of wonderment (so this is how the Germans do it! the Czechs said), and a little resistance, especially among older Communist Party members, who retained a residual distrust of Germans. But when asked about the bad memories he had of the takeover, one Skoda worker could only recall: 'the weak, filtered coffee they brought to the canteen! We demanded our old strong stuff back – and we got it', he says triumphantly.

VW was more than faithful to the terms of its contract. It invested over $3 billion, most of it between 1998–2002, when other car firms in the region were struggling. Annual output rose from 160 000 cars in 1991 to nearly half a million a decade later – a figure generally regarded as the minimum output for a non-specialist car plant to be economically viable. VW boasted other encouraging statistics: 83 per cent of its output was exported (accounting for around 10 per cent of the Czech Republic's total exports), of which two-thirds went to the West; and two-thirds of parts were locally sourced, as VW fired up a new subsector of local and foreign suppliers. The existing Favorit model was upgraded to a more modern looking Felicia, but the high point came in 1996 with the production of the Octavia, the first truly new VW creation under the Skoda brand. The internationally acclaimed Octavia was comparable with the VW Passat. Its release confirmed that Skoda had returned to world-class carmaking – and produced some tearful celebrations on the factory floor.

By 1997 Skoda had overtaken Fiat in Poland as the biggest carmaker in Eastern Europe. The Fabia sedan, which was built in 1999, won *Bild am Sonntag*'s prestigious Golden Steering Wheel award for best car in its class, and was named European car of the year by the UK's *What Car?* magazine. The progress was unceasing, with Skoda producing petrol engines and gearboxes for the entire VW group. And in 2002 there was a Skoda limousine, the Superb, built at a brand new plant in Kvasiny. Without VW 'it would have been a long and painful death', says Milan Smutny, a Skoda spokesman.

The changes at Mlada Boleslav are only part of the story. At the same time that VW took over Skoda, the German firm was negotiating a parallel deal to set up a plant in Slovakia. With the Cold War having ended, Slovakia was looking for ways to develop local industry in the wake of the collapse of the country's armaments business. Jozef Uhrik, a former boss of a local armaments company, was deputy director of the Federal Ministry of Machinery at the time, and recommended that the government should try to attract a passenger car plant to the country. Slovak officials started discussions with General Motors and VW. As in its talks with Czech officials, VW proved to be flexible and to have a long-term strategy. In 1991 the German firm signed an agreement to move into an existing plant just north of Bratislava, the capital. The deal was that VW would produce 30 000 vehicles a year, mainly Passats, and 20 000 gear boxes and gear box components. Things went rather better, says Uhrik, who became chairman of the new operation under VW. By 2002 the company was producing 225 000 cars a year, 300 000 gear boxes, and over eight million components (around 1.5 million of them in a new plant in central Slovakia). VW began with a staff of 1500; by the end of the decade it employed 9000 people. 'You could say that we exceeded the plan', says Uhrik with a smile.

The German firm's Slovak subsidiary began producing various VW Golf models in 1994, Boras in 1998 and Polos in 1999, and shifted

VW-Seat production from Spain to Bratislava in 2003. The plant became Slovakia's biggest and most profitable exporter. Indeed, the automotive sector, which VW dominates, accounted for 27 per cent of the country's total exports in 2002.

Just as significant as VW's investments in the Czech Republic and Slovakia has been the emergence of one of Europe's densest auto-components supply networks, stretching across Poland, the Czech Republic, Slovakia and Hungary. Around 270 suppliers operate in the Czech Republic alone, supplying not only VW's Mlada Boleslav plant, but the company's other plants around the world. The Czech Republic has attracted over half of the world's top 100 components manufacturers, including many first-tier subcontractors from the US such as Lucas, Delphi, Johnson Controls and Molex. The growth of an automotive supply pyramid in which car plants subcontract work and provide assistance to smaller firms has also stimulated domestic companies to raise their production, quality and delivery standards to international levels. Many of these local firms are now supplying other international carmakers. In fact Czech-based suppliers provide parts to 22 different makes of car around the world, generating $2 billion of revenue annually. The supply network is expanding in Slovakia too; over 60 major component manufacturers and research and development firms have come to the country on the back of the VW investment, and now do over $1 billion of business a year.

An estimated 130 000 people work in the newly invigorated auto sector in the Czech Republic (three quarters of them with suppliers), according to CzechInvest, the country's inward investment agency, and over 50 000 work in Slovakia. Hungary too has a thriving car components industry worth around $2.5 billion a year, which forms part of the so-called Prague-Bratislava-Gyor investment triangle, a newly industrialised slice of East-central Europe. The existence of such a supply network is a major reason why Peugeot, Toyota and Hyundai are all starting production in the Czech and Slovak Republics in the coming decade. These new plants will in turn make the supply base even more dense.

The arrival of VW gave East-central Europe much more than just a big foreign investor. It gave the region the chance to develop one of Europe's newest and most efficient industrial clusters, and therefore a stable investment base. With Skoda, VW turned a home-grown brand name into something to be proud of again. The crucial role that multinationals played in developing other failing local brands in Eastern Europe will be explored in Chapter five.

5
Whose Consumer Culture?

'East Europeans are attracted to the technical merits and value-for-money of a product, not its image. Advertisers in the West call this 'unsophisticated'. To me, it sounds very sophisticated.'

Moscow advertising executive.

The entry of western consumer goods into Eastern Europe after 1989 was far removed from the capitalist colonisation, or 'Coca-Cola-isation', so disliked by anti-globalisation campaigners. As this chapter will show, the relationship between East Europeans and western consumer goods manufacturers has gone through a number of distinct phases. At first, Eastern Europe had a heady love affair with western goods. Shortages were chronic, and consumers bought any western brand that they could lay their hands on. But the market soon took a different turn, as tougher economic conditions, nimble domestic producers and (in some cases) nationalist prejudice led shoppers to choose more affordable local products over bigger western brand names. The shift was clearest in Russia, where the collapse of the rouble in August 1998 suddenly pushed imported goods out of the price range of most people. This fact, and changing consumer tastes across the region in turn forced western multinationals to present themselves as local players. They did so by increasing their local production (by acquiring an existing company or building their own plant), employing local workers, keeping costs and prices low, branding their products with local-sounding names, advertising them with story lines that were familiar to their customers, and, most importantly, maintaining western levels of quality. As competition intensified, not only between multinationals and local consumer goods producers but also between the foreign firms themselves, the quality of locally produced goods improved so much that visitors to the region today may find it hard to distinguish products made in Eastern Europe from those imported from the West.

The entry and subsequent adaptation of western consumer goods companies was one part of the retail revolution in Eastern Europe after 1989. Equally significant was the arrival of large foreign-owned hypermarkets. These have had some negative effects in Eastern Europe, as elsewhere: suppliers are squeezed, small shop-owners go out of business, and town councillors are sometimes bribed to make cheap downtown land available. However, the second part of this chapter will argue that the benefits to consumers from the hypermarket invasion far outweigh any disadvantages, especially given the state of retailing in the region before the 1989 revolutions.

After 15 years of transition, many capitals in the region now boast glittering modern shops packed with affordable, high-quality products. Yet it is easy to forget about the lack of consumer goods in Eastern Europe under communism and the appalling quality of those that were on sale. The region was heavily industrialised and geared to production in general, and the needs of consumers were virtually ignored. Visitors to the Soviet Union or even (relatively) wealthier East-central Europe during the 1970s and 1980s were taken aback at how empty the shops were. Western tourists laughed at the clothes people wore and the funny box cars that trundled along potholed roads. Finding tasty food was almost impossible. Some Soviet towns had no supply of basic items such as eggs, and long food queues were a daily feature of East European life. An orange at Christmas time was a major family treat, and a mere plastic carrier bag from London's *Harrod's*, let alone the goods it might contain, was a coveted item.

Spend spend spend: the scramble for brands

When US burger chain McDonald's opened its first Russian restaurant in Moscow's Pushkin Square in January 1990, over 30 000 people turned up – not to protest against globalisation, but to queue for a Big Mac. For western consumer goods companies, the opening up of an East European market of 400 million brand-starved consumers was even more enticing. Few East Europeans possessed a TV set that wasn't decades old, or owned a pair of good-quality jeans, or had ever tasted an avocado or even a banana. Flashing a pack of Marlboro cigarettes on a Soviet road was enough for any hitchhiker to attract a lift within seconds. Beauty-conscious Bulgarian women spent their savings to acquire Nina Ricci or Estee Lauder make-ups, while Czechs scrambled onto the daily 5 am coach to Nuremberg, Germany, in search of Sony hi-fis. Everything from Procter & Gamble detergents to Danone yoghurts was greeted with hungry fascination.

It looked like the beginning of a capitalist rampage, and sales soared. One survey showed that one in four western firms were reporting annual sales growth of 50 per cent in Russia, and some companies saw their turnover double every year for much of the decade.[1] Fast-moving consumer goods (FMCG) firms reported similar growth in Poland, the biggest East European market in value terms, on the back of galloping annual GDP expansion of 5–7 per cent (see chapter 6). How was such sales growth possible when official average wages ranged from $50–250 per month (see Table 5.1)?.

The answer revealed a lot about the way social and economic life was organised in Eastern Europe in the early 1990s. Surveys almost always underestimated real purchasing power, since respondents, either out of habit or a genuine concern about nosey authorities, tended to conceal their true incomes. Many had hoarded local and hard currency during the years when there was nothing in the shops worth buying. The lack of a trustworthy banking system (to say nothing of anaemic capital markets) meant that when a few consumer goods did become available, a fridge or a piece of furniture became a good way to hold one's wealth.

Personal debt rose too, as banks began to lend to consumers (it doubled in Poland in the early 1990s), although debt levels were low compared to those of western households. There was also 'restitution', introduced most notably in the Czech Republic, which allowed owners, or their descendants, to reclaim property that had been confiscated by the communist regime as far back as 1948. Some of these lucky citizens suddenly came into possession of a factory or an apartment block, and lived well from the rents.

Official incomes were usually supplemented by a thriving grey or black market that accounted for an estimated 30 per cent of the

Table 5.1   Average monthly wages in selected countries (US$), 1991

Hungary	240
Poland	165
Czechoslovakia	129
Romania	120
Bulgaria	56
Russia	23

Source: International Labour Organisation.

economy, on average, in the region. Staff at one Warsaw unemployment benefits office regularly complained about sun-tanned yuppies
who would claim their payout before racing off in flashy new sports
cars. At the other end of the scale, anyone in the former Soviet Union
with a car was also a freelance taxi driver, as pedestrians commonly
hitched a lift (and still do) for a couple of dollars a ride. There were
plenty of 'in-kind' incomes to factor in too – rural households grew
their own fresh vegetables and bartered them to get an old motor fixed
or to have a free haircut, while many women sewed their own clothes.
Finally, housing costs typically accounted for a much lower share of
family budgets than in the West. Several generations often squeezed
into a single house or apartment, and rents and most utilities were
heavily subsidised by the state.

In addition, the multinationals had a rather distorted view of the
market, since they tended to focus on relatively wealthy urban consumers, and ignored the poorer provinces. In Russia, few salesmen ven-
tured beyond Moscow and St. Petersburg. Younger Muscovites in
particular seemed to love spending whenever possible, a trait perhaps
fuelled by their desire to be seen as equal in this respect to any west-
erner. One multinational company manager notes how as early as
1993–94, wealthy Russian men had swapped their track suits and train-
ers for Armani suits and were to be seen in night clubs with a bottle of
champagne in either hand and a female model on either arm, spending a small fortune. Given half a chance, young Russians were far
bigger spenders than the high-salaried western bankers in Moscow.
This spawned a genre of 'New Russian' jokes, based on splashing out
huge sums, often unnecessarily. 'In this market, you never advertise
something as cheap', said one market research analyst.[2] Mercedes' dealerships in Russia were among its fastest growing outlets in the world,
and when Reebok opened its first Moscow store in 1993, the company
found that its most expensive sports shoes sold the fastest.

One Scandinavian student in Russia witnessed this new, seemingly
irreconcilable cultural divide first hand, during an acrimonious split
with a local girl. He had met Irina in the small western Russian town of
Bryansk in the early 1990s. The town was starting to see western consumer goods, but few of the big brand-name clothes and make-ups had
arrived in the shops, and there were few western cars on the roads.
There was little to do in the evenings. The local disco had the smell of
sewage running through it, and the town's youth spent the nights
promenading in the park and by the fountain, all under the ever-
present glare of a Lenin statue that older residents refused to see torn

down. Street crime was low, although local gangs swaggered in the bars. Irina wanted desperately to make her way to the West. She had saved a thousand dollars, and her new Scandinavian boyfriend organised the visa. But if it was love at first sight, it wasn't to last.

He recalls how, although she was saving her money to go to the West, she insisted on buying the most expensive make-up. 'It must be Nina Ricci. I refuse to pay less than $20 for a pot of face cream. No woman is beautiful without the best creams,' she would say. After Irina ran out of make-up, a female friend of his kindly offered some of her own. Irina only wanted to know how much it cost, and declared that she would rather stay indoors than use anything but the best. It was the same story with lipsticks, eyeliner and everything else, says the boyfriend. 'She never washed it off – there were lumps of make-up hanging off her eyelids. And she would buy the most expensive shoes – something shiny and expensive – but her socks would stink, she never changed them! It was all exterior. Everything was status', he says. When they met a man with a BMW car, she would urge her girlfriend to make a date with him, regardless of how charmless or ugly he might be. 'But why not? He has a CD player in the car, go with him', she implored. None of this sat well with Scandinavian moderation, and the relationship ended.

Meanwhile, the rest of Russia was experimenting with the new choices on offer. Young people had the money and were better placed to succeed in the new conditions than their parents (whom they often supported, along with a grandparent or two). And the 20-somethings were ready to experiment with brands. This meant that big multinationals could be usurped in the Russian market by a smaller, nimbler competitor, either local or foreign. Dandy, a small Danish chewing gum maker, initially won a bigger market share in Russia than US giant Wrigley, for example. The fact that a product came from the West was also an important consideration, more so than the brand itself – a view held over from the days when a product's quality could be determined simply by knowing in which factory it was produced. For a while after 1991 Russians regarded a product made in the US or Germany as superior to the same product made by the same firm in Turkey, China or elsewhere in Eastern Europe. Curiosity was immense. 'Does Daz really wash whiter than white?' amazed housewives would ask.

The first signs that western goods and imagery could not simply be transported east became apparent in the advertising industry in the mid-1990s, and the different cultural perspectives required western corporations to tread carefully. Sometimes multinationals could get away with tweaking a global advert, thereby avoiding the cost of running separate campaigns for each country. However, one example from a report published by the Economist Intelligence Unit shows how this approach could carry dangers:

> A ruggedly handsome young man speeds down a desert highway on a powerful motorcycle. He stops at a roadside café and buys a packet of cigarettes from a machine. Roaring on, he encounters a gorgeous blonde having mechanical troubles with an expensive sports car. He fixes it in no time, and she gives him her phone number with a lingering, sultry look. Watching her drive off, he lights up with ruggedly bemused satisfaction. A narrator intones the brand and slogan.
>
> To most viewers around the world these 30 seconds of televised pantomime would read plainly enough. But a Moscow focus group offered some original deconstructions. Many thought the advertised commodity was the motorcycle (which they presumed was a Harley Davidson). Others wondered why the hero suddenly stopped to play a slot machine. Some who did follow the plot line concluded the cigarette was for losers since the girl left without the boy.[3]

Attempts to appeal to Russian sentiments could also miss the mark. In a light-hearted ad for Mars bars, which showed a typically Russian family sharing a meal with friends, the hostess cut up slices of its chocolate bars for guests. Many viewers felt that this patronised Russian family culture. East Europeans also had difficulty relating to ads with non-white faces. As Stephen Lee, Vice President for Strategic Planning at US food group Kraft Foods, points out, ads needed to have people 'who look like local people'. Wrigley started to do well in Russia after it introduced a new ad showing genuine local teenagers praising its gum, while a Turkish brand of jeans suddenly became popular after the manufacturer adopted a Russian boy band in its promotions. Unsurprisingly, local talent rapidly rose to the top of the big western advertising agencies, and western consumer goods firms soon started employing local agencies.

Although the new Russian yuppies continued to seek out over-priced goods, the emerging middle class had begun a sober reassessment of their buying patterns even before the rouble crash of August 1998. This stemmed primarily from tougher economic conditions and the improving quality of cheaper Russian-made products, but there was also a latent and often irrational nationalism at work. As Craig Mellow, an author and analyst of Russian business and politics, wrote: 'Russia's love-hate, inferior–superior, envy-despise relationship with the West is a central theme of its history. The dragon has awoken anew since the fall of communism'.[4]

Mars soon got a taste of the changing attitudes. The company was one of the first firms into Russia, building a distribution network to the smallest, remotest towns, and backing this up with nationwide adverts showing handsome, ambitious youths tucking into their *Snickers* bars. The impact was explosive. Sales soared throughout the country, leaving Nestlé, Cadbury and local rivals far behind. But many Russians who could barely afford basic foods soon tired of the Americanised image of the good life, and Mars became a target for attacks by nationalist politicians.

Russians embraced any local company that could hold its own against western goods. The rise of Vladimir Dovgan, a businessman from Vologda in north-west Russia, showed that local producers could tap into this patriotic sentiment, as long as they could raise the quality of their products to western standards and package them smartly. Starting with sales of vodka in 1996, his company branched out into over 2000 different product lines, from patés to chocolates. Russians lapped it up, charmed no doubt by the picture of Dovgan himself on the packaging.

Crash and backlash: consumers retrench

The August 1998 crash brought these issues into the open, testing both the attitude of Russian consumers to the multinationals, and the commitment of foreign firms to the local market. The rouble plummeted by around 75 per cent, making imported goods impossibly expensive for the fledgling middle class that multinationals regarded as the main buyers of western goods in the long term. Around 60 per cent of Russian families now found themselves on incomes of $150 or less per month, twice as many as before the crash. Middle-class incomes were ravished, and the average Russian's savings dwindled to a mere $40. The impact was everywhere to be seen. Advertising dried up, bars emptied out, and swanky Moscow restaurants that until recently had served overpriced food to the upcoming business elite started advertising cut-price 'crisis menus'.

As sales simply vanished during the rest of 1998, Western firms began scrambling to make sense of the sudden change in fortunes. Many adopted a belated cynicism about the market. Having predicted not long before that Russia might even overtake the US in spending power within a couple of generations, executives looked around for someone to blame. Of course the boom could not last, they said, with the benefit of hindsight – it was all froth and no substance. Some vowed never to trust the Russian market again.

Some western brands survived better than others in the immediate aftermath of the crash. Few Russians were so deluded as to believe that locally-made electronics goods were a match for German, Dutch or Japanese brands. Similarly, world famous food and drink companies such as McDonald's or Coca-Cola, although hurt in the crash, were always accorded respect by consumers. But most other western firms had to adjust very quickly, typically by slashing costs, postponing all investment decisions and laying off staff (although many did their best to avoid the latter). PepsiCo, 3M and Mars downsized and then waited to see how the economy developed. Many firms sent their most prized Russian managers to work in the west, and wait out the crisis (see chapter 1). Foreign firms in the dairy sector were especially vulnerable; competition from local firms quickly increased as newly price-conscious Russians became nostalgic for home-grown products. Dutch firm Campina and Italy's Parmalat both mothballed plans for new factories. There were even staff losses back home as a result of problems in Russia; margarine maker Raisio (Finland) announced layoffs in Finland and Sweden.

The moment of truth had arrived for both the multinationals and Russian consumers. If these firms really were committed to investing in Russia and offering affordable products, they would have to start (or increase) local production rather than simply importing their goods. Those multinationals that had longer-term plans to set up in Russia were forced to make a decision now. Setting up was no small undertaking; Russia's business environment was perceived as being notoriously hostile, a perception fuelled by countless stories in the western media about daylight robberies, murders and gangster-politicians. But multinationals could not escape the logic of cost, which led many of them to increase production in Russia. Before the crash, Danone imported around 80 per cent of the products that it sold in Russia, and charged prices 40 per cent higher than those of its local competitors. After the crash, the effective rouble price of Danone products tripled. The company's only hope of surviving was to crank up production at its Moscow plant and squeeze its profit margin to the limit. Now was the time to shift to no-frills, locally made products, and accept a smaller profit – or none at all – for the sake of survival and (hopefully) a larger market share in the future.

UK confectionery maker Cadbury and Germany's Stollwerck, which had shut down their plants for a month after the crash, restarted local production and soon reached pre-crisis levels of output (although sales revenue was obviously lower). RJ Reynolds, which had also halted production temporarily, introduced a low-price [Czar] *Peter Ist* cigarette brand, and ploughed a cool $120m into its St Petersburg plant. And Italian white-goods manufacturer Merloni, which had imported many of its products during the previous five fat years, boosted its local presence by buying the Stinol washing machine maker in Lipetsk for $120m. Even Mars's pet food sales did well – a surprise in a country where feeding a dog its own special food was deemed eccentric. Dandy, the chewing gum maker, declared soon after the crash that it was now planning to expand as fast as possible in Russia.

Winning hearts and minds: localising the brand

Those western consumer goods makers that did pull through in Russia did so with a combination of flexibility and acute sensitivity to the needs of local consumers. 'We want to establish our brand as something permanent and unshakeable, not something that changes shape every time the economy takes a turn,' said the managing director of one western drinks company. Showing commitment in hard times was part of the story, but the multinationals also had to contend with a cultural backlash, and found themselves in a battle for the hearts and minds of consumers. 'Western players ignore Russians' traditional preferences, and cultural cast of mind, at their peril,' declared John Rose, CEO of advertising agency Rose Creative Strategies.[5]

Maximillian Friedman, the former director of Conceptual Entertainment, a Moscow-based marketing company, observed that although there was an anti-western (particularly anti-US) backlash, most Russian consumers wanted a mix of Russian and western brands. They recognised that the West still represented quality, and therefore wanted the best of that. But at the same time, they wanted to learn from the West so that their home-grown products could eventually compete with foreign brands. Friedman notes:

> Underpinning the need for greater sensitivity is a belief that Russia's emerging consumer culture need not be wholly anti- or pro-Western. Western ideas and products have been very widely and unconsciously adopted by young people over the last decade and

have defined the consumer culture for the population as a whole. It is quite common for 60-year-old taxi drivers to listen to techno music, for instance.

Of course, some brands (Coca-Cola, McDonald's or Levi's) are obviously Western, and others (Lada or Stolichnaya vodka) obviously Russian. But there is a huge area in between, including Russian-sounding brands produced by locally based Western firms (such as *Peter 1st* cigarettes) and Russian brands with Western names (Yes!, Wimm-Bill-Dann). While it is important to introduce a local flavour to your product, it is equally important to know the limits to this approach. Coca-Cola's famed advert, which incorporated Coke into a Russian fairy-tale, grated on many viewers, who felt that a symbolically US product was out of place in a quintessentially Russian tale.[6]

Although the experience of western brands in Russia was extreme, the story was not so different elsewhere in the region. An initial lunge for western goods was followed by a backlash against high prices, and a growing preference for cheaper and much-improved local products, particularly during difficult economic times. This led to a fusion of local and foreign brands. Take the case of Kvass, a communist-era drink made from a fast-fermenting mix of water, rye and yeast, which made a comeback in 1998 as local producers started improving the taste with new flavours. Kvass became hugely popular among nostalgic 30–60 year-olds, especially in the Baltic states. Sales there outstripped those of Coca-Cola, which eventually bought one of the leading Kvass producers. Or take Traubisoda, a white grape soda popular in Hungary in the 1970s. The drink was relaunched by local-based businessman Saloman Berkowitz in 1993, using its old cartoon emblem that many middle-aged Hungarians remembered from childhood. As research by advertising agency Saatchi & Saatchi showed, Hungarians in the mid-1990s yearned for local products that could stack up against foreign imports. Similarly, the Czech Republic launched the 'Czech made' award in the early 1990s, with the aim of instilling pride in Czech products made to international standards.

The localisation of consumer goods reflected not so much the sudden rise of home-grown manufacturers but rather the decision by western investors to recast their brand portfolio. Some, such as Kraft Foods or washing powder maker Henkel, had from the outset adopted a strategy to promote local brands. Kraft imported its better-known global brands, such as *Milka* chocolate and *Jacobs* coffee, and sold them as premium products in the local market, but the company also picked up local brands through its acquisition of 11 mainly state-owned coffee and confectionery companies. Similarly, Henkel deliberately looked for local brands with a strong heritage that could be resuscitated, such as washing powders *Palmex* in the Czech Republic or *Tomi* in Hungary. Nestlé promoted the popular *Boci* plain chocolate bar in Hungary, while United Biscuits of the UK acquired Gyori Keksz, a Hungarian biscuit company with a brand dating back to the 1930s, rather than introduce its own *McVitie's* label. Those multinationals that had assumed that local brands would simply disappear (or even planned to kill them off) suddenly changed tack when it became apparent that sales of local brands were in fact holding up. Consumers had strong loyalties, sometimes to the seemingly least appealing products; Czechs continued to buy a drearily packaged coffee called 'coffee mix' up to the mid-1990s.[7] Multinationals even invented their own local brands. Danone launched *turo rudi*, a Hungarian sweet cheese and chocolate combination. Douwe Egberts introduced *Omnia*, an inexpensive coffee, into Hungary, and Kraft Foods responded with *Harmonia*.

Consumer goods manufacturers did not ride roughshod over local tastes and sentiments, but instead adopted and promoted anything of a domestic nature that was salvageable in the new economy. This reflected several considerations besides the obvious one of profitability. Western firms often simply wanted to avoid the hassles of building up a brand from scratch (although the lack of brand loyalty in the region meant that such a strategy could be successful). They were also sensitive to nationalist concerns that they were buying local firms in order to close them down. This did not happen. Indeed, several western managers say that taking over local production sites rather than continuing to import products helped multinationals to be seen as saviours rather than destroyers of jobs in their key sales markets. The new western owners invested huge amounts to modernise equipment, obtain more consistent quality, reduce levels of impurities, improve packaging and marketing, and add new lines, sizes and variations while retaining local tastes and names. Almost every FMCG category in Eastern Europe is now dominated by western-owned but locally-made brands. According to Marek Sebestak, Chairman of the BBDO advertising agency in Eastern Europe, most East Europeans see these brands as local, regardless of who owns the company that makes them.

And what of locally-owned firms? The successful ones have strong, high-quality brands and managers who have absorbed a few tricks of the trade about packaging and presentation from their western competitors. Pick, a salami maker based in Szeged, Hungary, does well at home and exports to the West. Budweiser beer, widely regarded by beer lovers as one of the best in the world, remains in Czech hands and is also exported. The Budejovicky Budvar brewery in southern Bohemia has successfully resisted the advances of the giant US brewer Anheuser Busch, which sells the blander *Bud* in Europe and its own version of Budweiser in the US.[8] Locally produced pharmaceuticals have given western competitors a run for their money; Etoran, an analgesic made by Polpharma, enjoys near-total brand recognition in Poland, and matches well-regarded western competition in both price and quality. Local firm Pliva dominates the pharmaceuticals market in Croatia, while Slovenia's Lek fared well for a decade and was eventually sold to Swiss drugmaker Novartis in 2002 for over $1 billion.

One of the most famous local start-ups is Russian dairy and drinks firm Wimm-Bill-Dann. (In a reversal of the trend to Russify brand names, the company was attempting to evoke images of English lawn tennis.) Unlike most western companies, Wimm-Bill-Dann focused on central Russia, Siberia and as far east as Vladivostok, and was able to outstrip the non-carbonated soft drinks of Coca-Cola and PepsiCo in sales and advertising spending. Wimm-Bill-Dann also dominated the local dairy sector as ordinary Russians retained a preference for 'their own' milk, kefir (sour yoghurt) or tvorok (cottage cheese). The company boasted annual sales growth rates of up to 40 per cent during the 1990s, and was valued at more than $1 billion when it was floated on the New York Stock Exchange in 2002. Its owners eventually sold out to UK food group Cadbury.

As well as having a better understanding of local consumer tastes, domestic firms also had other advantages. They usually paid staff less than western-owned firms did, and often had an easier ride from the tax or health inspectors. Coca-Cola often claimed that its costs were higher than those of local competitors throughout the region because the latter could get away with lower biological and safety testing standards. Managers at Kraft Foods recall how they always seemed to have to settle unpaid back taxes and social security bills and increase wages on taking over a new factory. Yet many locally-owned firms were unable to survive in a competitive market place, and fewer still were able to export. Forty years or more of communism had stifled the business skills of local entrepreneurs, a loss that could best be made good by learning from the recently-arrived multinationals.

Brand on the run: counterfeit goods

Getting the branding and advertising right in a volatile market such as Russia was only part of the learning process for western companies. In order to get their goods to the consumer, multinationals also needed a distribution strategy. There were few nationwide distributors anywhere in the region, and those that could reach remote areas were often run by criminal groups or inefficient state organisations. The huge distances that goods had to travel in Russia made western companies vulnerable to bureaucratic and criminal meddling, while in East-central Europe consumer goods firms initially found themselves using dozens of different distributors. As one confectionery maker in Poland lamented: 'How do you get four layers of wholesalers to pass on your price promotion? The answer is: you can't. A lot will simply pocket the difference'. Chewing gum producer Dandy created a nationwide distribution network in Russia virtually single-handedly, as did the larger multinationals. However, such efforts also ran into problems. Cigarette firm Philip Morris established its own fleet of vans in the Czech Republic with the PM logo painted on the side, only for them to become prime targets for carjacking.

An even more worrying form of criminal attack was counterfeiting, which could wreck consumer trust in a brand. In a region that barely understood the concept of property rights, western firms found it difficult to explain what was wrong with slapping a false western label on a jar of coffee or bottle of alcohol and selling it at a premium. Kraft Foods estimated that 30 per cent of Jacobs-labelled coffee sold in Russia was counterfeit. In the case of computer software, that figure could rise to a staggering 90 per cent. Even the state TV stations in Kazakhstan would show pirated Hollywood films, oblivious to the message displayed at the bottom of the screen prohibiting their illegal use.

Another common ruse was for local 'entrepreneurs' to register an internationally renowned brand name as their own, before the real owner had a chance to do so. In Russia, the notorious Sergei Zuikov registered more than 2000 Western trademarks, openly admitting that his aim was to sell them back to their original owners at an exorbitant price. In one case in 1998, Becton Dickinson, a US medical supplies firm, lost the right to its own trademarks because a certain Russian condom manufacturer had registered them first. He then demanded $100 000 from each of Becton's distributors for the right to use 'his' trademarks.

Users of counterfeit goods in the West typically claim that such piracy benefits the poor, giving them access to products that would otherwise have been unaffordable – an argument with which courts in Eastern Europe were often sympathetic. Even western political analysts could be seduced. One speaker at a conference in Sofia on music piracy admitted that during the lunch break he had bought counterfeit CDs on the street for a dollar a disc. However, governments across the region began to crack down on the product pirates in the late 1990s, not only because of pressure from foreign investors and bodies such as the World Trade Organisation, but also because governments themselves began to wise up to the dangers of counterfeit goods. Legitimate local firms were keen to protect their own home-grown brands, while scientists starved of state support were desperate to protect their inventions. Ukrainian computer programmers – among the best in the world – wanted to hold on to a decent job that could earn them a fair wage. The Russian authorities were concerned at the 40 000 alcohol-related deaths each year that stemmed from false labelling of substandard and dangerous drink, especially vodka.

Despite these obstacles, multinationals have been instrumental in creating sophisticated, high-quality consumer goods markets across Eastern Europe without junking local culture. Some of the changes may appear superficial or trivial; freedom surely means more than simply adding nuts, raisins and cream fillings to a bar of chocolate. Nevertheless, the extra attention given to the smallest details of consumer needs is helping to improve life for ordinary people.

A quiet revolution: retailing

Besides dealing with local competition, criminal gangs and economic volatility, western FMCG companies were closely linked with another, equally dramatic change in the social and economic landscape of Eastern Europe during the 1990s – the rise of the hypermarket. Sir Terry Leahy, CEO of Tesco, one of the largest retail operators in the region, describes the phenomenon as 'the quiet revolution'.

Not so long ago, a typical shopping trip in Eastern Europe was a logistical nightmare – time-consuming, expensive, and more a question of chance and good contacts than price and value for money. Shops typically had three different queues: one to see the product, one to pay for it, and one to collect it. Sales clerks trekked behind customers, not to assist, but to guard against shoplifting (although research by security firms shows that staff are more likely to steal than customers). Produce was kept behind counters, and shop assistants acted as if these were their personal possessions to dispense with as they saw fit, sometimes keeping them off the shelves for themselves, or selling them to friends and family. Cashiers added up prices with an abacus (and still do in remote areas of the CIS), and the security guard would check the customers' receipts on their way out to make sure that they had paid.

Much of this changed during the 1990s, not least because the supply of consumer goods multiplied exponentially, thereby shifting the balance of power away from the shop-owner. But even when an owner tried to run a shop intelligently, a simple lack of business experience and the inadequate supply infrastructure meant that many of the archaic, communist-era practices persisted for years. Staff barely greeted the customer (and even now rarely smile), and queues were long. Stock remained unmonitored, and displays were haphazard. Department stores would often display big-ticket items such as beds and wardrobes near the ground-floor entrance, as if they were 'impulse purchases'.

Old habits die hard. As one Tesco executive pointed out, local shops can be their own worst enemy, driving themselves out of the market. Although the opinion may appear harsh, most westerners living in the region have at least one absurd shopping story to tell – usually about appalling salesmanship. Take the corner shop in Prague where the author goes regularly to buy milk, coffee, water, bread and a newspaper. The shop competes with a (not very efficient) Austrian-owned Julius Meinl supermarket up the road, which often racks up queues of 30 or more people at the tills. That fact alone should give plenty of life to the smaller stores in the neighbourhood. But despite moaning about the new foreign competition, the shop owner supplies no plastic bags for his customers. When asked how the customer can carry half a dozen purchases, the assistant rummages in the back room and occasionally finds a huge cardboard box. Otherwise, the customer is able only to buy half the items that he wants. It's a ritual that occurs on almost every visit.

Sometimes a shopping trip can reach Monty Python levels of absurdity. One western businessman, a fluent Czech speaker who bought a glass door for his home sauna from a shop in Prague, recalls his conversation when he returned the following day in the hope of exchanging it for a wooden door:

Customer: 'I bought this glass door yesterday, but I want to swap it for a wooden door, please.'
Assistant: 'I'm sorry, it's not possible to swap.'

Customer: 'I have the receipt, and the manager said it was OK to swap.'

Assistant: 'The manager isn't here. You have to discuss the problem with him.'

Customer: 'When does he get in?'

Assistant: 'He's on holiday. He's back in two weeks.'

Customer: 'OK then, forget the swap, I'll just buy the wooden door as well.'

Assistant: 'I would prefer it if you waited for the manager.'

Customer: 'You don't understand. Forget that I ever bought a glass door. That's my problem. Think of me as a completely new customer. Now, I would like to buy a wooden door for my sauna – that one there!'

Assistant: 'You know, it's getting very complicated now. Can't you wait two weeks.'

Customer: 'It's not complicated. I want to buy that wooden door. Here's the cash! In my hand!

Assistant: 'No, I don't want to get into problems. It's better if you wait till the manager returns.'

Needless to say, the customer decided to stick with the original glass door. 'They do everything in their power not to sell their products', he concluded, as the Czech economy sank into recession.

The inability of many East European retail staff to connect with the customer, even in the new century, reveals a worrying need for further training and education, which is most likely to occur under the auspices of Western retailers. This began in a limited way when supermarkets such as Julius Meinl and German chain Billa – both from countries not exactly noted for their retailing flexibility – began expanding into Eastern Europe in the early 1990s. Bigger international players such as Tesco from the UK, Carrefour and Auchan from France, Ahold from the Netherlands and Metro from Germany, arrived in the mid-1990s, building supermarkets and hypermarkets in the major cities.

Tesco's arrival was somewhat inadvertent. A Hungarian manager working for Tesco in the UK had been contacted by an old friend in Hungary, who had acquired a local store and was seeking help in running it. Tesco told its Hungarian employee to give the Hungarian store a go and report back on the prospects for the retail market there. The news was good. The store had competent managers, and could benefit from western investment and logistical backing. This whetted Tesco's appetite, especially as growth in western markets was slowing.

Tesco's first acquisition was a 2000-square-metre site in the southern Hungarian town of Baja, which had formerly been a Soviet army base. When the British managers arrived with their construction team to build the store, they found 275 Kalashnikov rifles, several landmines and other military equipment that the Red Army had left behind in order to fill up their departing trucks with light fittings, floor tiles, windows, and anything else that might be of value back home. Soon the store in Baja was up and running, and hugely successful. Tesco subsequently expanded rapidly in Eastern Europe, acquiring the Savia and HIT supermarket chains in Poland, and SMarkt in Hungary. It also took over the Prior stores in the Czech Republic and Slovakia from K-Mart, and built numerous shopping malls. By 2003 Tesco had over 100 hypermarkets in the region.

The biggest challenge that Tesco faced at first was not improving service, but trying to fill its shelves with a reliable supply of goods that met its quality and safety standards. Supply chains were limited and highly bureaucratic, with hundreds of goods delivered directly to stores rather than through central depots. Tesco hunted down any local company that could meet its quality standards, or had the potential to do so, in a desperate attempt to fill the shelves. Local suppliers were invited to workshops where experts brought in from the UK taught them everything from packaging to the latest food technology. Once a supplier was up to scratch and could supply a single Tesco outlet, it would be expected to grow alongside the retailer and supply other stores in the country and abroad. A Slovak producer of sanitary towels and a Polish light bulb maker became suppliers to Tesco stores worldwide, while GTH, a Czech pasta manufacturer, saw its sales grow by some 1200 per cent over two years after becoming a major supplier to Tesco.

The eyes of many local suppliers bulged when they saw the size of orders that the hypermarkets were promising, and they rushed to service the new chains. Most were naïve and inexperienced. Hundreds of local firms agreed contracts at quality levels that they could not meet, and at prices that left margins so thin as to force them out of business. Not everyone rushed in without a thought for the long term, however. Zenon Suchanski, a Warsaw-based tea importer, seems an unlikely entrepreneur. In 1990, after working at the state tea trading firm for 20 years, he decided to make use of the new freedoms and set up his own tea firm. This sudden burst of energy surprised his family, since he was already 57 years old and they were expecting him to retire.

He began by importing tea from India, Sri Lanka and China in pre-packed and open cases, and then packaging and selling the products under his own ZAS brand. Although he had no start-up capital, he was able to buy everything on credit. By 1994 his was the number one tea company in the country, importing around 7000 tonnes a year. Having been established before the hypermarkets arrived in Poland, he was in a position of relative strength, and signed limited supply agreements with Dutch cash-and-carry chain Makro, Real, Biedronka, Auchan, Carrefour and several others. Spreading the customer base was his wisest move. 'Negotiations are really hard with these chains,' Suchanski says. 'They think that they can dictate the deal.' In most cases they can. Plenty of small Polish companies agreed to supply a single chain without having the brand name or customer base to counter the pressure from the retailer, and were wiped out as a result. He diligently guards his ZAS brand, which accounts for 75 per cent of his company's output (the remaining 25 per cent is produced for retailers' own brands). Half his output goes to the big hypermarket chains. 'You cannot be in the market without doing some business with them,' he says. His caution has meant that his company's annual revenues have halved since the hypermarkets arrived, from around $12m in 1994 to $6m in 2003, but he says that profits are still healthy. Suchanski says that he would rather lose a major client than sign a bad deal, and will never agree to supply a single chain exclusively. He once walked out of negotiations with a major French chain that told him all contracts were non-negotiable.

Customer care: servicing the client

If the arrival of hypermarkets suddenly made life tougher for many suppliers, consumers clearly stood to benefit, and they welcomed the new hypermarkets with open bags. Outlets mushroomed across East-central Europe, and it was clear that western retail chains had more than just novelty value. Market research surveys showed that consumers appreciated several tangible benefits. The most important were lower prices and better-quality goods, but shoppers also liked the wider product range, with around 50 000 lines in a store; helpful staff; bright, clean, well-organised stores; and long opening hours, in some cases 24 hours. Interestingly, shorter queues – a perennial demand of western shoppers – were initially not a priority among shoppers in the East, and only became so after the supermarkets and hypermarkets had already shortened them. Some of the new chains have created their own queues. When the Polus shopping centre opened in Budapest in 1996, for example, the lines stretched for three miles, and even in 2002, UK electronics retailer Dixons had to call in the police to manage the crowds attracted by opening-day bargains at its new Budapest store.

Enthusiasm for the new shopping culture shows little sign of abating. By 2001, only half a decade after the first hypermarkets were built, they accounted for 30 per cent of household spending on consumer goods in the Czech Republic (and were the preferred shopping venues for 40 per cent of Czechs), and 33 per cent in Hungary. International retail chains account for 40 per cent of consumer goods sales in Poland, up from 30 per cent in 1999, according to German market research group GfK. Hypermarket penetration in East-central Europe will gradually approach western levels, with up to twice as many outlets per capita as at present, as new consumer-finance schemes boost spending, and as higher car ownership allows more people to reach outlying shopping centres. Although three-fifths of Czech households surveyed by GfK regularly drive to the shops, Poles, with fewer cars per person, continue to shop in local stores.

Incoma, a Czech market research agency, reports:

> More than four-fifths of respondents need [a maximum of] 20 minutes to reach 'their' shopping centre [and] usually spend quite a long time on-site. Only a fifth of visitors [spend] less than an hour, while 62 per cent stay one to two hours [on each visit]. 19 per cent of visitors stay three or more hours .... Although it might seem that people are fed up by shopping centres already, the opposite is true. 38 per cent of the respondents say that they would like to spend even more time in a shopping centre.[9]

Many people go to the hypermarkets just to socialise. 'It's kind of creepy,' says Hana Lesenarova, a leading Czech journalist. When pranksters at a film school in Prague advertised the opening of an imaginary new western supermarket called 'Czech Dream' in 2003, thousands of people turned up hoping for some first-day bargains.

Incoma's research concludes that as a consequence of the arrival of western hypermarkets over the course of ten years to 2003 '...the proportion of satisfied customers had reached a very high level, usually exceeding 90 per cent', it noted. The highest satisfaction increase had been achieved with the price level of consumer goods (the proportion of satisfied customers increased from 24 in 1993 to 86 per cent) and with the range of goods (from 68 in 1993 to 95 per cent), the report concludes.[10]

The unprecedented attention given to the customer, resulting in innovations and efficiencies that were previously unheard of in the region, has clearly struck a chord. Tesco's Sir Terry Leahy notes: 'We track customers' views and tastes like an astronomer tracks the stars. In the retailer's universe how customers think and behave revolves around tangible issues: the type of food they eat and products they want; how, where and when they shop; the prices they can afford'.[11]

According to one analysis of the Czech market:

> The hypermarkets' mountain of consumer purchasing data allows them to arrange innovative promotions as well. Research shows, for example, that younger married males tend to go shopping on Friday, buy disposable nappies for their children, and drink beer in front of the television at home instead of in the pub as is typical of the older generation. The result, in this case, has been a Friday hypermarket promotion of bottled beer and nappies, with both products found together on the store shelves. Similarly, retailers experience a surge in purchases on the 10th and 11th of each month, when most workers receive their pay cheques. Capitalising on this anomaly involves fine-tuning what products get stocked. Globus (Germany) and other chains have considered increasing the space allocated to budget foods at the beginning of the month, with higher-cost meat and wine promotions in place for mid-month. At the same time, the increasing co-ordination between large retailers and banks through the use of debit and credit cards has allowed hypermarkets to smooth out these purchasing peaks and troughs, reducing the suppliers' influence over the process.[12]

The addition of multiplex cinemas, restaurants and other leisure activities to shopping centres means that shopping trips in Eastern Europe increasingly resemble those in the West. As standards are raised and competition among large retailers heats up, customers have become less passive and increasingly picky, particularly in the more developed markets of the region, and are registering a new impatience for other improvements, from speedier service to better parking facilities.

But for the time being most East Europeans still seek out the lowest prices. Tesco admits that its customers throughout the region continue to sniff out bargains and promotions across town and in rival supermarkets; loyalty to a particular outlet or chain still counts for little. A Polish government survey in 2001 shows that prices at foreign-owned chains are five to ten per cent lower than those charged by local retailers – because hypermarkets are more able to extract discounts from suppliers, or have them sponsor promotions, and can demand better credit terms. Increasing competition among big retail chains, as well as among consumer goods manufacturers themselves, has driven down prices, especially of foods. The food component of many countries' inflation baskets has fallen by two to three percentage points since the early 1990s before hypermarkets had arrived in force. Western retailers have helped to put more downward pressure on prices by selling 'own-brand' goods, often for 20–40 per cent less than the branded alternatives. Shallow-pocketed East Europeans are particularly keen on own-brand products such as milk or toilet paper, where there is little difference in quality with pricier brands.[13]

The retail revolution has yet to spread fully to the Balkans and the former Soviet Union. But it is not difficult to see how ordinary shoppers are likely to react. In Russia, the arrival of any big foreign-owned shopping outlet has a tremendous impact. In 1999 Swedish furniture retailer Ikea opened a store on the outskirts of Moscow that rapidly became one of its most profitable in the world, and a second store followed soon. Russia's emerging middle classes, tired of traditional heavy brown furniture, fell upon Ikea's light-wood designs. Ikea says that the average customer in its Moscow outlet spends around $70 per visit, about the same as in Ikea stores in Sweden. Several more Ikea stores are planned for Moscow and Russia's regions in coming years. Although Ikea, German hypermarket chain Metro and Ramenka from Turkey have been successful, few other large western retailers have taken the plunge in Russia, and most western-style retailing takes place through small franchising operations. According to Sir Terry Leahy Tesco has stayed out of the market largely because the company still sees plenty of growth potential in its East-central European markets. Other retailers are wary of the operating environment in Russia.

As with local producers of consumer goods, some local retailers in Russia have also performed well. Shortly after the 1998 economic crash, a group of Russians who had been trained at US management consultancy McKinsey took over a local pharmacy chain, and re-launched it with the trendy new name of '36.6' (a reference to human body temperature). The chain had expanded to 173 outlets by mid-2004. Mercator, a Slovenian retail chain that dominates its home market, has expanded into Croatia. But most local chains rely heavily on certain in-built advantages over foreign firms, one of the biggest of which can be the fact that local shopkeepers often pay little or no rent. Western retailers in Poland, for example, are asked to pay several times the rent that locals are charged, and often an additional one-off payment of some $70 000 for a single downtown unit. In Moscow too, westerners pay a heavy premium over their Russian competitors to rent centrally-located sites. GUM, a Russian department store, pays only $75 per square metre for its space; western rivals have had to pay up to $2500 for the same central Moscow location.[14]

Despite the vicious price wars between the foreign retail giants in Eastern Europe, smaller shops that charge higher prices can still survive as a result of their street-corner accessibility. Indeed, Tesco and other large hypermarket chains do not even regard such local stores as competitors. However, the western retail invasion has spelt trouble for many small local supermarkets that don't have a particular niche. Interkontakt, the leading Czech retail chain, was felled in 1999 by a combination of excessive debts and poor management.

Hypermarkets have made other enemies too, including local suppliers who do not have the negotiating power to resist the demands of large retailers or the capacity to supply them on an international scale. Anger among these suppliers has fuelled political protest; the parliaments in Poland and Slovakia in particular have tried to introduce laws to limit the proportion of imported goods being stocked. However, western-owned chains are increasingly sourcing products locally anyway – around 90 per cent of sales in Tesco stores across the region are of locally-produced goods. There have also been attempts, particularly in Poland, to limit total hypermarket space and slow down (or even halt) the growth of new outlets through zoning restrictions. However, municipalities have often opposed such proposals, since big stores can create some 500 permanent jobs, plenty of building contracts, and auxiliary services such as cleaning and security for a town.

Even the big multinational manufacturers that can strike international deals with the major retailers are feeling the heat, especially from supermarkets' own brand labels, which are produced with far smaller profit margins. 'They are deciding on our margins,' says the director of one leading alcohol producer in the Czech Republic. 'During special promotions there's sometimes no profit at all.' One manager at German drinks group Eckes complains about a major retailer soliciting bids for premium shelf space at customer-eye level. The German firm's Fernet drink lost out to a generic rival, whose sales then rocketed.

For the losers, the expansion of hypermarkets in Eastern Europe has been a traumatic development. Unfortunately, however, local manufacturers and retailers have often squandered their advantages of low rents and an existing customer base. Those local producers who have been up to the challenge have become international companies under the pressure and encouragement of competition. Older consumers may find the changes disconcerting, and the swish efficiency of the shopping malls may exclude the poorest shoppers, who prefer local kiosks and outdoor markets. But most people welcome the lower prices, broader ranges, greater convenience, longer opening hours, shorter queues – even the occasional helpful smile from the staff – and a finely tuned sense of what the customer wants. As Chapter Six will show, the free application of supply and demand across the economy has been crucial to the region's recovery and has transformed the lives of millions of people. Sentimental western observers who would like a return to the quaint, slow-paced shopping experience of the past should listen to a Slovak mother recall the humiliation of waiting three hours on a Christmas night in the hope of buying three oranges for a family treat.

6

The Economy: Shock Therapy and Creative Destruction

'It requires a Damascene conversion for an official to see currency speculators as Mandeville's bees in the social garden of Eden and not just as Mafia thugs'[1]

The assumption

When Poland became the first country in the region to try to turn a communist economy into a free-market one virtually overnight, its leaders were making one of the boldest leaps of faith in 20th-century economic history. In modern times Eastern Europe has had a handful of world-famous political revolutionaries, such as Vaclav Havel, Boris Yeltsin and Lech Walesa. Far less well-known are the revolutionary economists, whose contribution to their countries has arguably been just as outstanding. Foremost among them is Poland's Leszek Balcerowicz.

When Tadeusz Mazowiecki became Poland's prime minister in September 1989 as part of a power-sharing agreement between Solidarity and the communists, Balcerowicz got a call asking him to become finance minister and lead the country's economic reforms. 'I was on my way to the UK to lecture in non-Keynesian theories of economics', he recalls, and at first he declined the offer. 'My wife was against it', he remembers. But they then spent the whole night discussing the pros and cons. As an academic, he had never been in the political spotlight, and this job would put him at the centre of an international stage, and into the economic history books.[2]

He eventually agreed, but his task was daunting. Most people in Eastern Europe began life in the global economy after 1989 with little understanding of how basic market mechanisms worked. The idea that prices of goods and services reflect the relationship between supply and demand was far from obvious. Prices had been fixed by central planners, and any excess of demand over supply manifested itself not in rising prices but in lengthening queues – giving rise to countless jokes about life under socialism.[3] Industry was geared towards massive overproduction, a situation that became chronic when traditional markets in the Soviet Union collapsed. Poland was in a better situation than many other countries in the region, having been exposed to some market mechanisms before 1989, mainly in agriculture, but ignorance about supply and demand was still prevalent. Poland also had other macro-economic worries; like Hungary, Bulgaria and Yugoslavia, it was burdened with an unmanageable foreign debt, amounting to $40 billion (including unpaid interest). Most of this had been amassed during the 1970s, in part to pay for limited imports of western consumer goods and technology in a failed attempt at economic reform.

By the end of the decade Poland's economy was in its death throes. The government could not meet the $2 billion annual cost of servicing its foreign debt, while the budget deficit was out of control and was being financed by printing more zloty. This drove down the currency's real (black market) value, and led to a build-up of hyperinflationary pressure, which was being held back only by artificial state control over prices. There were shortages of basic goods such as soap and meat. Industry was dysfunctional and was undergoing 'spontaneous privatisation', a polite phrase for theft, as managers began looting the assets. On top of all this, the government faced immediate wage demands from the same Solidarity trade union that had just helped to form the new government.

For Balcerowicz, the only course worth pursuing was the most far-reaching of all: to let the existing economic system collapse, and allow consumers and producers to meet freely and exchange goods and services by mutual agreement. This sounded good in the textbooks, but more cautious economists balked. Were policy-makers really going to abandon a system that, despite its malfunctions, was understood by everyone, and then assume that the 'invisible hand' of the market would somehow bring goods to the shops at prices that people could afford? Could the radical economists in the new government assume that a population drilled for decades to leave all economic decisions to the state would make a quick enough mental adjustment for the new system to work?

While the rest of Eastern Europe was engulfed in political revolution, Balcerowicz was frantically putting together his own economic revolution, which would be launched on 1 January 1990. It was 'a romantic endeavour [in which] political divisions disappeared', says Balcerowicz of the atmosphere at the time. By 29 December 1989, the only missing part of the plan was the $1 billion of financing that western governments had promised but not delivered. Balcerowicz called Michel Camdessus, the managing director of the International Monetary Fund (IMF), and told him that Poland was 'doing every-thing that we had declared in our programme, but the West is delay-ing its support'. He forced the Deputy Secretary of the US Treasury, David Mulford, from his sick bed in a Brussels hotel to help. Mulford set about lobbying recalcitrant contributors, and much (though not all) of the money arrived in time.

Moment of truth

A formidable and exacting intellect, Balcerowicz has a clinical and cal-culated approach to economics, and is famously unswerving in the cause of reason and logic. On New Year's Eve 1989 he was remarkably calm, given the magnitude of what was about to happen the next day. His view was that although a radical approach was risky, it was better than a series of gradual measures that he believed would definitely fail. But it was impossible to know what would happen; when prices would stop rising, or what the correct exchange rate should be. One could make only 'directional forecasts', Balcerowicz says. 'Even if I failed, it would have been better than not trying.'[4] International institutions, western governments, creditor banks and other reformers in the region all had an interest in seeing the Polish experiment succeed, and, along with a bewildered population, they watched.

The next day the 'Balcerowicz plan' was unleashed. Import controls were swept away, and prices for around 90 per cent of all goods were deregulated, allowing sellers to set their own prices according to the demand around them. Many Poles who had previously stored piles of useless zloty and foreign currency at home, because there was nothing worth buying, now chased the few goods on offer. Inflation soared far above the expectations of either the Polish reformers or their western advisors, including the IMF, putting many goods out of reach of those who relied on their meagre wages to survive. Prices doubled within a couple of months, then doubled again, and again. Average annual inflation in 1990 was 586 per cent. The long communist-era queues had vanished, but it would take a further half decade to bring the annual inflation rate below 20 per cent.

Hyperinflation went hand-in-hand with a massive devaluation of the zloty, which brought the currency below even its black-market rate. To maintain confidence in the currency and help dampen raging price rises, the government fixed the zloty to the dollar, adding further constraints to a collapsing economy. Balcerowicz imposed tight fiscal policies to get the budget into balance within a few months. He resisted inflation-linked wage demands, and began taxing 'excessive' wage rises in state enterprises. The unions were furious, but accepted the limits on wages, whereupon Balcerowicz realised that these were insufficient and tightened the screws some more.

Polish industry was thrown into disarray. Huge state enterprises were unable to survive without centralised handouts, and simply stopped production. Industrial output imploded, falling by 36 per cent over the next two years. *Under*-employment under socialism became full-blown *un*employment, a previously unknown phenomenon, and the jobless rate hit double figures by 1991. As the upheaval mounted, and state funds began to run out, the government considered making use of the $1 billion IMF-organised stabilisation fund that Balcerowicz had put together with such urgency a few months before. The country was in turmoil, and the patience of workers in the railway, mining and other industries eventually ran out. In 1992 they took to the streets, and the country witnessed some of the biggest strikes in Europe's history. Had the attempt to sweep away a communist economy overnight been just too risky, and a terrible miscalculation? Where was the 'invisible hand' of market forces that the economic textbooks talked about?

But something remarkable was also happening amid the chaos. Mark Allen, the IMF representative in Poland at the time, remembers looking out on the huge square outside the Stalinist Palace of Science and Culture in Warsaw, which had been used for May Day parades under communism:

It started with people selling items purchased in the Berlin supermarkets, largely foodstuffs that had been novelties or scarce in previous years. Bananas, a considerable rarity in the past, were sold one by one in this market. The car-trunk trade was joined by people selling their surplus assets. Pensioners sold clothes and other odd items either draped over their arms or from a plastic sheet spread on the ground. Then people began to bring tables and chairs to sell from and the first booths were erected ... Poles would go East and purchase foods on whose resale they could turn a profit. [They also bought] tools and industrial parts, precision drawing equipment and toys. These catered to the impoverished side of the Polish market that could afford to buy cheap Russian goods that had previously been scarce, but could not afford the relatively more expensive, higher quality western products. The whole market was a visible exercise in the power of arbitrage...

Often people who had accumulated some capital and business connections from the early street trade rented retail space that the local authorities had made available or that state enterprises no longer needed ... Car dealerships and innumerable groceries, clothing shops and the like opened up, and the city was transformed.[5]

The old communist ministers still in government immediately tried to contain the shambolic street traders, but Balcerowicz stepped in. 'You will not touch those people – they're the reason we're doing [the reforms]', he told them. Poland's economic liberalisation had – as the theory predicted – also spawned a wave of small enterprises (either privatised or newly formed), including some in the previously unheard-of services sector. By 1991 there were over a million small businesses registered.

After U – collapse and recovery

After Poland, other countries took the plunge. All witnessed a similar dramatic collapse of output, and the vast majority experienced hyperinflation as well. It was like 1920s Germany and the Great Depression rolled into one (see Table 6.1). Russia's inflation rate topped 1500 per cent in 1992.[6] The three Baltic states went from triple-digit inflation in 1991 to quadruple-digit price increases the following year. The situation was even worse in war-torn areas. Georgia's inflation rate touched 15 000 per cent in 1994, and prices in Serbia during the 1992–5 Balkan war rose by 16.5×10^{12}.[7]

Similarly, it took even the most advanced countries in the region in East-central Europe over a decade to regain their 1989 levels of output (although the quality of the goods being made had certainly improved in the meantime). These countries did not even resume economic growth until 1994–95. Russia's economy contracted by over 40 per cent between 1991–97, whereupon it experienced the flimsiest recovery before crashing again in August 1998. Ukraine, the second most populous country in the region, completely failed to restructure its industry and agriculture, and saw its economy shrink in every single year of the 1990s. By the end of the decade the Ukrainian economy was barely one third as big as it had been in 1991.[8]

Table 6.1 **Output decline in the region**

| | *The transition recession: 1990–2000* | |
	Consecutive years of output decline	*Lowest registered GDP (% of 1989 peak)*
Czech Republic	3	85
Poland	2	82
Hungary	4	82
Slovakia	4	75
Bulgaria	4	63
Estonia	5	61
Russia	7	55
Latvia	3	51
Ukraine	10	37

The Great Depression 1930–34

	Consecutive years of output decline	*Lowest registered GDP (% of peak year)*
France	3	89
Germany	3	86
UK	2	94
US	4	73

Source: World Bank; EBRD.

The rate of unemployment, a shocking notion for many who had become used to socialism's commitment to full (though often pointless) employment, was suddenly in double figures. Although former Yugoslav states had experienced unemployment in the 1980s, for countries such as Slovakia with jobless rates above 20 per cent, it was a new phenomenon. Regional disparities in employment within countries were even more marked; one in three workers in parts of eastern Slovakia, for example, were unemployed, compared to near full employment in Bratislava, the capital.

Many voters across the region blamed the reformers, who became widely despised.[9] The IMF, which had resolutely called for tighter spending and spending cuts to keep down inflation, was none too popular either. Shock therapy was often viewed by economists as a form of Schumpeterian 'creative destruction'. Others talk more prosaically of a U-shaped transition, as old firms went bankrupt and new companies and owners emerged in their place. How quickly the U-bend turned upwards depended on how fast old enterprises could recover or new companies could be formed.

Although the emergence of small enterprises and cross-border 'suit-case traders' initially helped to galvanise economies in flux, the prospects for the huge, loss-making state industries were less encouraging. Despite having obsolete machinery, some made gallant and occasionally successful attempts to export to the West, with the help of a weakened domestic currency. But their products were substandard, and local consumers now had a choice of imported goods. No longer part of a complex central plan, the big firms had no source of finance, little information about their customers, no means of extracting payment from debtors and no experience in setting prices. Inter-enterprise arrears and barter trade spread through the economy like a virus. Politicians found it hard to face the painful reality that even with state handouts, low wages and a devalued exchange rate, these enterprises would not be able to survive in the long term. They were a world away from providing the modern production methods, the latest management ideas and the economies of scale that the emerging market economies of Eastern Europe would need. So who could provide all this?

White knights?

One answer was western multinational companies. As we have seen in previous chapters, the multinationals shook up the brittle socialist enterprises that they acquired across the region, helping to transform large chunks of the economy in the process. The vast majority of foreign investment to date has gone to Poland, Hungary, the Czech Republic and Russia. By 2003 these countries had received a total of $161 billion between them, accounting for over three-fifths of the region's total (see Table 6.2). On a per-capita basis, Slovakia, Slovenia, Croatia and Estonia are among the largest recipients of FDI.

Although multinational companies have had a major impact in all of these countries, their governments took different approaches to macro-economic management, and had different views as to the role that foreign investment should play in economic regeneration. Poland's economic recovery began early. Voters blamed Balcerowicz for the turmoil, and he was dropped from the government following the general election in October 1991, but his boldness paid dividends, and international confidence in the new Polish economy began to rise.[10] In 1991 the Paris Club of sovereign creditors wrote off $15 billion of Poland's debt, half of the total it owed to the Paris Club;[11] three years later the London Club of commercial creditors granted a 45 per cent

Table 6.2   Foreign direct investment

	(Cumulative total 1990–2003)	
	Cumulative FDI inflows 1990–2003 (US$bn)	Cumulative FDI inflows per capita 1990–2003 (US$)
Poland	54.7	1433
Czech Republic	40.3	3931
Hungary	37.8	3757
Russia	28.3	196
Kazakhstan	15.8	1054
Slovakia	10.5	1930
Romania	10.4	466
Croatia	9.3	2096
Azerbaijan	8.0	973
Ukraine	6.7	141
Bulgaria	6.4	828
Slovenia	4.1	2040
Estonia	4.0	2971
Lithuania	3.8	1110
Latvia	3.4	1449
Serbia & Mont.	3.3	311
Belarus	1.8	185
Turkmenistan	1.4	229
Georgia	1.3	300
Bosnia & Herc.	1.2	282
Albania	1.1	348
FYR Macedonia	1.0	519
Uzbekistan	0.9	35
Armenia	0.9	298
Moldova	0.7	172
Kyrgyz Republic	0.4	90
Tajikistan	0.2	34
Total/average	**258**	**632**

Source: The Economist Intelligence Unit.

write-off worth $13 billion, and Poland started fully servicing the rest. The ratio of foreign debt to GDP fell from an unserviceable 84 per cent in 1990 to 33 per cent in 1996, and the government's total domestic and foreign debt fell to 50 per cent of GDP during the same period, below the Maastricht limit of 60 per cent. The lighter debt burden helped Poland to begin a broad economic recovery in 1992, two years earlier than its regional neighbours. From 1995–97 the economy grew at a ferocious annual rate of 6–7 per cent, driven largely by the strong domestic market that Balcerowicz's reforms had let loose.

Yet with the exception of carmakers Fiat and Daewoo, PepsiCo, International Paper and a few other big western corporations that arrived early, Poland was generally slow to attract foreign direct investment (FDI). By the middle of the decade cumulative FDI had reached $4.6 billion, or a paltry $120 per head. Western firms remained worried about Poland's political instability given the infighting within the ruling parties and especially delays to a debt rescheduling deal. The foreign companies that did come were more interested in tapping Poland's booming consumer market than in looking for an export base. This changed after 1997, when a centre-right, Solidarity-led coalition took office and began privatising large enterprises in earnest. Foreign firms were the only buyers with deep enough pockets to take them over. Between 1998–2002 around $34 billion of FDI poured into almost every sector of the economy, tripling the per-capita total compared with the level in 1997. As Poland's extraordinary private consumption boom faltered at the turn of the new century, the country began to rely increasingly on these strong FDI inflows, and the exports that they helped to generate, in order to sustain growth.

Hungary took a different path, partly because the relatively benign form of socialism in the 1980s had allowed some private businesses to operate, and even to form joint ventures with western firms. The shock of price liberalisation after 1990 was consequently milder than in Poland, and Hungary's governments were more stable as a result. In contrast to Poland, Hungarian governments decided to service rather than reschedule the country's foreign debt, selling leading state companies in order to raise money. Hungary sold much of its manufacturing sector, bringing in well-known western electronics companies such as Philips and General Electric, and it attracted carmakers Suzuki, General Motors and Audi with ten-year tax holidays and specialised investment parks. By the mid-1990s Hungary had also sold its fixed-line telecom monopoly, utility companies and leading banks. The country attracted the most foreign investment in the region in every year until 1996, when it was overtaken by Poland, a country four times its size.

However, as the FDI poured in, the centre-right government that was in power in the early 1990s became lax about its own spending. By 1994 the budget deficit was running at over seven per cent of GDP, and the current-account deficit was almost ten per cent of GDP, putting pressure on the currency, the forint, and creating fears of a major devaluation. It fell to Lajos Bokros, a former central banker who became finance minister in 1995, to implement his infamous 'Bokros package' of spending cuts in March of that year. The package was an attempt to rein in heavy spending by social ministries, and set the tone for future budget negotiations. Bokros acted in unison with Gyorgy Suranyi, the new head of the central bank, who implemented a 'crawling peg' exchange-rate mechanism that involved a gradual and controlled devaluation of the currency by slightly less than the inflation rate. The introduction of temporary customs duties aimed at curbing the current-account deficit caused inflation to shoot up to 28 per cent in 1995, and the sudden tightening of the fiscal and monetary screws caused GDP growth to fall to one per cent that year. As Poland began to boom, Hungary entered a two-year period of austerity that led to some public protests. Bokros lasted even less time in his post than Balcerowicz, resigning after a year in a dispute over healthcare spending. He wasn't missed, but the economic discipline he introduced paid off. From 1997 onwards the Hungarian economy began to grow by some 4–5 per cent annually. And unlike in Poland, the recovery was export-led, driven by the hundreds of foreign companies that had adopted Hungary as a regional base.

The Czech Republic adopted a far meeker approach to economic reform, despite the radical rhetoric of its government. The Czech part of the then Czechoslovakia entered the 1990s in relatively good shape. It was not burdened with foreign or domestic debt, its budget was roughly in balance, and its balance of payments was under control. On the other hand, the country had experienced a far stricter form of central planning than Poland or Hungary, and Czechs had almost no experience of market economics. As elsewhere in the region, industrial output initially fell sharply, by nearly 26 per cent in 1990–91. But there was a countervailing growth in small businesses as shops, bars and hotels were privatised after October 1990, and the state relinquished control over retail and wholesale prices. This was followed by a nationwide voucher privatisation scheme, in which citizens could bid for shares in state enterprises using vouchers that they had received virtually free of charge from the government (see chapter 7).

Rather than using the relatively good economic starting position to force loss-making industry to restructure, the Czechoslovak government pampered uncompetitive enterprises with three quick devaluations of the currency, the koruna, in 1990. Later the 'voucher-privatised' companies were further protected by a state-dominated banking system that funnelled easy loans their way, and by the absence of a workable bankruptcy law (see chapters 4, 7). By 1995, only 838 Czech companies had been put into bankruptcy, compared with almost 6500 in Hungary.

There appeared to be a tacit social contract: in return for low public-sector pay demands, the government would do its best to protect jobs. By the mid-1990s unemployment was at a remarkably low three per cent, compared to the double-digit (and rising) jobless rates in neighbouring countries. Even better, the Czech economy was humming along with annual GDP growth rates of 4–6 per cent and single-digit inflation.

The seemingly effortless transition suggested that the Czechs were different (and possibly cleverer) than their counterparts in the region. That impression was created in no small part by the all-knowing Vaclav Klaus, the finance minister (1989–92) and subsequently prime minister (1992–97), who had the relatively rare distinction of being both a well-versed economist and a persuasive politician. Klaus became one of the few leaders in the region to win two consecutive elections, and was roundly applauded abroad as well. The praise did not last long, however. Because of the lack of serious restructuring, Czech industry was losing money at an alarming rate. The cracks in Klaus's system became visible in the growing current-account deficit, which rose above seven per cent of GDP in 1996. Moreover, the rising import bill did not reflect the cost of new technologies needed to restructure industry (as Klaus had claimed), but rather the growing domestic demand for western cars and consumer goods. Currency speculators served warning with an attack on the koruna, the anchor of Klaus's economic stabilisation policy, forcing it down by 15 per cent in 1997. Having been seemingly the most successful in the region, the Czech economy spent most of the last three years of the decade in recession, while the rest of the world was booming. Klaus was ousted from power, and the Czechs finally felt the economic pain that Poland and Hungary had faced head-on years before.

For much of the 1990s the unwelcoming attitude of the Czech government to foreign multinationals was symptomatic of a general unwillingness to subject protected state companies to greater discipline. Many local politicians felt that Czech industry and its bosses had little to learn from the West. Klaus had pointedly refused to provide tax breaks to big foreign investors, arguing that the country boasted enough attractions already. It was a reasonable point to make in theory, but it was not borne out by events. Investors didn't come in force until 1998, when the newly elected Social Democratic government quickly sold off the state banks that had been instrumental in preserving the industrial status quo, and began pitching more assertively to attract major western corporations. Some $30 billion of FDI flowed in between 1998–2002 largely as a result of these efforts, sweeping the Czech Republic past the cumulative total in Hungary, and making the country the highest FDI recipient in per capita terms in the whole region. The recovery in Germany, coupled with the remarkable expansion of the VW-Skoda plant (see chapter 4) and other foreign-owned, export-oriented companies, helped to pull the country out of recession.

Although the lion's share of foreign investment went to Poland, Hungary and the Czech Republic, multinationals arguably had a much greater and more direct impact in some of the oil- and gas-exporting countries of the former Soviet Union, such as Kazakhstan and Azerbaijan. Energy exploration and development and the construction of export pipelines were almost exclusively undertaken by the international oil majors. The economic equation in these countries was simple: GDP growth depended on oil, and only multinational companies (often in a joint venture or consortium that included the state oil company) could bring it to market.

The multinational presence was more limited in Russia. Despite its initial attempt at broad-based economic regeneration, Russia's first reform government in 1991 could do little more than cut away the power of communist enterprises and their bosses (no small feat in itself). However, the reformers proved unable to replace the old system with anything much more productive. Instead, power fell into the hands of a circle of domestic business tycoons whose prime objective was to acquire and consolidate control over chunks of industry, without necessarily investing in or developing these businesses. Western investors had little say in these proceedings and generally stayed clear of all but the oil and gas industry, where they were forced, through the lack of production-sharing agreements and opaque privatisation deals, into joint ventures with local firms. Ownership of the main assets remained in the hands of the state or the big tycoons. The oil- and gas-dependent economy meant that Russia did not recover until the turn of the century, when international oil prices rose again, pushing the current account into a healthy surplus and the budget back into the black. Meanwhile, the rest of the economy was left sorely under-funded.

Costs and benefits

This chapter has shown how the region went through an economic upheaval in the early 1990s, starting with Poland, and how different countries began attracting western multinationals to invest as part of the process of economic recovery. But to what extent did their arrival really help these economies?. Multinationals have clearly benefited specific companies and industries. Most micro-level surveys clearly demonstrate that multinationals are generally more efficient than local enterprises, export more and tend to encourage free trade – the fastest route to growth. However, the macro-economic effects are less clear-cut, and the remainder of this chapter will discuss whether multinationals have also helped the economy as a whole. Academics have long debated the pros and cons of multinational companies in emerging economies, and this debate has spilled over into Eastern Europe. The macro-economic impact of FDI is difficult to measure. Foreign companies had a strong presence in the faster-growing, more open economies of the region, notably Poland, Hungary, the Czech Republic, Estonia and later Slovakia, and were absent from economically backward or politically troubled states in the CIS and, until recently, the Balkans. But did the multinational presence cause these economies to grow more rapidly, or did strong rates of GDP growth attract foreign investors? Poland, for example, was doing well on account of its large domestic market long before large numbers of western investors arrived, while tiny Slovenia was growing steadily with relatively little foreign help. Yet Hungary and Estonia boomed only after the multinationals entered the market, while the non-oil CIS economies have attracted little FDI and most remain in the doldrums. High levels of FDI and rapid economic growth may well be too closely interrelated and mutually re-enforcing to allow for a definite conclusion.

Although the link between FDI and economic growth may be inconclusive, there are plenty of other pros and cons on the macro-economic level to weigh up. One debate concerns the initial inflows of foreign investment themselves. These have helped to stabilise East European economies, since selling state-owned companies to foreigners brought revenues to the state treasury and helped to plug large current-account deficits. But the FDI inflows resulting from the larger deals threatened to push local currencies towards levels at which exporters would struggle to compete internationally. A second question is whether the presence of multinationals improve a country's public finances or balance of payments once the initial investment has flowed in. Many governments lost out on budget revenue after granting generous tax incentives to attract foreign investors in the first place, and some multinationals decided to repatriate profits to their home country rather than re-investing them in the region. Thirdly, the impact of multinationals on foreign trade also needs to be examined. Foreign investors may have underpinned the export performance of many countries in East-central Europe through higher value-added production, reflecting their greater investment than local firms in research and development (R&D). But they were also responsible for the vast majority of imports too. A final question is whether multinationals have benefited other firms in the economy or just themselves and a small number of partners, while accelerating the demise of smaller, weaker local enterprises.

Stabilising inflows

Selling state-owned assets to foreign corporations allowed governments across Eastern Europe to raise substantial amounts of money relatively quickly and cheaply without jeopardising economic stability by running up excessive debts or deficits. Indeed, FDI inflows helped to secure otherwise shaky budgets and cover current-account deficits during highly volatile periods. Some economists point out that multinational investors were also partly the cause of the current-account deficits in the first place, because they imported many goods too.[12] However, the important issue is not the existence of a current-account deficit – indeed, this can be a positive sign of restructuring – but how it is financed, and economists generally agree that cash from multinationals setting up operations is one of the most stable ways of covering an external gap.

Early privatisation helped Hungary through its difficult austerity period and enabled the country to cover its twin deficits at a time when raising taxes would have been politically and socially too painful. FDI inflows also enabled Hungary to reduce its external debt from over 50 per cent of GDP in 1995 to less than one third of GDP two years later. This contributed to a credit rating upgrade in 1996, which in turn reduced the country's future borrowing costs. A few quick asset sales to foreign investors in 1992 enabled Slovenia to build up its foreign-exchange reserves and escape a currency crisis that the country faced when it became independent the previous year. Similarly, Croatia was threatened with a damaging currency depreciation during its post-war recovery as its foreign reserves dwindled and the budget deficit widened out of control. Deutsche Telekom eventually saved the day in October 1999, paying $875m for a 35 per cent stake in local fixed-line telecom monopoly Hrvatske Telekomunikacije. Towards the end of the decade Bulgaria, Romania and Lithuania all boosted their foreign-exchange reserves through privatisations, while Poland retired nearly $1 billion of government bonds following the sale of fixed-line monopoly TPSA to France Telecom in 2000.

Other methods of selling state assets (such as voucher privatisation in the Czech Republic, Russia and Azerbaijan, or management-employee buyouts in Bulgaria and Slovakia) raised much less money for governments. Another alternative – selling shares to international portfolio investors – would have deprived governments of the extra cash that strategic investors paid in order to exercise management control, and would have deprived the companies themselves of the foreign know-how that they desperately needed. Multinationals therefore proved to be a vital source of finance for the region's cash-strapped emerging market economies.

The entry of foreign investors has also had some potentially destabilising effects – one of which is the risk that large FDI inflows will push up the value of local currencies, harming the export competitiveness of locally based manufacturers. In an attempt to avoid this problem, central banks arranged for billions of dollars of incoming investment to be paid into offshore banks in recent years or used the cash to repay international debts, circumventing foreign exchange markets altogether. Such manoeuvres didn't always convince currency traders, who continued to revalue the exchange rates. But the problem was not an upward valuation of the currency per se but rather overshooting, which is primarily the fault of panicky currency traders rather than the corporations that were investing.

Twin deficits

Another point of concern was that although privatisation proceeds provided much-needed budgetary support, the state lost out on potential revenue by providing generous tax holidays (typically for ten years, and sometimes more) to big international, usually greenfield, investors. (Local enterprises, much to their annoyance, were usually not eligible for such breaks.) In 1999 foreign companies in Hungary paid only 13 per cent of their gross profits in taxes, around half the rate paid by domestic companies, the difference being equivalent to 1.7 per cent of total government revenue.[13]

The multinationals argued that without their investment these companies would have been much less profitable (or more likely loss-making), so there would have been no profits to tax anyway. Foreign investors also claimed that the higher wages that they paid meant that governments were generating higher income tax revenue than they otherwise would have done. Still, multinationals did very well out of the tax incentives they received, and they fought bitterly to hold onto them when the EU called on the eight first-wave East European accession states to scale back the incentives in line with its more restrictive state aid rules. At the very least, lower profit tax revenues have to be seen as part of the price to be paid to attract FDI.[14]

Although privatisation proceeds helped to finance current-account deficits, the longer-term effect of FDI on a country's balance of payments might not be so beneficial if multinationals repatriate future profits to their home countries through dividends or transfer pricing deals. Profit repatriation tends to be low initially, as the foreign investor retools and develops the local business it has acquired, but inevitably rises once the major investments in capital and machinery have been completed and the local company's growth has levelled out. Corporate head office will ultimately want most of the profits of its foreign subsidiaries to be sent home.

However, Eastern Europe still seems to be some way from that point (see Table 6.3). One survey conducted in Hungary in 2002 indicates that repatriation remains modest overall, with 50 leading foreign investors claiming to have repatriated a relatively low 23 per cent of their profits on average by 2000.[15] Such surveys should be treated with some caution, but nonetheless indicate a general picture – Philips, for example, reinvested all its Hungarian profits in most years. There are some exceptions to this pattern. One French pharmaceutical company in Hungary paid dividends amounting to 31 per cent of its post-tax profit in 1995, and 97 per cent the next year, thereby repatriating $47m (compared to an initial investment of $200m). Dividend

Table 6.3 Direct investment income outflows (per cent of FDI inflows)

	1997	1998	1999	2000	Profit outflow as % of FDI stock 2000
Czech Republic	4	10	17	18	3.9
Hungary	21	47	43	50	4.2
Poland	21	12	6	8	2.1
Slovakia	1	9	13	2	0.9
Slovenia	24	43	85	73	4.6
Bulgaria	n/a	10	1	11	3.2
Romania	2	8	5	7	1.1

Source: Vienna Institute for International Economic Studies.

payments back to the parent company may not be the only financial outflow. Foreign investors have been known to use internal transfer pricing schemes, with the local subsidiary overpaying for inputs from elsewhere in the group. However, relatively low levels of profit tax in the region (assisted by tax holidays) mean that such transfer pricing mechanisms are just as, if not more, likely to work in the other direction, with foreign firms trying to report higher profits in a low-tax country such as Hungary.

Export-led growth

Multinational corporations have also had a profound influence on the changing foreign-trade patterns of East European economies following the spectacular collapse of exports in 1990–91. Exports from Eastern Europe dropped by 62 per cent in volume terms in the first three years of transition, only regaining 1989 volume levels nine years later. The situation was even worse in the CIS; export volumes in 1998 were a mere 15 per cent of 1990 levels.

However, the collapse of exports was followed by a remarkable recovery and re-orientation of trade to the West as EU markets opened up. By the mid-1990s around 70 per cent of Poland's exports were going to the EU, compared to 32 per cent in 1989, and by the end of the decade the Baltic states were sending 50 per cent of their exports to the West, mainly the EU, up from a mere five per cent in 1991. Between the mid-1990s and the end of the decade, the Czech Republic's share of the total imports of its EU trading partners rose from 1.94 per cent to 2.54 per cent; Hungary's share rose from 1.65 per cent to 2.65 per cent; Poland, which relies more on its large domestic market rather than exports to drive economic growth, nonetheless saw its market share rise in line with EU growth; and Slovenia, with relatively little foreign investment, saw its EU market share decline.[16] This export capability is vital given that only six out of 27 countries in the region have domestic markets significantly bigger than ten million consumers.

There was one other inescapable fact about exports from Eastern Europe: they were dominated by western investors. Nearly 90 per cent of export sales from Hungary by the end of the decade were from the subsidiaries of western multinationals. The figure for Poland and Czech Republic was around 60 per cent and rising every year, while exports from Slovakia and Estonia depended heavily on a single western firm (VW and Elcoteq, respectively). This was equally true in commodity-based economies such as Kyrgyzstan, which relies largely on a Canadian-owned gold mine for export revenue.

Why multinationals export so much more than domestic enterprises is not too hard to understand. Productivity levels at foreign-owned companies are generally estimated by economists to be two or three times higher than in local firms, and western corporations also have established markets in which goods produced by its local subsidiaries can be sold. Perhaps more important than the volume is the type of exports from multinational company subsidiaries. The view that multinationals in the region are principally interested in low-value-added production based on cheap labour is unfair with higher-value production being a principal focus of multinational companies in the region.[17] Foreign-owned firms spend much more than local companies on research and development (R&D), for example. Few local firms invest much in R&D, and those that say they do are usually just buying new equipment or trying to meet minimum legal product standards, rather than genuinely innovating. Only one in six domestic Polish companies, for example, introduced a single product innovation between 1998–2002.[18] This reflects a lack of both money and a long-term strategy. As a result, much of the region's extraordinary intellectual wealth is squandered, remaining in under-funded universities or left to rely on meagre state subsidies.

By contrast, countless multinationals in electronics, pharmaceuticals, carmaking and other high-tech sectors have large R&D facilities in the region over the past ten years. Big names such as Electrolux, General Electric, Sanofi, Ericsson and Motorola have ploughed tens of millions of dollars into research centres in Hungary, employed thousands of top scientists and contributed substantial sums to the National Academy of Sciences. Moreover, these companies have reversed an exodus of the brightest scientific minds from Hungary, which in the mid-1990s was losing over 200 scientists a year, according to the academy. The story is similar in Estonia, and, increasingly, in the Czech Republic and Poland too.

Critics point out that although multinationals may be driving exports, they have also brought large volumes of imports into Eastern Europe, especially in the case of consumer goods firms looking to build market share (see chapter 5). Even export-oriented foreign-owned manufacturers are responsible for importing significant amounts of components that go into the finished product for export, or new machinery to retool the factory. Since imports are subtracted from exports in expenditure-based calculations of GDP, large import volumes could potentially act as a drag on growth in Eastern Europe.

However, foreign-owned firms tend to import less as they complete the restructuring of their local acquisition, and as suppliers and service providers move in-country (or local suppliers are found). Again, the case of electronics manufacturer Philips in Hungary is instructive. In 2002 the company imported some 40 per cent of its cost of sales and exported around $2 billion worth of products, making it a net exporter to the tune of $1.2 billion that year. The Economist Intelligence Unit has calculated that the elasticity of exports to FDI penetration in East-central Europe was 1.36 in 2001, meaning that exports rose by some 36 per cent more than the increase in the proportion of FDI as a percentage of GDP. To put it another way – more FDI means disproportionately more exports.

Help your neighbour

As we can see, western corporations have helped to finance budget and current-account deficits, invested more in high technology, and played a central role in encouraging export-led growth. But have they also helped domestic firms to grow? The debate over such broader effects (commonly referred to by economists as 'spillovers') is a fierce one. In theory, multinationals spread their superior skills, technology and know-how to domestic firms, while at the same time forcing local competitors to raise their own performance. Foreign investors may also have less direct influences: for example, workers and managers trained in a top multinational (such as the hundreds of East Europeans trained each year in western law and accounting firms) may subsequently take up jobs with local enterprises, thereby spreading their knowledge. In addition, the reforms to the business environment that were required to attract foreign multinationals also helped domestic companies. When Slovakia introduced its 19 per cent flat tax for companies in January 2004 to attract western capital, domestic firms also saw their tax bills fall. And when multinationals lobbied for transparent regulations, lower trade barriers and the alignment of customs procedures with EU norms, local firms looking to export to EU markets also benefited. For sure, there is some divergence in interests; investment incentives went to foreign investors rather than to locals, while murky tenders have generally given local firms an advantage over multinationals. However, measures to improve the operating environment have generally helped all legitimate businesses, whether foreign or domestic.

A number of empirical studies have questioned the extent of such spillovers, arguing that local firms gain no benefit from the entry of a multinational in their sector, and may even lose.[19] On one level, such findings should come as no surprise – after all, why would a foreign investor want to help its competitors in the same sector? Competition is all about efficient firms eliminating weaker rivals (especially those with few business skills who acquired their company in a rigged privatisation contest). In addition, much of the research that questions the existence of spillovers tends to overemphasise manufacturing, while downplaying or even ignoring the greater influence of new foreign-owned service companies, such as telecoms firms or banks, which constitute much of the foundations of a modern economy (see chapter four).

Even in the case of manufacturing, such surveys often fail to capture the fact that although multinationals might hurt the local competition, they boost the performance of the local suppliers that they train, equip and sometimes even finance. As one recent analysis concluded: 'Productivity is positively correlated with the extent of potential contacts with multinationals' customers but not with the presence of multinationals in the same industry ... a ten percent increase in the foreign presence in downstream sectors is associated with a 0.38 per cent rise in output of each firm in the supplying industry'.[20] Moreover, local firms that meet the global supply standards set by a foreign company often export their goods to that company's other global subsidiaries, as local suppliers to Volkswagen and Tesco have done. By one estimate, for every additional dollar invested by a western firm in an emerging economy, a further $1.50–2.30 is invested by local enterprises.[21]

The operations of Philips in Hungary are again a good example. The company employs 5000 people directly in the country, plus a further 10 000 through outsourcing agreements, and sources around 60 per cent of its supplies locally, either from western suppliers based in Hungary or local firms whose performance and quality meets international standards. By signing long-term supply agreements with Philips, local firms have greatly reduced their financial risk and have managed to obtain bank credits that would have otherwise been out of reach. The quality of these local firms' operations has also improved. 'Achieving simple quality levels such as getting supplies in the right quantity, time and place required considerable work. Failure to do so was usually accompanied by a plethora of excuses and the blaming of others', says Willem van der Vegt, the former Philips CEO in Hungary. He adds: 'We brought jobs, salaries and paid taxes. We brought our sub-suppliers to Hungary, or we used local suppliers for relatively simply inputs such as plastic components and metals.

There is a danger that these spillovers may not spread far enough, and that multinationals may be creating enclaves of fast-growing foreign-owned manufacturers and their small band of suppliers, with little connection to the rest of the economy. On this view, those domestic firms without a link to the international production system and new technologies may simply slide into terminal decline. Although such a scenario could potentially emerge, it is still too early to draw firm conclusions. Relationships between multinationals and local enterprises can take years to build, and the former shows no sign as yet of shunning willing and competent partners. Indeed, the opposite may be the case; multinationals are especially keen, but unable, to find local firms with which to work.

It is true that partnerships with multinationals are not the only way for local companies to upgrade their production processes and raise quality. Slovene-owned firms, for example, have been successful at importing and incorporating technology without a commercial relationship with a big foreign investor.[22] But Slovenia may be the exception: it was the most advanced country in the region in 1990, partly because many managers had picked up western business experience during the 1980s, and it remains the richest transition economy today. Or maybe Slovenia was ahead of the game, which begs a further question: did the multinational competition enter the region too quickly, without allowing local firms time to restructure? Other things being equal, some local firms might well have been in a stronger position to compete with the foreigners had they had more time – and of course more money. But other things are seldom equal; financial clout is, in general, one of the great strengths of western corporations and a reason for wanting their investment. Besides, there was a limit as to how long employees would be willing to wait and how much taxpayers would be prepared to pay before they saw results from their home-grown 'champions'. Indeed, prolonged periods of protection generally left domestic enterprises in an even worse state, ultimately making bankruptcy inevitable rather than staving it off, and in the process eliminating the possibility of finding a well-resourced foreign buyer.

The fate of these struggling enterprises, and their relationship with the new, foreign investors that arrived on the scene, ultimately came down to politics. The region's economic reformers, who wanted to instigate 'creative destruction', also had a particular perspective on how free markets and foreign investment would help overall recovery. The reformers would abandon domestic enterprises to the ravages of the international market, but at the same time this openness would encourage multinationals to commit more fully to the domestic market, by setting up major plants, research and development facilities, and local supply networks. The reformers reasoned that a sound rule of law, relatively uncorrupted institutions, free trade and low inflation would persuade a multinational to integrate its local business more fully into its global operations, thereby providing desirable spillovers of technology and a virtuous circle of investment that state-sponsored socialism failed to generate.

Their opponents, on the other hand, insisted on forcing multinationals into joint ventures with local firms, or wanted to slap tariffs on imported components in order to force foreigners to buy supplies locally. Although such policies could give multinational subsidiaries short-term, localised benefits in the form of import protection and even a monopoly, they made foreign investors more cautious about the market in general. This approach was the wrong way to generate the kind of spillovers that the reformers envisaged. Multinationals feared that their joint-venture partner might steal proprietary technologies and create management conflicts. They worried that locally purchased inputs would be of lower quality than those that could be imported. As a consequence, foreign firms invested less in such countries, and kept their subsidiary there at a safe distance from the rest of their global network. Neither the host country nor the investor would gain much if the market was not large enough to compensate for the foregone international links.

That was a pity. Multinationals have probably helped to drive these economies forward at a healthy speed. Not everyone has benefited – those who cannot keep pace have fallen by the wayside. But the overall effect of foreign investment, at least from the evidence so far, seems to be positive for exports, investment and GDP growth. It may still be too early to draw definitive conclusions. Much more analysis is needed, particularly into the relationship between foreign investment and GDP growth especially if some multinationals start to leave these markets for lower-cost locations in coming years. But the evidence so far looks fairly compelling.

The often hostile reaction of host governments towards multinational companies generally had little to do with macro-economic considerations. As the next chapter will argue, the failure to restructure industry, or to bring in a western corporation to do so, was essentially a political decision, and was often guided by local vested interests looking to enrich themselves at the expense of the local population.

7
The Good, the Bad and the Ugly: Reform, Privatisation and Corruption

'It was privatisation in a Franz Kafka sense'
Milos Zeman, former Czech prime minister.[1]

Multinationals in Eastern Europe in the 1990s found themselves operating in a political and legal environment that was often rigged against them. Despite being better qualified to rehabilitate many failing state enterprises, foreign companies were often excluded from privatisation deals. As this chapter will show, although many foreign corporations have regrettably been involved in nefarious activities such as bribing state officials, these actions pale next to the wholesale plunder of some East European economies by local businessmen and power brokers, who left the taxpayer to pick up the bill.

Countries such as Hungary and Estonia welcomed foreign corporations soon after 1989, but many East European governments (at least initially) wanted to keep them out for a variety of reasons, including nationalism, fear or, in some cases, sheer incompetence. It took over a decade for Russia to allow private ownership of real estate or to allow western oil firms to sign production-sharing agreements – the standard legal framework for long-term oil investments in emerging markets. For a while the Czech Republic espoused a 'Czech way' to privatise industry, implying that western companies had little to offer the country. Smaller, wealthier Slovenia was also defensive about selling enterprises to foreigners, a stance that it briefly relaxed after independence, but was not seriously breached until 2002, when Switzerland's Novartis acquired pharmaceutical company Lek for over $1 billion. Some politicians in East-central Europe resisted sales of state assets to companies from Germany, the old enemy, while Latvians and Lithuanians bitterly opposed Russian firms taking over their oil refineries.[2] The broad-based democratic coalition in office in Romania from 1996–2000 desperately wanted foreign investment, but wasted years arguing over which party should run the privatisation deals. It was not until the reformed communists returned to power in 2000 that many key privatisation deals were completed.[3]

Although this mix of nationalism, fear and incompetence could be powerful, there was often a more basic motivation behind the defensive or downright hostile attitudes that many countries had towards foreign investors. Keeping foreigners out of a country's large enterprises gave local elites the opportunity to grab the assets for themselves and become rich beyond their wildest dreams. As political scientist Joel Hellman argues:

> Actors who enjoyed extraordinary gains from the distortions of a partially reformed economy have fought to preserve those gains by maintaining the imbalances of partial reforms over time. ... In each case the winners from an earlier stage of reform have incentives to block further advances in reform that would correct the very distortions on which their initial gains were based.[4]

This process occurred either directly through privatisation, or indirectly as a result of a weak legal system, but the outcome was the same. Perhaps the most spectacular example of the whole period was the sale of part of Russian gas monopoly Gazprom to its managers in 1994 for less than one per cent of the stake's estimated market value.[5] The region is also brim full of stories of foreign investors who failed to navigate the labyrinthine corridors of power and lost millions of dollars as a result. Sometimes the problems were small – for example when the authorities in Minsk, Belarus, built a construction fence around a local McDonald's restaurant, forcing customers to walk an additional 100 metres to the entrance. On other occasions, however, the consequences could be catastrophic. The failure of the Russian government to rein in local oligarchs and assert the rule of law contributed to the 1998 economic crash, which cost western investors billions of dollars – not to mention the Russians who saw their local-currency savings become worthless.[6]

The first part of this chapter will illustrate the various problems facing both western multinationals and beleaguered local populations by describing events in Slovakia, the Czech Republic and Russia during the first decade of transition. In particular these included the direct sales of leading Slovak enterprises in 1994–98 to friends of Vladimir

Meciar, the prime minister; the poorly regulated voucher privatisation programme in the Czech Republic in 1991–93; the theft in the same country of the Nova television station from Central European Media Enterprises (CME); the loans-for-shares scheme in Russia in 1995–96; and the sham bankruptcy of Russian oil company Sidanko in 1999, which cost BP hundreds of millions of dollars.

The second part of the chapter will examine how multinational companies have interacted with officials; the extent to which major foreign firms have been involved in bribery; whether it is the investor or the official who has initiated the bribe; and whether the practice can ever be justified by the nature of the environment in which foreign companies are operating.

Who wants to be a millionaire?

The problems of Slovak privatisation in the 1990s are emblematic of much that went wrong in the region. The exclusion of multinational companies from Slovakia between 1994–98 was central to building and maintaining a crony-capitalist system based around a powerful governing party and its leader.[7] Meciar, a lawyer and former boxer, was Slovakia's dominant political figure, after leading the country to independence following the break-up of the former Czechoslovakia in January 1993. With the exception of a few months in opposition in 1994, he remained prime minister until October 1998. During this period he asserted ever-increasing personal control over the economy. One of his first acts as prime minister was to cancel the privatisation programme that his government inherited from the former Czechoslovakia. Although with hindsight the Czech system of voucher privatisation also turned out to be a failure, Meciar embarked on a more blatant form of cronyism, practically giving away the country's largest companies to a small circle of political supporters. For example, gas storage company Nafta Gbely was sold in 1996 to an obscure shell company for a mere $5.6 million, although the firm made a profit of around $36m in that year. The terms of this and other such deals were kept secret at first, although it was generally known that many well-connected investors were able to buy the assets with the help of low-interest, long-term loans from the state. Needless to say, few loans were ever fully repaid, and rather than investing in the firms, many of Meciar's friends merely stripped the assets and funnelled the money to offshore bank accounts. Between 1995 and 1998, the National Property Fund, the body charged with privatising state assets, recorded over

$3 billion worth of privatisation sales, but when a new, broad-based coalition of democratic parties took power in 1998, the Fund had a mere $1 million in its bank account, and was unable to explain where the majority of the money had gone.

By creating an inner circle of multi-millionaires who owed their entire fortune to prime ministerial patronage, Meciar was attempting to build an impregnable power base from which to manipulate or control all other institutions of state. Foreign multinationals, with their deep pockets, global reach and independence, were clearly not so easily pushed around and were therefore largely excluded from privatisation. Despite the fact that Slovakia, like most of the region, was crying out for western expertise and capital, only seven out of nearly 800 companies sold in 1995–96 involved any foreign investment. The situation changed after 1998. Mikulas Dzurinda, the new prime minister, saw multinationals as playing a key role in restoring democracy and anchoring the country firmly in the West. In clawing back an estimated $3 billion of lost assets, the new government not only replenished the state treasury, but also undercut Meciar's financial power base – one that might have allowed him, even in opposition, to continue meddling in state institutions.[8]

The story of privatisation in Slovakia (and in much of the rest of the region) is best encapsulated by the sale of VSZ, a giant steel works in the eastern Slovak city of Kosice (see also chapter 3). In 1994 Meciar approved a decision to sell 15 per cent of VSZ to a shell company named '*Manager*', which was set up on the very day of the share sale by Alexander Rezes, the minister of transport and a friend of the prime minister. *Manager* then acquired further shares through other shell companies, financing the purchases with VSZ's own funds, until it controlled 47 per cent of the steel mill. Rezes had little knowledge of the steel industry and probably even less interest in it, but his acquisition of VSZ made him a player. He was seldom seen without a bodyguard, and enjoyed the glamour of suddenly becoming the country's richest man. He indulged in an extravagant spending spree with the company's money, but did little to upgrade VSZ's core operations.

VSZ became a hodgepodge of 27 mostly non-steel businesses, including a leading bank, newspapers, a fleet of limousines and several football clubs, many of which were also to be financially drained. In fact it was impossible to know what the company owned or controlled. As one share trader commented: 'it's like investing in a black hole.'[9] Rezes shamelessly used his political authority as transport minister to protect his investment, for example by approving tariff discounts on the railways that saved VSZ – and cost the railways – some $30m a year.

VSZ was not a bad company even under communism, although it needed to upgrade its technology and find new foreign markets. But by 1998 the firm's debts had reached almost $500m, and its losses for that year alone were $263m, as cash was siphoned out under Rezes's ownership (his spectacular villas in Spain gave some indication as to where the money was going). Inevitably VSZ was soon on the brink of collapse, having breached the terms of one of its foreign loans. With over 24 000 people working at VSZ, and at least 100 000 people in eastern Slovakia indirectly depending on it, no Slovak government could afford to let the company go bankrupt. But a creditors' committee led by ING Bank decided that enough was enough and threatened to do just that unless Rezes and his allies left the company. With Meciar now out of power, Rezes had lost his protector. ING appointed Gabriel Eichler, a Slovak émigré who had worked as a corporate turnaround expert in the US, to sort out the company. His task was to ease out the managers, separate the loss-making peripheral businesses from the steel works, which would then be restructured, and find a foreign investor who would turn the company into a major regional steel producer.

Eichler had his work cut out. He was not the government's man (although the Dzurinda cabinet reluctantly accepted him), and he recalls being told by local managers that they had been betting on whether Rezes's men 'would shoot me on the first day or second day'. But Eichler would not be intimidated and refused to have bodyguards, in the hope that this would endear him to ordinary people, not least the workers at the mill. 'The previous president [Rezes] was like a feudal lord', he says. Many local workers assumed that Eichler would be yet another gangster-businessman. The shopfloor trade union that was loyal to Rezes was hostile towards Eichler, while other VSZ unions were lukewarm at best. VSZ was riven with tax liabilities and complex cross-shareholdings. As Eichler tried to stabilise the company's finances, tax and finance ministry officials descended like vultures to audit the firm, and pored over the books for two years. The EBRD, which was a shareholder in VSZ, had recently soured on Slovakia over another deal and was not on hand to lend support.

Eichler faced outright hostility from Rezes's friends on the board. 'No one really wants you here', they told him at the first shareholders' meeting he attended. They had good reason to worry, since he was exposing rotten practices at every level of the firm. Senior managers had been taking 'plastic bags [of money] to Switzerland every week', he recalls. The chief financial officer operated a private company on the side, supplying raw materials to VSZ at jacked-up prices, and steel was being supplied to middlemen who never paid for it. By simply cutting out these operators, Eichler managed to triple VSZ's monthly cash flow. Despite rising opposition to Eichler within VSZ, the western creditor banks were determined to keep him in place, even though their only leverage was the threat of foreclosing on the company altogether – a move that was in no one's interests, including the banks'. 'If Eichler goes, everything goes', said one of the bankers at the annual general meeting in 1999.

Unfortunately, foreign investors were hardly rushing to the rescue. The reaction from one international steel maker – 'fix it, renationalise it, then maybe we'll look at it' – was typical. Aside from the fact that the European steel industry was already oversupplied, VSZ's political entanglements alone were enough to deter even the most hard-nosed operators. The only potential buyer was US Steel, a Pittsburgh-based company that had never owned a major subsidiary outside the US, let alone one located in a small, troubled East European country. US Steel and VSZ weren't complete strangers, because they had formed a small tin plate joint venture a couple of years previously, but three separate attempts to cajole the US firm into buying the entire company came to nought as the top brass in Pennsylvania repeatedly lost their nerve.

However, Dzurinda, the new prime minister, was determined to see the restructuring through and get the company into western hands, and his support for Eichler kept the project on track. Dzurinda believed that selling VSZ to a western firm would send a message to Meciar and his allies that crony capitalism in Kosice was a thing of the past, and would show western governments and investors that Slovakia had ridded itself of a particularly nasty case of it. After all, if a conservative American company was to choose eastern Slovakia, why should other, more experienced investors not come too?[10]

US Steel was therefore offered a completely clean company after the steel operations that it wanted were separated from the rest of VSZ in a legal manoeuvre involving the transfer of some 28 000 separate assets. The government got its investor and some money back, the bankers were repaid in full, and there were no redundancies. US Steel paid $425 million for the mill, which covered all debts, and agreed to invest $700m in the mill over the next ten years. As for Rezes, he died shortly afterwards, leaving an estimated $20m fortune to his family.

In many ways, the VSZ saga is at odds with the image of the slick, expansionist US firm turning around a sick, incompetent East European operation. US Steel in fact acquired a strong company that after two years of Eichler's restructuring was making an annual profit of $80m. The workers were highly skilled, and mid-level managers performed well once they were given the freedom to act responsibly. One Slovak director was even transferred to Pittsburgh to run a large US division of the firm. By contrast, the American newcomers were 'hard-nosed, good old American steel workers' without much cosmopolitan flair, says Eichler. They could be dictatorial and often clashed badly with the locals. But their attitude changed when they understood the high quality of the business that they had acquired, and US Steel-Kosice has since gone from strength to strength. The Slovak operation soon became the US company's most profitable unit anywhere. The real question, Eichler asks in frustration, is not 'why they came, but what took them so long'. And the answer was political risk. From the Slovak point of view, the deal was not only about business, but also a means to help preserve the country's newly won democracy.

Vouching for security: Czech privatisation

While Meciar orchestrated the bare-faced pillage of his nation's wealth, a similar story was being played out, if more subtly, in the Czech Republic – for so long the West's favourite transition economy. The Czech approach to plundering was to twist a seemingly fair and equitable method of transferring the nation's industry to private hands – voucher privatisation – to achieve the very opposite of the scheme's original aims. The Czech government allowed this to happen despite calls from multinationals, international institutions such as the IMF and the EU, and many Czech politicians, to establish transparent, enforceable laws and regulations.

The central idea of voucher privatisation, which was launched in 1991 in the former Czechoslovakia and continued in the Czech Republic (but not Slovakia) after the country split in 1993, was to create a nation of shareholders almost overnight by issuing vouchers for a nominal registration fee to all Czechoslovak citizens, who could then use them to bid for shares in thousands of state-owned enterprises. Because some companies would be more in demand than others, voucher holders would be required to bid for the companies in several rounds, until an equilibrium price was reached, at which point the shares would be transferred. The voucher scheme had several advantages. It was intended to educate the population in such concepts as supply and demand, private ownership and the operation of stock markets; it was viewed as a just form of restitution, returning nationalised assets back to the people; and it also provided an escape route for politicians who did not want to be accused of selling the country's so-called 'crown jewels' to foreigners, the only investors with hard cash. Vaclav Klaus, the finance minister at the time (and later prime minister), had been quick to see the potential political advantages for himself of voucher privatisation. The scheme would allow him to boast of a Czech innovation in state asset sales, and to point to his signature on every voucher book. Such considerations were sure to boost his standing in the upcoming 1992 general election, he believed.

However, the scheme also had numerous flaws, one of which was that it would raise almost no money. Fortunately, unlike countries such as Hungary, Czechoslovakia had a relatively low foreign debt, and its balance of payments and budget were in good shape (see chapter 6). Policymakers therefore felt that the country could forego the injection of funds from foreign investors. In addition, there were many other large state enterprises such as Tabak, the cigarette monopoly, or Sklo Union, a glass works, where stakes would be sold for cash to a strategic foreign buyer. A more critical problem was that the scheme was launched without a clear regulatory structure in place. Share trading lacked transparency, there were few rules on disclosure of information, and there was no legal protection for minority shareholders. But Klaus, an economist, simply wanted to get the assets out of state hands as quickly as possible and then let the markets do the rest – an astounding leap of faith given how undeveloped the markets were at the time.

The scheme had other shortcomings. Despite the voucher give-away, citizens were far from enamoured by the idea, and at first failed to take up their voucher entitlement. Their lack of interest partly reflected ignorance about capitalism, and specifically about how to judge the value of one company over another. But the Czech public was also deeply sceptical about politicians and their clever schemes, a view that western advisers did not fully appreciate at the time, but which subsequently proved to be rather far-sighted.

The project was teetering on the brink of failure, and was threatening to end Klaus's political career, until Viktor Kozeny, a 28-year-old, Harvard-educated Czech émigré, arrived on the scene. Returning to his homeland in 1991, Kozeny set up the Harvard Capital investment fund, which offered to invest people's vouchers using the expert research of his firm. Other funds cropped up too, some of which were run by the state-owned banks, but the Harvard name seemed to convey academic excellence and integrity (although the fund had no connection to the university), and it garnered trust among Czechs.[11] The privatisation programme took off after Kozeny made a simple offer to voucher holders: any investor in the Harvard fund would be guaranteed a ten-fold return on their vouchers after 'a year and a day', a typical time period in Czech fairy tales. Here, indeed, was another fairy tale. Although the offer in itself was not wildly implausible (Harvard was offering a ten-fold increase not in the value of the companies being acquired but rather in the nominal cost of buying the voucher), it proved to be virtually worthless.

The immediate consequence of Kozeny's announcement was that Czechs streamed into Harvard Capital offices to hand over their vouchers, thereby saving the voucher privatisation project. Soon the young entrepreneur was in control of some of the biggest enterprises in the country. But Harvard and other such funds were either unable or unwilling to assert effective shareholder control, and managers at the companies (or even the fund managers themselves) began stripping assets through a variety of transfer payments practices, such as charging inflated fees for financial advice. Such manoeuvring left minority shareholders, and not least the voucher holders themselves, holding near worthless pieces of paper.

It got worse. Many of the investment funds that had hoovered up the vouchers, becoming part-owners of major state companies in the process, were themselves still owned by state banks. So while managers and investment funds were gouging the newly acquired companies, the state-owned banks (and by extension the taxpayers) were supplying cheap credits to keep these companies afloat. The tight system of cross-ownership provided a neat and secretive way by which the government could continue to exert control over industry, despite seemingly wishing to be shot of it. Ultimately, Czech voucher privatisation amounted to a massive con perpetrated by various political insiders, who became extremely rich, while crumbling industries remained in state hands in all but name.

Failure to regulate the system was the main undoing of voucher privatisation. As writer and journalist Robin Shepherd points out, the government had failed to understand, or deliberately ignored, the distinction between 'private possession' and 'private property'. The former, he argues, may simply involve dumping state holdings onto an unsuspecting public. Without effective laws and regulations to defend private ownership rights, privatised assets end up in the hands of those with 'the biggest stick' or the best connections. The institutional framework in the Czech Republic was so weak that the legal transfer of shares proved to be irrelevant. Failure to enforce private ownership rights meant that there was nothing to stop poorly regulated investment funds taking over a company and stripping its assets, while untrained, under-funded court officials dithered for years over ownership disputes without clear legislation on which to base a decision.[12]

One of the most devastating critiques of voucher privatisation came not from opposition economists but from Vaclav Havel, the president of the Czech Republic at the time. The animosity between Havel and Klaus is well-known. The latter often attacked Havel, a philosopher, playwright and former dissident, for his woolliness and his ramblings about civil society and Christian morality. Yet the president could not have captured the economic, political and ethical failings of Czech privatisation better than he did in a speech to the Senate following the collapse of the Klaus government in November 1997. Havel superbly deconstructed Klaus's distorted version of capitalism:

Intoxicated by power and success, and fascinated by the discovery, or rediscovery, that a political party can be turned into a marvellous springboard for a climb up the career ladder, many began – in an environment that took the law so lightly – to turn a blind eye to this and that, until they were faced with scandals casting doubts on the principal reason for our pride – on our privatisation.... The declared ideal of success and profit was turned to ridicule because we allowed a situation in which the biggest success could be achieved by the most immoral ones, and the biggest profits could go to unpunishable thieves...

[The problem was that] the transformation process stopped halfway, which is possibly the worst thing that could have happened to it. Many businesses have been formally privatised, but how many have concrete, visible owners who seek increasing effective[ness] and who care about the long-term prospects of their companies? It is no exception to see companies whose executives are unable to say who their owners are, or how they are supposed to account to the owners for their managerial performance. But how can we expect the desired restructuring of companies, and of whole branches of our economy, when there are so few clear owners, and when so many of those who represent the owners see their role not as a task, mission or commitment but simply as an opportunity to transfer the entrusted money somewhere else and get out? A rather strange role, to my mind, is often played by our banks: they indirectly own companies that are operating at a loss, and the more the companies lose the more money the banks lend them.[13]

It would be left to the next government, the general public and multinational companies to clear up the mess.

Contrary to the popular view, the Czechs and Slovaks did not take alternative paths to reform; the differences were in form rather than substance. Academic Abby Innes writes:

> Where Klaus's ideological dogmatism allowed a covert corruption of privatisation and reversion to patronage, Meciar went quite publicly for the clan-economy, the placing of party men in crucial industrial, bureaucratic, educational and media positions, and the clientelistic distribution of state assets to loyal followers, signalling clearly that to be a 'party man' was once again the way to get ahead. …Where Klaus refused to legislate for state accountability, Meciar legislated for unaccountable recentralised power. … Both regimes carved up state influence between themselves and their coalition partners.[14]

Television game show: the battle for TV Nova

Although the unravelling of voucher privatisation harmed ordinary Czechs rather than multinationals (who had been largely unable to participate in the scheme), some foreign investors suffered badly from the weak regulatory environment in the Czech Republic. Foremost among them was Central European Media Enterprises (CME), a US television company controlled by Ronald Lauder.

CME entered the Czech Republic in 1994 under an agreement with a group led by local entrepreneur Vladimir Zelezny, who had been a dissident playwright under communism, and was a member of the revolutionary Civic Forum in 1989. Zelezny and a band of intellectual friends had won a licence for a new TV station and set up TV Nova. CME agreed to finance the acquisition of the licence and the set-up costs on condition that the station take all its programming from a Lauder investment vehicle. TV Nova was an instant success. The channel had initially promised serious programming, but saw its viewing figures skyrocket on a diet of US soaps, popular quiz shows and naked female weather forecasters. Within a couple of years TV Nova's annual operating profit was over $50m. Zelezny, as chief executive, became a rising star not only in the Czech Republic but in CME itself.

But all was not well. CME soon smelt a rat, suspecting rightly that Zelezny was breaching their agreement by quietly taking programme content from his own production company that he had recently set up. Zelezny then managed to persuade the Czech broadcasting council to allow licence holders such as himself to apply for changes to the original terms of the licence, enabling him to cut Lauder and CME out of the programming process altogether. It was a shameful case of asset-stripping, which took place with the implicit collusion of the broadcasting authorities. CME kicked Zelezny out and sued him for $23m, the theoretical value of his shares in the near-defunct CME-backed subsidiary. But Zelezny, as the licence holder, simply withdrew his licence from CME altogether and began to run Nova on his own, refusing to take CME programming and therefore depriving the US company of advertising revenue. The move destroyed CME's investment in the Czech Republic, the only profitable part of its East European media empire, and threatened to bankrupt the entire company. During the course of 1999 CME's share price collapsed from an all-time high of $16 to $1.50, scuppering the planned $600m sale of the US-based parent company to a Scandinavian broadcaster.

The Czech broadcasting council failed to act, merely telling both parties in 1999 to resolve their disputes without interrupting programming. CME won a preliminary ruling in an Amsterdam arbitration court, which ordered Zelezny to restore CME as the exclusive service provider, but the ruling was ignored. Lauder then took out a series of advertisements in the New York Times and the Washington Post, warning foreign companies not to invest in the Czech Republic, which, he claimed, was encouraging investment but failing to protect it. The Czech government read little into this outburst, and most analysts put it down to sour grapes.

Lauder then decided to sue the Czech government itself for breaching a bilateral investment treaty with the US aimed at protecting foreign investment. There followed a series of over 50 rulings and appeals in Czech and international arbitration courts against both Zelezny and the Czech government. Finally, on 14 March 2003 a Stockholm arbitration court ruled that the Czech authorities had indeed failed to protect CME's investment, and ordered the state to pay $353m in damages to CME. The Czech government accepted the verdict, and paid up.

Local courts also found in favour of CME, and began a hunt for Zelezny's assets. Police raided his Paris home, looking for his art collection, and chased down bank accounts in Liechtenstein and Prague. But Zelezny was far from finished. In 2002 he was elected to the upper chamber of the Czech parliament, where he hoped to gain immunity from prosecution, and, despite facing six criminal charges, decided to stand for the European Parliament in 2004, winning a seat. Fred Klinkhammer, the chief executive of CME in Eastern Europe, whose task was to get CME's money back after the company had pulled out of the country altogether, described the situation thus: 'it was like being in the dentist's chair with Zelezny holding the drill, but me holding him by the balls.'

Russia for the Russians: loans for shares

While the attempt to create a tiny oligarchy in Slovakia was ultimately defeated owing to an inspired defence by the Slovak population of its new-found democracy, it was nonetheless a close-run thing. Such a battle never occurred in Russia, where a similarly outrageous asset give-away, known as the 'loans for shares' deal, did succeed.

The scheme was hatched in 1995 by a group of successful business-men in their 20s and 30s, led by Vladimir Potanin. It was aimed at helping Russian President Boris Yeltsin, who was facing possible defeat by the Communist Party candidate in the 1996 presidential election, and who also had a gaping hole in the budget to fill. The businessmen offered to lend the government $2 billion in return for management rights over leading state-owned enterprises, mainly in the oil, gas and metals industries. Since these firms were, in effect, controlled by their old communist directors anyway, the government in Moscow felt that it had little to lose from allowing these brash upstarts to have a crack at the old enemy. A highly complicated financial plan was presented to both the Russian people and the western press as a temporary arrange-ment to help cover the budget shortfall, and was accompanied by all the legal paraphernalia of open tenders. In reality neither the govern-ment nor the new tycoons expected the loans to be repaid. They weren't, leaving Potanin and the other businessmen owning assets worth an estimated 20 times the price they paid. There was a vicious scramble among the tycoons to share out the assets, but the key point was that the deal had created an oligarchy in Russia within a year. Yeltsin, meanwhile, was financed through the 1996 election, which he won.

In a postscript to the 'loans-for-shares' carve-up, British oil company BP was to suffer the consequences of operating in the East European shark pool without fully understanding the political subtext. In the original loans for shares agreement Potanin had sold a 33 per cent stake in oil company Sidanko to Alfa Group, a company owned by fellow oligarch Mikhail Friedman, for $40m. But Potanin later realised that he could sell a 10 per cent stake in Sidanko to BP for a much higher $571m. He therefore bought the 33 percent stake back for $100m from Friedman, who, unaware of BP's interest, thought it was a good deal. Friedman later realised that he had been outfoxed, and an almighty battle broke out between the two oligarchs. 'We never wanted to go to war with BP, we wanted to go to war with Potanin', Friedman reportedly claimed.[15]

The oligarchs resolved their dispute in typical Russian fashion – by manipulating the country's complex legal system and putting pressure on judges. Friedman was to take his revenge on Potanin by focusing on Chernogorneft, a profitable subsidiary of Sidanko, but with some debts to its name. Through his own oil company TNK, Friedman bought out two-thirds of Chernogorneft's creditors, and then forced the subsidiary into bankruptcy with the help of a local court. BP and other foreign creditors, including George Soros and the EBRD, were furious but could do little about it. Worse, just before the creditors' meeting a Siberian court reduced Chernogorneft's debt, thereby diluting their voting power as creditors. With Chernogorneft's assets set to be sold at a bankruptcy auction, Friedman moved swiftly. The western investors initially blocked the auction with a court injunction, but at the last moment the court reversed its decision. An auction was held in a faraway Siberian location, enabling TNK to grab Chernogorneft for a mere $176m. This left the remaining shareholders, including BP, with a virtually worthless Sidanko.[16] BP was out of its depth, unable to navigate a legal system that gave more power to creditors than shareholders. 'They don't feel comfortable in our wars – PR, legal and others. That is the whole problem', noted Potanin afterwards.[17]

Perhaps the most important point to emerge from the Sidanko saga was not that western investors needed better lawyers, but that the rules of the game themselves had been drafted specifically with such outcomes in mind. Loans-for-shares 'tenders' were run by the eventual winners of the tender. As Konstantin Kagalovsky, a representative of the Menatep group, which participated in the sales, notes: 'The key was to ensure that the law banning foreign participation was intentionally vague.' So if foreign firms sought a loophole to allow themselves in, they could be taken to court, and 'with a law so open to interpretation and the home court advantage, Menatep would stand a strong chance of winning... The whole point was to transform the decision for foreign firms from a purely legal question... to a political one',

Kagalovsky says. In fact, Kagalovsky wrote part of the loans for shares law himself.[18] As John Hewko, a western lawyer in the region, came to realise, reforming the legal system wasn't a case of pointing out short-comings in the law. It isn't mere legal inexperience 'when Russian banks start rescinding currency swaps and forward contracts on the grounds that they constitute "illegal gambling", and when the courts begin to rule [erroneously] that force majeure events have occurred (the force majeure event being that one party to the transaction has no money)'.[19]

Such problems, although extreme in Russia, could be found almost anywhere in the region. Tenders in the Czech Republic were typically run with few clear guidelines, bids and decisions were kept secret, and ministers were under no obligation to consult affected third parties. Selection panels were fronts for pre-determined political decisions (which could be awkward when a well-meaning committee selected the 'wrong' winner). There was seldom an investigation or audit. There were no 'Chinese walls', and barely a concept of conflicts of interest.[20]

Some of the most glaring conflicts of interest were not even illegal. Quentin Reed, an analyst at the Open Society Institute, a non-govern-mental organisation that lobbies against corruption in government and business, points out in a PhD thesis that Czech officials were simply unaware that a conflict of interest was a problem. He cites the case of Jaroslav Lizner, the head of the central securities register of the voucher privatisation scheme, who used his inside knowledge of the bidding prices to make parallel deals with interested bidders, and was caught taking a $300 000 bribe. In his court defence he argued that the money he took was a commission for facilitating a deal – thereby failing to display even the most basic realisation that such activities were corrupt in principle.[21] The Czech government 'conveniently forgot to pass a law on privatisation funds', says Zdenek Bakala, a financial advisor on many privatisation deals. As one of several examples, he cites the cre-ation in 1992 of the R-M System, an over-the-counter share trading mechanism. 'What was that if not a scam to transfer ownership secretly without even recording the price of the purchase?' he asks. 'It was so simple. They said: "Let's just turn the lights off for a while, and then turn them back on again", and the assets were gone'.

Transparency and bribery

How were multinational companies expected to operate in this legal twilight zone? Plenty of them braved the new East European markets early on, won privatisation and other tenders fair and square, never had to contend with any high- or low-level political interference, and were never asked to pay a bribe to a minister or an inspector. Yet many foreign corporations do stand accused of employing sharp practices, lobbying to keep out the competition, setting up elaborate (and non-too-subtle) transfer pricing schemes to evade local taxes, and indeed initiating the bribes. This is despite the existence of the US Foreign Corrupt Practices Act, which makes the paying of bribes to officials abroad illegal, and the recent adoption by the EU of OECD guidelines on the issue. Such legislation clearly puts the onus on the western multinationals, not local officials, to ensure a clean transaction.

James de Candole, a director of CEC Government Relations, one of the most respected political lobbying firms in the region, says that multinationals play hardball just like any other firm. Foreign companies argue that there may simply be no alternative but to pay a bribe if they want to win a tender, but at least they do a better job of running the company afterwards. Whether the end justifies the means, as far as the general public is concerned, is highly debatable. Marek Jacoby, an analyst at Slovak think tank Mesa 10, says that foreign investors routinely engage in low-level bribery to win public procurement contracts. He says that many of the offenders are companies from the US, despite its anti-corruption laws. Jacoby says that even if there is a scandal in the local press, the bribe payers calculate that it will quickly blow over.

Off-the-record discussions with firms, politicians and political lobbyists across the region support this view to some extent. Indeed, there is something of a template for painless bribery, as the description of one US bank's approach reveals.

The bank wants to win the tender to advise on the privatisation of a $150m–200m food company. The bank's director meets 'Pavel', the 50-year-old head of a food industry association. He has spent most of his working life perfectly happily in low-paid jobs in the industry, but has become a little disoriented by the changes and new possibilities after 1989. If the bank wins the job, it could earn $1m–2m in fees. Pavel has no real understanding of finance or the privatisation process, but he does have industry knowledge. He also has a much more important asset – he's an old friend of the minister running the privatisation. The bank invites Pavel onto its proposed team as a 'consultant'. He arrives at the bank's plush modern downtown offices, slightly awed by the professional western aura of the boardroom, and the executives rushing around in expensive suits. He's happy to be a part of the deal. The bank's director says: 'Pavel, let us talk about your fee. If we get rich we want you to be rich too. So how about a percentage of our fee – say 10 per cent?' It's a ludicrous amount for a bit of advice on the food industry, but that's because there's more to it. He must not only deliver the deal but also cover any other expenses that he might come across in his relations with the minister. Pavel calculates around $100 000 for the minister and $20 000 each to three members of the decision panel. That leaves Pavel with around $40 000, a huge reward for being a mere conduit for a few illicit payments. Pavel agrees. And of course there is no trail of payments to either the bank or the minister.

The picture of the beleaguered foreign corporation just trying to do the right thing while all around is corruption and intimidation may not be entirely accurate, but nor is it wholly false. The trouble, according to some observers, is not that western companies initiate such payments, but that ministers or bureaucrats solicit them. Jan Vrba, the former Czech trade minister (once described as 'the best minister that the Czechs ever had'[22]), insists that the source of corruption is local, and that much of it comes from political parties.[23] Vrba, who was involved in about 40 privatisation sales to foreign investors, can cite no instance of a multinational company behaving improperly or unfairly, or even taking advantage of ministerial ignorance. His discussions with Siemens – a company often accused of making nefarious payments – never even hinted at the slightest suggestion of a bribe. Bribes, he says, were paid because they were asked for.

This would hardly come as a surprise. Can one realistically expect a politician earning the equivalent of $500 a month not to ask for a financial sweetener that would allow him to buy a new house, or provide a private education abroad for his children? Who could not sympathise with Russia's young reformers, who risked life and reputation to dismantle the communist system with no financial gain for themselves, only to watch oligarchs amass billions of dollars on the back of their work?[24]

Paying down the line: dealing with bureaucrats

The solution to such problems lies in government transparency. Given how easy it is to pass on a bribe, only an open decision-making process, in which ministers' decisions can be easily tracked and assessed, is likely to scale back the practice. Unfortunately, combating bribery is not just a matter of dealing with senior ministers. The market for bribes goes right through the system. 'There was always a raft of private deals going on below the main deal', says Bakala, 'and few people saw anything wrong with this'. Paul Melling, a partner at law firm Baker & McKenzie in Moscow, says that throughout the region 'bribery options are built into the legislation, and a lot of power is given to relatively low-level officials in law', allowing them to line their pockets. 'Why else is there a waiting list to be a customs officer, or a member of the traffic police – not from love of public service', Melling says. The going rate for getting a job in Azerbaijan's customs office is believed to be around $10 000 – around 10 years' wages.[25]

Along with customs officers, members of tax, health and safety inspectorates (especially fire inspectors) are notorious for seeking additional incomes, although often these are not for the inspectors themselves but for the organisation or department for which they work. Kraft Foods, a US group, was constantly being hit in the late 1990s by the fire authorities in St Petersburg, Russia. Stephen Lee, Kraft's Vice President for Strategic Planning, recalls one fire inspector asking the firm to buy the municipality a new fire truck in exchange for a health and safety permit. 'It would have made our lives easier if we had, but we did not oblige,' he says. Similarly, the fire service in Hungary carried out regular bi-weekly fire risk investigations at the factory of detergent maker Henkel, which is noted for its high standards of safety (see chapter 2). Each time the inspectors arrived they asked for a contribution to the fire service, says Gunter Thumser, Henkel's Executive Vice President for Central and Eastern Europe. In a survey of 1000 small enterprises carried out by Russia's Centre for Economic Reform in 2000, 46 per cent said that fire inspectors appeared at least once per quarter, as often as racketeers. The report added that 'a number of government organs, independent of their official duties and theoretical benefits, have, in reality, become organisations whose single function is the extortion of bribes'.[26] As one Russia analyst quipped: 'Given the frequency with which state fire inspectors visit local and foreign firms, Russia should be the safest country in the world.'

There also seems to be no end of ways in which local tax offices can fleece foreign investors. Tax inspectors often have revenue targets to reach, and they are keenly aware that major western multinationals can be sensitive about bad publicity. 'Any question of [non-payment of] taxes and we pay it. [In this respect] we're more Catholic than the Pope', Lee remarks. Television manufacturer Thomson Polkolor got a visit from a burly, six-feet five-inch tall member of the Polish tax police, who claimed quite outrageously that the company had breached a rule dating from the period of martial law in 1981, which prohibited price increases for certain products.

Such money-scamming devices eventually take their toll on the investor, not least because they require firms to beef up their accounting departments and hire expensive tax advisors in order to defend themselves. Yet despite the inconvenience, most multinationals say that it is better to resist the bureaucrats, and accept that it may take several months longer to receive a licence or register a company, rather than pay up and encourage further demands. It is not unheard of for Western firms in Russia to pay a $1000 fine the official way rather than a $50 bribe to the local inspector. The bureaucrats soon learn that they won't squeeze any money from the firm, and stop trying.

Unfortunately, such enlightened self-interest may be possible only in countries where legal safeguards exist, and where refusing to pay merely delays business rather than ruins it. Where the rule of law is weaker, foreigners are under pressure to pay their way through the bureaucracy, as there is no recourse to a legal system for protection. A World Bank survey of corruption in the region in 2000 notes that in countries with high levels of 'state capture' – that is, where a small, possibly criminal clique runs the government – foreign firms headquartered in-country are far more likely than domestic companies to be engaged (or at least compelled to engage) in corruption, either as a giver of bribes or as an attractive target for officials.[27] This is particularly the case in Russia, Ukraine, the Caucasus and Central Asia. For example, getting a shipping container through the port of Odessa in Ukraine requires several hundred dollars in bribes and the employment of a local dealer with friends in the customs service. There is little way around this. According to the head of the Odessa office of shipping company Maersk, 'much depends on the customs officer's mood on a given day. Sometimes they charge outrageous fees, and then the next week they forget what they were'.[28] What most galls multinationals is that inspectors usually give a clean bill of health to local companies that seriously contravene health, safety and other rules. 'We would be more than happy to be treated equally to a local competitor', says one food and drink investor in Romania. 'That way our competitors would have to implement proper health and safety regulations and pay their taxes, like we do. They would find it rather harder to compete then.'

There is plenty of confusion as to what constitutes a bribe. Melling says that the dividing line is truly fuzzy, and he draws various distinctions. The certification official who wants to have two versions of every sample, one of which he takes home for himself, is corrupt – firms may only send a properly invoiced sample to the address of the certification office. But food inspectors may receive free samples as a gift from a food factory that normally gives all its visitors such samples. Alternatively, a payment to officials to expedite a registration probably violates US corrupt practices legislation; but buying flowers for all the women in the registration offices, which may constitute an essential part of developing good relations there, would probably be all right.

It can also be easy to confuse an overly rigorous approach by a tax office with an attempt to extract a bribe. Polish authorities are typically guilty of excessive scrutiny; a single firm can be subject to detailed investigations by the tax office, the tax police, the social insurance agency and the customs service. As one tax accountant puts it: 'the general criticism of these organs is not that they're unreasonable, but that they're unimaginative – they spend lots of time going over and over small sums'. Investigations into alleged transfer pricing have become more effective and rigorous, and many disputes have ended up in courts. Yet local courts, even in Russia, increasingly find in favour of the western company in disputes with the tax office. These cases are won not by paying off the judge, but by having one's paperwork in order.

Things can only get better

So where is the pressure for change coming from? Some foreign investors in the region have mounted spirited campaigns to improve the legal environment. However, probably more significant has been the realisation by government officials and also local tycoons that a system of greater openness and fairer treatment of investors – not least minority shareholders,[29] would lead to faster membership of international organisations such as the EU and the World Trade Organisation, and also boost the value of local companies. In East-central Europe, the EU has also played a crucial role in pressuring governments to clean up their legal acts. It has carefully monitored legal reforms in at least ten transition economies and held the ultimate carrot of eventual EU membership over the applicant states. Financial self-interest among local tycoons has also been key, especially after they had won in the crazy scramble for assets. Russian oil firm Yukos found that adopting western accounting methods and disclosure standards enabled it to raise vast sums on western stock markets and boost its market value threefold in a couple of years, and therefore set the standards for other major players in the market. Similarly, the disclosure by Russian juice maker J7 that one of its owners had a criminal record, far from harming the firm, was taken as a sign of greater transparency and helped to open up international financial markets to the company. As lawyers constantly point out, plenty of best-practice codes had been floating around for years, but what made the difference was the simple realisation that co-operation and transparency was where the money was.

Multinational companies may not have done much more than to add their voices to the general call for reform. But they have played a direct role in changing attitudes at the lower levels of the bureaucracy, as a result of their daily interaction with officials, and their long slog to improve laws that were drafted in ignorance or haste. Through foreign companies' diligent attention to detail, patient explanation, and the specialist expert knowledge that only committed investors could have acquired, the more effective laws, customs and best practices began seeping into the business environment. Willem van der Vegt, who until recently headed Dutch electronics company Philips in Hungary, was one of thousands of multinational managers who made a real difference on the ground. Enlightened self-interest led Philips to create a taskforce to help reform the Hungarian customs system. 'The key lesson to get across was that an honest mistake didn't mean that the company was trying to evade taxes, and it was unnecessary to freeze the firm's bank account', he says. At the same time Philips helped the customs office upgrade and computerise its information system.

Western companies took responsibility for the daily drip-feeding of their expertise into Eastern Europe's multifarious bureaucracies. It is no coincidence that the most ignorant, pedantic, inconsistent and inexperienced officials were found in countries with the least exposure to normal international business practices. Companies in Slovakia in the late 1990s, for example, typically reported that it was not so much bribery and corruption that concerned them as officials' simple lack of exposure to western practice, resulting from low levels of foreign direct investment. The business landscape began to alter as the multinationals took it upon themselves to invite officials to their offices, and show them how their business worked in practice. Eastern Europe began to change less as a result of sweeping exhortations from the West for local politicians to come clean, but rather through the unglamorous daily grind of multinational company work on the ground.

As John Hewko recalls speaking at an international conference on reform in Ukraine, which has attracted relatively little western investment to date:

> I summarised the key specific changes to existing Ukrainian law that were needed to facilitate private-sector financing. The response: eyes

glazing over. I finished, received polite applause and the western experts and Ukrainian panellists continued their discussion in the most general of terms about ... the need to implement market reforms and stamp out corruption.[30]

Actions of multinational investors may well speak louder than the well-meaning words of public officials – a point that might be considered with greater attention by those genuinely interested in helping developing countries out of poverty not just in Eastern Europe and the CIS, but throughout the world, and one that will be looked at in more detail in the final chapter.

8
Conclusions: The Road Ahead

'In the movie Manhattan, Woody Allen's character talks about the hotel, where the food was dreadful, and there was not enough of it, either! The critics of multinationals often make similar complaints'[1]
– Jagdish Bhagwati

I am sitting in the plush lobby of a top Prague hotel, near Wenceslas Square. At a table in the corner are three young businessmen, probably in their late thirties, quietly discussing a forthcoming meeting over morning coffee. They are sharply dressed in dark blue, faintly pin-striped suits, crisp white shirts and sober ties. Their English-made shoes are a well-polished black, and worn over black socks. They wear taste-ful, expensive watches. Their hair is well-groomed, not trendy. They look healthy but not overly tanned by beach or sunbed. I assume that they are multinational company managers from Western Europe or the US, since they have none of the characteristics of stereotypical local businessmen – ill-fitting brown or purple suits with white socks, an awkward lack of confidence, and an over-eagerness to impress each other (or the waitress). But as I move a table closer to eavesdrop, I realise that they are Slovaks.

Admonishing myself for crass typecasting, I am left to conclude that executives in much of the region have now fully absorbed the manner-isms and trappings of multinational companies. They dress, talk and act the same as their western counterparts, which in itself might have been quite unusual as recently as five years ago. But there is something more than absorption and imitation. There is identification. The new generation of multinational executives from Eastern Europe aren't just replicating western behaviour, but are an intrinsic part of the game. When Peter Skodny, a Slovak (see chapter 1), can joke about his consulting colleagues around the world all looking and behaving like 'androids', a more fundamental development is occurring. Multi-national business people in the region have formed something of a new culture – with similar codes of dress, behaviour, ethics, skills, obligations, risks, rules and exacting standards to those that have long been common in the West.

The new East Europeans have more in common than good salaries and ambition; they also share a certain pride and status. An East European who says that he works for Volkswagen, Microsoft, Procter & Gamble or Coca-Cola is making a powerfully loaded statement that evokes numerous complex assumptions and reactions, just as it might if someone says that he studied at Harvard or Oxford, or if an English-man has a double-barrelled surname. The members of this multi-national society recognise one another in airport lounges and at conferences. Their business cards confer acceptance by their peers, and their abilities and integrity are taken for granted, not just at home but across the world. They socialise together and meet their spouses through each other. They enjoy good salaries, bonuses, health insur-ance, international travel and top hotels, and in turn (generally) don't fiddle their expenses, and don't do private deals with company money. Basically, they are trusted by their peers, and in turn they trust the institution that employs them.

All this is significant because most East Europeans in 1989 sorely lacked basic pride and confidence in their institutions. Communism compromised independent organisations, from the local rambling club to the church, forcing them all into the party's ideological embrace. As a result such bodies were corrupted by state interference and corroded by mistrust. This chapter will not delve into the endlessly analysed issues of civil society, except to note that much of the region still lacks the sort of autonomous private institutions – where membership is voluntary and overlapping and based on reciprocal consent with government – that underpin a healthy, pluralistic society. Attempts at reforming post-communist societies by creating vibrant institutions run into a seemingly insoluble conundrum: how can governments encourage something that might sooner or later oppose them? As political scientist George Schopflin writes:

'Central and Eastern Europe was witnessing the replay of an age-old dilemma, the problems of modernisation from above. If modernity is equated roughly with the functioning of a civil society conscious of its autonomy vis-a-vis the state, then the state is hardly the best-equipped body to act as midwife. Unfortunately there is nothing else. ... the state would need to exercise an extraordinarily high degree of self-limitation ... In practical terms this is all but inconceivable. Once the state has gained control of an area of activity, involving opportunity for power, privilege and patronage, it will not give them up without a struggle'.[2]

If such institutions cannot evolve from above or below, how can they be developed? One answer to the dilemma is to import them. Since 1989 multinationals have brought their attitudes and economic prowess into Eastern Europe with impressive speed and power, and in doing so have become an effective force in developing at least one small aspect of civil society that the region so desperately needed. As sociologist John A. Hall notes: 'The chances for civil society are on balance improved by the historic rejection of import-substituting industrialisation. The possibility of a rise in levels of economic growth and an increase in connections to the external world will both lend support to civil society'.[3] Although it could be argued that multinational corporations are merely part of the fabric of centralised power in Eastern Europe, the very short time in which they have been operating in the region, and their exclusion from many privatisation deals in favour of local investors (see chapter 7) suggest that this is not the case.

Broadly speaking, multinationals have provided Eastern Europe with two hugely important things in the last 15 years: large, independent companies that are willing and often able to resist arbitrary political force, and a link to the global capitalist system. Although relations between governments and foreign investors have generally been harmonious in much of the region, the very presence of politically and economically powerful multinationals serves as an important check on potential abuse of power by governments. Local firms can also defend their interests using good contacts in government, but only multinationals have the ultimate sanction against bullying politicians of being able to pack up and leave, with the loss being absorbed in a consolidated global balance sheet. Governments will therefore be more wary of overplaying their hand with foreign investors than with local firms, since a high-profile multinational departure could damage a country's reputation and deter future investors.

Vladimir Meciar, the former Slovak prime minister, may have displayed all the symptoms of control freakery, but he never seriously touched Volkswagen, the country's biggest foreign investor. President Putin has had leading Russian oligarchs arrested or driven into exile, but has kept his hands off the multinational companies in the country. Multinationals may also be less vulnerable than domestic firms to the threat from local mafia gangs, which in some areas of the region seem to wield more influence than the authorities. And when the gangs do strike, foreign companies have other cards to play. In one case a Russian manager in a multinational was being intimidated by a local mob that wanted a distribution deal with the firm. Although his life was threatened, he refrained at first from informing his superiors, fearing the sack. When eventually he revealed all, the company simply relocated him and his family to the New York office for three years, until the threats died away. The gang was dealt with by the company's own security firm.[4]

Multinationals have also introduced the values and performance standards of global business to Eastern Europe. For the pinstripe-suited Slovaks and many others in the region, these attributes are a major attraction, since foreign-owned companies are the channels through which ambitious young executives can live a western or international lifestyle. These firms have brought not only modern technology but also the latest working methods, global brands and an international reputation.

However, multinationals are not agents of morality. Their purpose is primarily to seek profit, which can have both positive and negative effects on the people, communities and countries with which they come into contact. The previous chapters of this book have demonstrated how the independent clout and corporate assumptions that multinationals have brought to Eastern Europe have benefited not only the locally-employed managers and staff of these companies, but also entire societies and economies in the region. Foreign direct investment (FDI) gives host economies the chance to enjoy the sort of turbo-charged development that local enterprises, governments or international institutions may not be able to deliver. However, the international and independent perspective of essentially profit-driven multinationals can create problems as well as opportunities.

Employees may gain wonderful career opportunities, with the chance to train and work abroad, but they could also find that their skills have become obsolete, and be forced to work longer and harder than before, and with greater risk of getting fired (see chapter 2). Local projects and charities may find that meddle-free corporate sponsorship is a welcome alternative to relying on local power-brokers, or the investor may choose to remain remote from the community and out of touch with its needs, snatching its oil reserves or poaching the best workers from nearby businesses (see chapter 3). Multinationals may restructure or reinvent industries (see chapter 4), but they may also perpetuate monopolies or shift manufacturing operations abroad if wages rise too far. Foreign companies can introduce exciting consumer products and reinvigorate local brands, but there is also a risk of them dominating the market with imports, and eliminating popular local brands from their portfolios (see chapter 5). Retailing has seen the good and the bad too. Foreign-owned hypermarkets have made shopping cheaper and quicker, and have widened the range of products available, while making millionaires out of ambitious local suppliers; but such outlets have spelt the end for inefficient corner shops across the region.

Although the economy overall benefits from multinational-led exports and investment, there is a growing fear among politicians that foreign firms huddle in enclaves and have little contact with the rest of the economy, repatriating rather than reinvesting their profits. Foreign firms have helped to build modern international economies in Eastern Europe, but the perception remains that they are liable to turn a small country into a tiny cog in a vast supply chain (see chapter 6). And although multinationals campaign for transparency in government and even help to train local bureaucrats, they can play hardball too, bribing ministers and lobbying for changes in the law that would limit competition (see chapter 7).

What went right?

Although this book has argued that multinationals have been an over-whelmingly positive force in Eastern Europe since 1989, such an outcome was not preordained. Four key factors were at work. First, much of the region had a system of checks and balances in place, albeit not necessarily in a formal constitutional sense, that helped to constrain multinational behaviour. Second, East Europeans had the right set of skills and adequate levels of education. These fitted well with the needs of foreign investors, while allowing the workforce to absorb the potential benefits of the investment. The third factor was the widespread reaction against communism, which naturally suited the interests of western corporations. Finally, the opening up of Eastern Europe in the 1990s coincided with an increasing awareness among Western firms of their wider corporate social responsibilities.

Perhaps the most important of these factors is that multinationals in Eastern Europe have generally operated within an informal system of checks and balances provided by the EU, international financial institutions such as the EBRD and the IMF, national and local governments, the bureaucracy, trade unions, the media, competitors, consumers and voters. Although civil society itself was weak in the early 1990s, governments were still powerful, and multinationals still had to operate within rules increasingly set by the EU or the IMF. Consumers, although not acting as an organised unit, were also a force to be reckoned with when it came to choosing the brands they wanted or where to shop. As this book has demonstrated, all these groups influenced the activities of multinationals (and one another) in numerous important ways – sometimes in support, sometimes in opposition, sometimes directly, sometimes indirectly. A sufficient degree of plurality has emerged in many parts of the region over the last 15 years to prevent the most rapacious form of multinational company behaviour from sweeping the region, while opening up the markets to the positive influences of foreign investment.[5] For example, host governments offered generous tax breaks to foreign investors, but also drafted privatisation contracts prohibiting layoffs for five years, or requiring environmental clean-ups or local sourcing. And multinationals rushed to develop existing local brands rather than destroy them after gauging the pronounced and somewhat unexpected preferences of East European consumers.

The existence of checks and balances between local actors could also favour multinationals, by curbing the excesses of the state or of certain vested interests. The mass political demonstrations in Slovakia, Bulgaria and Romania in the mid-1990s were as much about demanding the political, economic and business opportunities on offer from the West, such as EU accession and foreign investment, as they were about ridding these countries of corrupt government. The EU, the IMF and reformist governments also performed a balancing act. They forced austerity packages on unwilling populations, helping to stabilise the business environment. At the same time these institutions helped to prise open domestic markets, against the wishes of local vested interests, allowing new foreign and domestic firms to enter these markets.

In the case of more authoritarian countries where pluralism is less well-developed, foreign investors have either stayed out altogether, or (in the case of some energy firms) harnessed the power of an autocratic state while turning a blind eye to the possible negative side-effects that their investments may be having. In general, however, the variety of influences on multinational behaviour has made it easier for much of the region to absorb FDI, ensuring that the presence of foreign companies has contributed to a virtuous cycle of economic development.

The second reason why Eastern Europe has absorbed FDI well is that multinationals and host countries each had skills to offer the other. Under communism the region had been relatively well educated in areas such as mathematics, engineering and computing. Populations had become adept at technical improvisation, especially keeping broken or obsolete machinery in operation, and were therefore able to appreciate and make maximum use of the modern equipment that suddenly entered their factories. At the same time, the skills that these countries lacked most – good management, and basic knowledge of marketing, finance and human resources – could easily be provided by multinationals, through expatriate western managers and training programmes. Communism had left holes in precisely the areas that the advance troops of capitalism were best-positioned to fill.

A third reason was the measure of ideological compatibility between privately owned multinationals and many East European citizens, who had an abiding dislike and distrust of central planning from the communist era, and were potentially natural allies of capitalism and the West. Consumers in the region initially coveted western goods; workers distrusted their trade unions; and big foreign investors were often looked upon not as predatory invaders, as communism had warned, but (rather unrealistically) as a panacea that would make everyone as rich as their western neighbours overnight. The desire of East-central Europeans in particular to join the EU and NATO also worked to the advantage of multinationals which sought new markets with relatively low political risk.

Not everyone has welcomed the multinationals. Distrust of western capitalism was also widespread in 1990, encapsulated by 'homo Sovieticus', the typical communist man, who had absorbed anticapitalist ideology, lost out in the transformation, and continued to oppose adamantly the symbols of the West. Even after a decade of change, unreformed communist parties remain strong in many of the former Soviet states, as well as in the Czech Republic, which is now an EU member. The disturbing rise of nationalist sentiment in Romania, Poland, the Balkans and elsewhere is another indicator of an enduring distrust in some quarters of most things western. But such sentiments tend to be held by those who are weaker, poorer, older and less dynamic than the winners from transition, and although governments cannot discount their concerns at election time, these groups are in general less influential.

A fourth and final reason why Eastern Europe absorbed FDI well was the fact multinational companies were starting to moderate their behaviour by the time they entered the region. Much has been written about the role of multinationals in Africa, Latin America and elsewhere during the 1960s and 1970s, and their behaviour, in respect of their wider social responsibilities, was at times far from exemplary. By the 1990s, protests in the West against some of the activities of big corporations in developing countries were gathering force, and threatening (though not always fairly of helpfully) the image of well-known brand names such as Nike, Nestlé and others.[6]

These developments intensified with the emergence of a diverse anti-globalisation movement that used modern communications and the internet to become more organised and more alert to perceived abuses by multinational companies world-wide. Scores of anti-corporate, anti-globalisation books became best-sellers in the 1990s. Moreover, a younger generation of executives in those companies were themselves becoming more aware of their corporate social responsibilities. Thus when these companies entered Eastern Europe, such ethical issues were already firmly on the agenda in the West, and brands could still be vulnerable to popular activism back home.

That said, one can easily overestimate the power of such pressure groups. A brief visit to the run-down, underfunded office of an environmental group in the region, staffed by committed volunteers struggling to counter a perceived abuse by energy giants, provides a sobering reminder that the balance of power remains with the corporate entity.

Where to now?

The influence of multinationals has not been felt evenly across the region. Foreign companies initially focused on the three big economies of East-central Europe – Poland, the Czech Republic and Hungary – and the energy sectors of Russia, Kazakhstan and Azerbaijan; they were prominent in per-capita terms in Estonia, and slowly extended their exposure to the other Baltic states; and they have made a late rush into a radically reformed Slovakia. They wanted to pile into the non-oil sectors of Russia, but a difficult business environment, insider privatisation, and the country's economic independence from the West (a consequence of huge oil and gas reserves), have kept many multinationals away. Their presence has also been patchy in the Balkans, the European CIS – Belarus, Ukraine and Moldova – and most of Central Asia.

In other words, the majority of the region has still not been fundamentally affected by multinational enterprises. Moreover, in the countries that have received large amounts of FDI, multinationals have tended to gravitate to the western-most regions closest to the EU, or around the capital cities. Despite the best efforts of governments to attract them to areas of high unemployment, foreign investors have gone where market forces and not social needs have been most compelling.

So what is the future for multinationals in the region? In the key East-central European countries, membership of the EU will not radically alter perceptions of business opportunities. Western companies had long anticipated the benefits of freer trade stemming from EU integration, and have invested accordingly. Further investments will, however, be driven by the host country's economic policy and growth rates, rather than politics. An Economist Intelligence Unit report on the implications of EU enlargement notes: '... FDI inflows in central and eastern Europe are very sensitive to the policy framework – in addition to market access and wage costs – and this, rather than the mere fact of joining the EU, is what largely influences investment decisions'.[7] If the region's more advanced states were to become increasingly bureaucratic, then multinationals would be more likely to steer clear, regardless of their EU membership. EU accession could even make these countries less attractive, by adding greater social and environmental costs, and restrictions on state aid and tax incentives.

More important than EU membership for foreign investors in East-central Europe are rising wages, which are forcing those multinationals that rely heavily on low-cost labour to rethink their strategy. Multinationals that have set up a plant and gone through the painful start-up and retraining process are less inclined than portfolio investors to hotfoot out of a country unless there are overwhelming reasons to do so. However, these reasons may be starting to emerge as labour in East-central Europe becomes more expensive relative to that in the Balkans and parts of the CIS, and in particular relative to South-east Asia. Just as Western Europe lost investment to lower-wage countries in the new Europe, foreign companies may shift some of their plants in Hungary, the Czech Republic and Poland to Ukraine, Romania, Serbia or Asia. The shift of production to cheaper locations may even bypass East-central Europe altogether, going from the US or Western Europe directly to the Balkans, for example.

Such considerations are especially relevant in East-central Europe's electronics sector, which rapidly became dominated in the early 1990s by big western companies. France's Thomson took over Polish TV set manufacturer Polkolor; Philips set up in Hungary, as did Sony in Slo-vakia; IBM, Ericsson, Flextronics, General Electric and Siemens estab-lished large plants in the region; and Elcoteq, a Finnish producer of handsets and other mobile phone equipment, became one of Estonia's biggest companies. A huge brouhaha erupted in Hungary in 2002 when IBM and Flextronics shifted production of hard disks and Microsoft X-box consoles respectively to China, with the loss of almost 5000 Hungarian jobs, and politicians in East-central Europe will almost certainly have further opportunities to voice shock and alarm at the perceived perfidiousness of foreign investors.

The fear of losing such investments is understandable, but also parochial and shortsighted. First, although concerns about departing multinationals are couched in nationalist terms, locally-owned firms may also need to seek out cheaper locations if they are to survive in a globally competitive market. It is also rather hypocritical of countries in East-central Europe to lure investors away from higher-cost Western Europe on the basis of low wages, and then to deny countries further east the right to do something similar. Lower-skilled production is likely to migrate from East-central Europe to poorer countries in any case. Since rising wages generally come with rising productivity and skills levels, politically stable countries such as Hungary and the Czech Republic should be well-positioned to attract higher value-added investments in areas such as high-tech manufacturing or research and development.

A complex process is underway in which multinational companies are looking to locate different types of production in different areas, depending on the required skills and wage levels. The challenge for countries in East-central Europe is to make their shift up the value-added production ladder a smooth one. If well-managed, the change won't bring upheaval. Following IBM and Flextronics, Philips moved some operations – the production of computer monitors – from Hungary to China in 2003, but the Dutch firm also announced that one of its Hungarian plants would start producing higher-value cathode ray television sets, which were previously made in France. Even the French factory did not lose out; it began making upscale flat screen TV sets. Estonia might have had even more to worry about in 2001, when Ericsson decided to phase out the local produc-tion of mobile phone handsets, forcing Elcoteq, its subcontractor, to lay off one-third of its workforce. But Estonia's open economy and flexible workforce meant that Elcoteq soon located other production there.

New frontiers

The Balkan states should also eventually benefit from this process. What has kept multinationals away from most of this sub-region has been more its violent recent history rather than any inherent economic backwardness (with the possible exception of Albania). As ethnic tensions recede, the legal environment improves, and road and rail links are upgraded, it will be the turn of these poorer countries to attract investment based on the combination of relatively low wages and high education levels. The Balkans will also be guided towards economic reform by the beacon of EU membership; Bulgaria and Romania are already preparing for membership in 2007, and Croatia should follow soon afterwards. The rest of the Balkans is now connected by a variety of free-trade agreements, and as the EU expands it will become less tenable economically for other Balkan states to pursue a non-EU integration development path.

A similar scenario could play out eventually in the countries of the western CIS – Ukraine, Belarus and Moldova – if these states can make the profound political transformation that is finally taking place in the Balkans. With the western CIS most probably decades away from creating open, well-regulated, democratic societies, many multinationals will continue to stay away for now. Those that do take on the risks of a weak business operating environment will rely for survival less on the rule of law than on good political connections. The few foreign investors in dictatorial Belarus, for example, are particularly vulnerable without the unswerving support of President Aleksandr Lukashenko. Ukraine is somewhat less autocratic, but getting on the wrong side of the ruling party can cause plenty of difficulties, as Belgian-owned Kredyt Bank found during its endless battles with the local tax office in Lvov. Relying on political patronage is generally not a good solution for long-term investors. Autocratic ruling elites may be short-lived and their decisions arbitrary, and corporations that do business with them may find themselves out of favour when a regime changes.

The outlook for Central Asia and parts of the Caucasus differs from that for the Balkans and western CIS in two key respects. First, these countries show few signs of becoming democracies in the foreseeable future, so there may be little point in investors holding back and waiting for political improvements. Second, investment will continue to come from international oil and gas companies that are well-versed in dealing with, and indeed benefiting from, authoritarian regimes. Their principal approach will be to limit exposure to the rest of the economy, and to secure deals that demand rapid, front-loaded repayment of their investment as soon as the oil revenue comes in. Multinationals will feel that they can exert little pressure by themselves in favour of greater democratisation; rather than play by rules that don't exist, they will either play the game like the locals or not invest at all. The lure of foreign investment will, at best, serve as a small incentive for local elites to democratise, and will not be a catalyst for rapid reform. The situation may not be hopeless though; the 2003 revolution in corrupt, resource-poor Georgia may be an indicator of a more positive future for the region. But political revolution is only a first step, since authoritarian societies leave behind complex power arrangements that are not easily changed. (Serbia provides an example of such difficulties: the assassination in 2003 of Prime Minister Zoran Djindjic demonstrates how hard it can be for a society to implement reforms, even when a democratic leader is in power.) Even the most optimistic multinational will step into the CIS cautiously.

The costs, benefits and future of multinational companies in Eastern Europe have been presented throughout the book, but there is one further important counter argument that needs to be addressed. This book has made the assumption that countries in the region should open themselves to western corporate investment because it is deemed to be good for them. Yet it could equally be argued that every country has the right to choose to protect its culture and economic lifestyle from western influences. If such protectionist countries believe that the local culture could be overwhelmed by the presence of foreign brands, foreign management and an obsession with 'the bottom line', then it is their sovereign right to take that stance. The question is whether such decisions are made openly and fairly, based on a balanced assessment of the economic, social and cultural risks and rewards, or merely reflect entrenched elites protecting their own status. It takes some leap of imagination to say that political leaders in Uzbekistan, Turkmenistan or Belarus are generally keeping foreign investors away in order to preserve their indigenous cultures, and not simply to defend a dictatorship.

A subtler case is presented by Slovenia, the wealthiest post-communist country, whose lukewarm attitude towards foreign investors has irritated many multinational managers, particularly brewers, bankers and pharmaceutical firms. Slovenes are proud of their country, with its beaches, mountains, beautiful capital and high standard of living. Why should they be obligated to sell up to western multinationals if they can develop their economy at a reasonable pace on their own? Significantly, this is not necessarily a view held only by an entrenched leadership;

Slovenia is the one country in the region where multinational investors say that it can be difficult to find locals who specifically want to work for them. But this is a view that has receded with time.

The art of the possible

An American diplomat in Hungary was once asked why the US and Western Europe were not introducing a new Marshall plan for Eastern Europe, similar to the one devised by the US for Western Europe after the Second World War. 'Oh, but we are doing that', he replied, and referred to the billions of dollars that multinationals were investing into Hungary. His point was that the region needs operational know-how rather than Marshall-style Aid. Similarly, an IMF official in Bulgaria, which had struggled to find investors, confided: 'What this country really needs is a couple of big multinationals to come over and sort out this mess'.[8]

Does the experience of multinational companies in Eastern Europe point to ways in which their power can be better harnessed to combat poverty, empower communities and spread best business practices in other post-communist states in the former Soviet Union, and in poorer countries in Asia, Africa, Latin America or the Middle East? It is possible that the experience of Eastern Europe is unique; its communist past and advanced level of education may have made it particularly well placed to receive multinational companies – a situation that might not apply elsewhere. Yet it is also possible that the experience over the last 15 years could still point to ways to help other countries. The rest of this chapter will explore some of the wide variety of ideas and approaches to such problems. These include setting global standards of corporate behaviour regarding transparency, environmental disputes and labour relations under the umbrella of international bodies such as the UN; giving local businesses a leg up into the global economy by allowing them to benefit more fully from foreign investment; and working alongside developing country governments on important social and infrastructure policies such as bringing telecommunications and private finance to remote villages.

The first point to make is that any such process would have to be commercially and politically realistic in order for large corporations to be involved. Profit-seeking multinationals can hardly be expected to invest in any meaningful way if the commercial returns do not warrant it. Tax breaks and other incentives offered by the host government (and sometimes the foreign company's home country as well) can help to swing an investment decision, but such considerations won't always be decisive, and merely slanting the playing field may not address the underlying reasons why a country has trouble attracting investment.

Nor is it fair or feasible to expect these global firms to contribute directly to political liberalisation in host countries, beyond calling upon multinationals to adopt basic western norms of corporate social responsibility wherever they invest. Except for the occasional subtle nudge here and there, it is hard to imagine how western corporations can significantly influence the political behaviour of an authoritarian government without seriously compromising their own commercial interests, or even being accused of acting as an agent for a foreign government. Is steel group LNM in a position to encourage democracy in Kazakhstan simply because of its importance to that country's economy?

Others argue, of course, that lack of transparency and democracy also works in favour of the investor, especially in the mining, oil and gas sectors. But several such firms have at least made a start, by signing up to a 'Publish What You Pay' campaign, backed by hundreds of non-governmental organisations (NGOs), that calls on investors to reveal all net taxes, fees, royalties and other payments to developing country governments, thereby putting pressure on the authorities to account for how that money is subsequently spent.

Similar international frameworks, setting minimum standards and best practices, could be applied to environmental issues, though businesses say that dealing with technical or scientific issues in a public arena can be politically fraught and prone to misunderstanding and manipulation. For their part, pressure groups fear that deep-pocketed corporations would capture the process, thereby neutralising the protestors. And workers in poorer countries could benefit from a globally co-ordinated approach to spreading best employment practices to be found in multinationals. In many respects, as Chapter 2 argues, they have treated their workers in Eastern Europe relatively well, bringing decent pay and dignified working conditions, and as a result have added pressure to local enterprises to follow suit.

Multinationals argue that while they may be willing to set what they regard as realistic global norms of employment, they also fear that militant activists in the West would make absurd demands, such as paying first-world minimum wages irrespective of local purchasing power and skills levels. Multinationals also fear the entrenched and hostile positions towards corporate mobility held by many unions in the West, which tend to regard a job brought to Hungary or Kazakhstan only in terms of a job lost in the US or Germany, for example, and therefore understandably resist the creation of jobs elsewhere. Clearly workers of the world do not unite, and those in developing countries are often seen less as comrades and more as a threat. A localised view of workers' interests (in which multinationals are accused of playing divide and rule with their global workforces) makes it much harder for corporations and unions to start a sensible dialogue.

Nevertheless, all these risks should not deter attempts to move forward. In a globalising and confusing world there is increasing need for internationally legitimate bodies, like the UN, to create a mechanism for resolving disputes and apportioning responsibility that is seen to be fair and objective, without necessarily deterring the much-needed investment itself.

Setting global frameworks for appraising and settling differences may be one avenue to explore, but the East European experience shows that the governments of host countries also have a key part to play. As noted in Chapter 2, a country's workforce gains most from multinational investment when educational standards are high enough for locals to absorb the new technology brought in. Reaching this level may not require specific training on the machinery itself. Governments and international agencies could work to enhance reading, maths, foreign languages or computing skills within the education system with an eye to the needs of the multinational companies, and in consultation with them.

Governments in host countries should also recognise the gains from the creation of industrial clusters, or 'eco-systems', in which a major multinational draws in suppliers and sub-suppliers (see chapter 6). The experience of Eastern Europe shows that multinationals will gladly work with local firms that meet (or can be brought up to) the required standards. Problems arise when host governments oblige rather than encourage investors to work with lower-quality local suppliers; in Eastern Europe the imposition of local sourcing requirements on foreign investors has been counter-productive, since it only serves to discourage initial investments. Where finding adequate local supplies is problematic, multinationals could at least take a small step in the right direction by organising mentoring programmes or even internships for local entrepreneurs, without necessarily making a commitment to purchase the local firm's goods. There are plenty of retired multinational company managers who can teach local entrepreneurs exactly what is required to become a supplier or business partner. The EBRD already has a similar mentoring scheme as part of its TurnAround Management Programme, which has been effective in the CIS. Alternatively, multinationals can go the extra step by pledging to bring in other western investors from their home country, either in the same industry or in other sectors. US Steel has done this in Eastern Slovakia, thereby acting as a 'reference' for a host country or municipality.

Multinationals can also co-operate more closely with host governments, as well as with international organisations, in undertaking socially important infrastructure projects, such as providing or improving telecommunications links to villages. Telecoms operators could offer special mobile phone packages for use in the poorest villages under the aegis of an internationally recognised development programme; this would hugely empower the poorest people, while not necessarily being a financial burden on the company. International banks could, in conjunction with established development banks, set up micro-finance operations alongside their normal practice of lending to multinationals or governments, bringing expertise and much-needed funding to the poorest communities. Chapter 4 has shown how the lives of ordinary East Europeans were transformed by the provision of advanced telecommunications and retail banking services.

Other social goals, such as helping excluded minorities to enter the workforce, could be furthered by a variety of small projects, such as US Steel's links with the Roma population in Slovakia. The corporation's home government could even offer tax credits for such policies, though it remains to be seen whether companies are equipped to take on particularly complex social problems beyond simply adopting a policy of non-discrimination in the workplace.

There are other more subtle but no less far-reaching ways in which multinationals, along with governments and international non-governmental organisations, can provide assistance both within the less advanced areas of Eastern Europe and globally. These include fostering co-operative habits at work, and educating a new generation in the application of law. As John Hewko notes (see also chapter 7):

> The influence of many legal training programs funded by the international development community absolutely pales in comparison with the impact of foreign investors and foreign accounting and law firms. No amount of reform programs and resources could have even remotely been able to affect the quality and level of the accounting, auditing and legal professions as did the private sector.

If the goal is to increase the quality of the legal and accounting profession in a given country, there is no faster or more efficient mechanism than to encourage in that country a critical level of foreign investment and foreign law and accounting firms.[9]

The preceding discussion suggests that it might not be too difficult to persuade multinationals to go outside the strict dictates of corporate strategy and support development-oriented, but nonetheless profitable, projects. George Lodge, a professor at Harvard Business School, has suggested a World Development Corporation (WDC) under the auspices of the UN, involving leading multinational companies from around the world working with international development agencies of all kinds. 'Rather than merely applying superficial aid, the WDC would work to change the very system that has caused poverty in poor countries in the first place. Here again, the profit motive would come into play,' Lodge says. He concludes: 'Corporations possess the competence for the job – in the form of skills, technology, and access to global markets and credit'.[10]

International organisations including the UN have a role to play in bringing these other actors together and harnessing the power of multinationals within a realistic framework of co-operation. A 2004 report commissioned by the UN itself admits that 'many critical resources for private sector development are under the radar screen of development, since they are not carried out by the traditional development players and do not occur under the explicit label of development.' But the report also notes that 'the primary responsibility for achieving growth and equitable development lies with developing countries'.[11] Establishing a new alliance for development based on greater co-operation among all key actors is within grasp. In this respect, the experience of Eastern Europe is instructive. Vaclav Havel, the former president of the Czech Republic – a country that has benefited hugely from the arrival of multinational companies in the 1990s – alluded in 2000 to the fact that globalisation requires profound new thinking about the priorities and means of achieving the world's goals:

We often hear about the need to restructure the economies of the developing or the poorer countries and about the wealthier nations being duty-bound to help them accomplish this. If this is done in a sensitive manner, against a backdrop of sound knowledge of the specific environment and its unique interests and needs, it is certainly a worthy and much needed effort. But I deem it even more important ... that we should begin to also think about another restructuring – *a restructuring of the entire system of values* which forms the basis of our civilization today. This, indeed, is a common task for all.[12]

Notes

Introduction

1 G. Schopflin, 'Politics in Eastern Europe 1945–1992' (Oxford: Blackwell Publishers, 1993) pp. 274–5.
2 Such was the sense of fantasy and possibility at the time that Czechoslovakia's new president Vaclav Havel, an avid rock music fan, even appointed Frank Zappa as a cultural envoy, before being persuaded by state officials to withdraw the selection.
3 C. Skalnik Leff, 'The Czech and Slovak Republics-Nation Versus State' (Oxford: Westview Press, 1998) p. 2.

Chapter 1

1 C. Freeland, 'Sale of the Century: Russia's Wild Ride From Communism to Capitalism' (New York: Crown Publishers, 2000) p. 269.
2 Business Eastern Europe newsletter 29 April 1996, published by The Economist Intelligence Unit (EIU), Vienna.
3 One Czech executive in 1992 was concerned that he wasn't being taken seriously by his western suppliers, and asked a manager at a US consultancy for some advice. The response was harsh but probably fair: 'Change the purple suit and ditch the white socks', he was told.

Chapter 2

1 Disclosed by Ivan Miklos, Slovak Economy Minister and Deputy prime minister, at Economist Government Roundtable Conference, in Bratislava 1999.
2 C. Freeland, 'Sale of the Century: Russia's Wild Ride From Communism to Capitalism' (New York: Crown Publishers, 2000) pp. 329–30.
3 W. Pankow and E. Kopatko, 'Workers and Unions in Post-Communist Ukraine', p. 188, cited in 'Workers After Workers' States: Labour and Politics in Postcommunist Eastern Europe' (ed.) Stephen Crowley and David Ost (US: Rowman & Littlefield Publishers, 2001).
4 Izvestia 26 November 1999, cited by Crowley, ibid p. 215 'Workers After Workers' States: Labour and Politics in Postcommunist Eastern Europe'.
5 S. Crowley, 'Labour Quiescence in Post-Communist Russia' in 'Workers After Workers' States: Labour and Politics in Postcommunist Eastern Europe', p. 217.
6 D. A. Kiderkel, 'Winning The Battles, Losing the War: Contradictions of Romanian Labour in Post-Communist Transformation', p. 114, S. Crowley in 'Workers After Workers' States: Labour and Politics in Postcommunist Eastern Europe'.
7 R. Rose, S. White and I. McAllister, 'How Russia votes' (Chatham New Jersey: Chatham House Publishers, 1997) p. 216.

8 D. Ost, 'The Weakness of Symbolic Strength in Labour and Union Identity in Poland 1989–2000', in Crowley, ibid p. 80.
9 Interview with Richard Falbr, Prague, 16 July 2003.
10 L. Vinton, 'Managing Human Resources in Eastern Europe', The Economist Intelligence Unit, Vienna (EIU), p. 158.
11 ibid p. 140.
12 ibid p. 145.
13 Business Eastern Europe newsletter 5 Jan 1998, The Economist Intelligence Unit, Vienna.
14 Summary Company Monitor, Ahold-Czech Republic June 2003, Research by Lenka Simerska, commissioned by FNV Mondiaal, Netherlands Trade Union Federation, pp. 6–8.
15 Business operations report Romania, 23 October 1998, The Economist Intelligence Unit, Vienna.
16 L. Vinton, ibid p. 174.
17 Business Eastern Europe newsletter 15 June 1998, EIU, Vienna.
18 Business operations report Romania, ibid.
19 L. Vinton, ibid p. 117 Such pig-headedness was far from an isolated case. Another training course for five Turkmen engineers, held in Germany, produced one particularly good student who soon became chief engineer in Ashgabat. But he refused to pass on his new skills to other engineers back home as now 'it was beneath his status to get his hands dirty and work with the machines'.
20 PriceWaterhouseCoopers Training and Development Survey in the Czech Republic 2001, p. 28.

Chapter 3

1 United Nations report: Kazakhstan: Special Report on HIV/AIDS and Drug Addiction, 10 August 2003.
2 ibid.
3 The Economist 24 January 2004, p. 57.
4 L. J. Oswald, 'Multinational corporations' responses to environmental risks in transitional economies University of Michigan Environment and Business Newsletter, no. 2, September 1996, p. 1.
5 World Bank Extractive Industries Review December 2003: 'Striking A Better Balance', p. 19.
6 Mountains of Gold: Kumtor Gold Mine in Kyrgyz Republic, CEE Bankwatch Network, Budapest, May 2002, p. 36.
7 T. Popper, Regional Environmental Centre, Budapest Newsletter, vol. 10, no. 4.
8 'Report on the Cyanide Spill at Baia Mare, Romania' June 2000, United Nations Environmental Program, UN Office for the Co-ordination of Humanitarian Affairs, p. 3.
9 U. Kazarian, Caucasus Environmental NGO Network (CENN) Daily Digest, (An Official Testimony To the BTC Hearing in Borjomi and Tbilisi) 17 September 2003, p. 4.
10 ibid p. 3.

11 'Azerbaijan–Georgia–Turkey pipeline systems: An evaluation of the public disclosure and consultation process in Azerbaijan, July–October' CEE Bankwatch Network, 2003, p. 4.

12 'Baku–Tbilisi–Ceyhan Pipeline Review of Land Acquisition and Compensation Process', Interim Report Tbilisi, Oxfam, CEE Bankwatch, Association Green Alternative, 2003, pp. 24–5.

13 Stated in a press conference at EBRD Annual General Meeting London in April 2004.

Chapter 4

1 T. Whipple, 'Creating a capitalist Czechoslovakia: After the Velvet Revolution', p. 152, cited in C. Skalnik Leff, 'The Czech and Slovak Republics-Nation Versus State' pp. 262–3 (Oxford: Westview Press, 1998). By the late 1990s, Klaus the free-market ideologue had given way to Klaus the politician. In the very early years of reform, Klaus had staunchly believed that government should intervene in the economy as little as possible, even if this meant that foreign investors might become the new owners of Czech enterprises. Unfortunately his early rhetoric was not always matched by later policy.

2 For a thorough analysis of Czech privatisation and the troubles at Skoda Plzen, see Gerald A. McDermott, 'Embedded Politics: Industrial Networks and Institutional Change in Post Communism' (Ann Arbor: University of Michigan Press, 2002).

3 Poland's Central Bank President was arrested in 1991 for giving dodgy guarantees to private firms; Ukraine's Central Bank was accused of misusing some $700m of IMF money in 1999.

4 S. Fries and A. Taci, 'Banking Reform and Development in Transition Economies' p. 1, EBRD Working paper no. 71, June 2002.

5 'A Survey of Finance in Central Europe', p. 6, The Economist, 14 Sept 2002.

6 Author interview 27 November 2003.

7 Top managers at Citibank's Polish subsidiary, Bank Handlowy, left to join PZU, the leading domestically-owned insurance company. In addition, some Russian oligarchs have taken to hiring top western managers (sometimes paying more than their multinational competitors) to run their banking operations.

8 EBRD, ibid pp. 3–4.

9 R. W. Campbell, 'Soviet and Post-Soviet Telecommunications', p. 21 (Boulder CO: Westview Press, 1995), cited in Jurgen Muller 'Restructuring the Telecommunications Sector', p. 196.

10 International Telecommunication Union.

11 Some Poles have developed a shameless habit of string-pulling. While the author was interviewing the finance director of TPSA, a multi-billion-dollar company carrying out one of the region's toughest restructuring programmes, the latter was interrupted by a call on his mobile from an acquaintance he had met at his local social club. The caller said that his home telephone line was down, and asked the finance director to sort it out for him.

Chapter 5

1 A survey of 75 multinationals doing business in Russia in 1997, conducted by the Economist Corporate Network, Vienna 1997.
2 C. Mellow 'Consumer Marketing in Russia: Beyond Nouveau Riche', April 30 1997, The Economist Intelligence Unit, Vienna, p. 14.
3 ibid p. 51.
4 ibid p. 16.
5 Business Eastern Europe newsletter, 25 March 2002, The Economist Intelligence Unit, London.
6 Business Operations Report, Russia, December 1999, The Economist Intelligence Unit, Vienna.
7 The dull packaging could also be intentional. Given the tendency of western ads for washing powder to compare the product with a mythical 'ordinary' washing powder, a Czech manufacturer launched a new line of 'ordinary washing powder', in the familiar plain white box seen in western ads, thereby attempting to gain some free publicity.
8 The two brewers have been involved in a decade's-long dispute over the right to use the Budweiser brand name. The Czech brewer says that the name dates back to the 13th Century, originating in the town of Budejovice. Anheuser Busch claims to have been the first to patent the name. The two companies are locked in some 80 lawsuits and proceedings before courts and patent authorities around the world. Budvar has the upper hand in Europe, while the US brewer has exclusive rights in the US. The UK sells both brands.
9 Incoma press information, 8 September 2003.
10 ibid.
11 Speech to conference on EU enlargement, Vienna, December 2001.
12 Business Eastern Europe newsletter, 10 December 2001, The Economist Intelligence Unit, London.
13 P. Barrett, Managing Partner of Retail Academy Hungary cited in trade journal, *Elelmiszer*, 11 July 2002.
14 J. Arnold, 'Distribution and Retailing in Eastern Europe: supplying the new consumers', p. 50, The Economist Intelligence Unit, Vienna, 17 April 1998.

Chapter 6

1 M. Allen IMF representative in Poland 1990–3. IMF staff paper, vol. 48, special issue 2001.
2 Author interview with Leszek Balcerowicz, 29 March 2004.
3 One of the consequences of the end of communism has been the sad demise of the countless witticisms and bitter jibes made about the system by those living under it. Jokes such as: 'What's 100 metres long and eats cabbage? A queue for meat' typified the sort of social satire that market-based economic systems have yet to equal.
4 Author interview, ibid.
5 M. Allen, ibid.
6 Russia embarked on a similar shock therapy programme in 1991. Balcerowicz met Boris Yeltsin, the Russian president, who asked if prices would double or

treble following liberalisation, as his economists had predicted, or would increase tenfold, as Yeltsin feared (another example of Yeltsin's uncanny sense for the reality of the moment). Balcerowicz advised him to err on the side of pessimism. According to Balcerowicz, Yeltsin then summed up: 'This is for us the most difficult moment since the end of the Second World War. Whichever way our reform goes, whether in victory or defeat, will be relevant for the entire world ...' in Balcerowicz 'Socialism, Capitalism, Transformation' (Budapest; Central European University Press, 1995) p. 367.

7 It took the greater part of 15 years to tame rising prices across the region. In 2003, the average inflation rate for East-central Europe and the Baltics was under three per cent; in the Balkans 6.7 per cent; and in the CIS just under ten per cent.

8 It is difficult to ascertain exactly how far industrial output fell. Before 1990 the tendency was to exaggerate output in order to fulfil a five-year state plan; after 1990 the priority changed to hiding production in order to evade taxes. Another distorting factor was the burgeoning grey and black market, estimated to be as big as 30 per cent of the official economy in many cases, and even as high as 60 per cent. Economists took to using electricity consumption as a proxy for output levels. Although those figures paint a slightly more dynamic picture of the region's economies than the official output statistics, the drop in electricity output was nonetheless also dramatic.

9 The key economic reformers after 1989 – notably Balcerowicz, Lajos Bokros in Hungary, Vaclav Klaus in the Czech Republic, Yegor Gaidar and Anatoly Chubais in Russia, Ivan Miklos in Slovakia and Viktor Yushchenko in Ukraine – tended to be supremely self-confident, laptop-tapping intellectuals who spoke flawless English. They all sang from the same free-market song sheet, calling for price liberalisation, the reduction of inflation, tight fiscal and monetary policies, low taxes, free trade, stable currencies, rapid privatisation and as much foreign direct investment as possible. Well down their list of priorities were job protection, welfare benefits, and subsidised utilities and rents. They were adored by Western investors (and a few educated urban East Europeans) but were villains to the great majority of their respective populations. Bokros was one of the most disliked politicians in Hungary; Balcerowicz needed bodyguards as governor of the central bank; and some writers have pointed out that the red-headed Chubais made it all but impossible for any other redhead in Russia to become a successful politician, such was his negative image.

10 Balcerowicz's successors as finance minister, whether in centre-left or centre right governments, were to support the same strict policies in practice (if not in rhetoric). Balcerowicz returned to government in 1997 as a member of the Freedom Party, a small new grouping, and later became governor of the central bank.

11 In 1990–1 the indefatigable Balcerowicz lobbied almost every western decision-maker he could find to help reduce Poland's debts. He even brought up the subject when he met the (Polish-born) Pope John Paul II, who wanted to know if it was possible to create a just market economy in Poland. Cited in Balcerowicz, 'Socialism, Capitalism, Transformation' (Budapest; Central European University Press, 1995) .

12 J. Mencinger 'Does Foreign Direct Investment Always Enhance Economic Growth?', KYKLOS vol. 56, 2003, p. 502.

13 G. Hunya, 'The Recent Impacts of Foreign Direct Investment on Growth and Restructuring in Central European Transition Economies', Vienna Institute for International Economic Studies, Paper no. 284, May 2002.

14 The debate is further complicated by the argument about whether these corporations would have invested without generous incentives. Many companies say that they would. Volkswagen did not receive huge tax breaks in Slovakia, for example, and surveys of multinational investment decisions in the region tend to show that the availability of investment incentives, though important, was seldom the crucial factor. Rather, incentives were viewed as an indicator of a government's general attitude towards improving the business environment.

15 L. P. King and B. Varadi, 'Communist and Post Communist Studies' issue 35, 2002, pp. 1–21.

16 Eurostat Comtext database, quoted in Hunya, ibid.

17 The term 'cheap labour' is a vague and relative concept. East-central Europe is a cheap place to produce higher value-added goods, but is more expensive than South East Asia as a place to produce textiles.

18 CASE-Doradcy, cited in Business Eastern Europe, 20 October, 2003.

19 See S. Djankov and B. Hoekman: 'Foreign investment and productivity growth in Czech Enterprises' The World Bank Economic Review, vol. 14, no. 1, 2000, pp. 49–64.

20 UN/ECE Economic Survey of Europe, 2001 'Economic growth and foreign direct investment in transition economies'. As noted, there could be reverse causality involved.

21 B. K. Smarzynska, 'Does Foreign Direct Investment Increase the Productivity of Domestic Firms', World Bank Policy Research Working paper 2923, October 2002, pp. 3–4.

22 J. Mencinger, ibid. He notes that the ratio between the share of FDI in GDP to fixed capital formation in GDP is particularly low in Slovenia, implying that Slovenian firms get their technology elsewhere.

Chapter 7

1 Author interview with the prime minister, April 2002.

2 In October 1999 Lithuania sold a 33 per cent share and management control of its Mazeikiu port oil refinery complex to a US firm, Williams, in the hope of preventing Russian interests from wielding too much influence over the economy. But Williams was unable to guarantee regular flows of oil, since it depended on Russian oil companies for supplies, and in 2002 the US firm was forced to sell its shares in Mazeikiu to Yukos, Russia's largest oil firm. Surprisingly, there was very little protest from the Lithuanian parliament – a testament to how tensions in the Baltic region had subsided since the refinery was first sold. Few such prejudices existed in the Baltics when it came to Scandinavian investors, who dominate the Baltic investment league there. In many respects the Baltic states see themselves as more Nordic than post-Soviet.

3 The turning point in Romania's post-revolutionary economic development arguably came in July 2001 with the sale of Sidex, the giant Galati-based

steel works, to the Indian-owned LNM Group (see Chapter 3). This was a deal truly worthy of international congratulations.

4 J. S. Hellman 'Winners Take All: The Politics of Partial Reform in Postcommunist Transitions' World Politics 50.2 (Baltimore: Johns Hopkins University Press, 1998) pp. 232–33.

5 Developments in Russian Politics, Stephen White, Alex Pravda and Zvi Gitelman (eds) (Basingstoke: Palgrave, 2001). Chapter by John P. Willerton Jr. pp. 35–6.

6 Citibank, for example, was to write off some $325m as a consequence of the 1998 Russia crisis.

7 A good indication of how Meciar's Movement for a Democratic Slovakia (HZDS) lacked a coherent ideology, and based its government on patronage and favours, became apparent when the party went into coalition with an extreme left-wing workers' party and an extreme right-wing nationalist party. No mainstream parties of left or right would work with Meciar.

8 It is worth noting that Slovakia was the only EU candidate country from Eastern Europe that had its application to start membership negotiations rejected for political rather than economic reasons.

9 'From Common To Private: 10 Years of Privatisation in Slovakia' Mesa 10 (Bratislava: Centre for Social and Economic Analysis, 1999) p. 146.

10 US Steel has since been campaigning to attract other American firms to the region (see Chapter 3).

11 Officials at Harvard University were infuriated by the apparent insinuation of their support.

12 R. Shepherd, 'Czechoslovakia: The Velvet Revolution and Beyond' (London: Macmillan Press, 2000) pp. 82–4.

13 V. Havel, Speech to the Senate, 9 December 1997, website: www.vaclavhavel.cz.

14 A. Innes, ibid p. 270.

15 C. Freeland, 'Sale of the Century Russia's Wild Ride From Communism to Capitalism' (New York: Crown Publishers, 2000) p. 352.

16 Five years later BP and TNK would make up. Chernogorneft was re-integrated into Sidanko, which BP still partly owned, and BP merged its Russian business with TNK in a deal worth some $4.2 billion, the largest foreign acquisition in Russia.

17 Business Eastern Europe newsletter, 13 December 1999, The Economist Intelligence Unit, Vienna.

18 Freeland, ibid p. 184.

19 J. Hewko, 'Foreign direct investment: Does the Rule of Law Matter' Rule of Law series no. 26, April 2002, Carnegie Endowment for International Peace, p. 17.

20 Ivor McElveen, an advisor to the Czechoslovak Industry and Trade Ministry in 1990–1, recalls being struck by the lack of government accountability. He gave the new minister, Vladimir Dlouhy, a copy of the book 'Yes Minister', an English political satire, to help him deal with parliamentary questions, which were a complete novelty at the time.

21 Q. Reed, 'Political Corruption, Privatisation and Control in the Czech Republic: a Case Study of Problems in Multiple Transition' Doctoral thesis (Oxford: Oriel College, September 1996) p. 275.

22 Described by Quentin Reed, Open Society Institute.
23 In one of the few publicised cases, Klaus's ODS party was heavily criticised for organising a party fundraising dinner in 1994 that was attended by state-owned companies paying around $3500 each. In other words, these companies were using state money to finance a private political party. Klaus's government fell in November 1997 after the media reported allegations that Milan Srejbar, the winner of a tender to buy a steel company, had indirectly donated money to the ODS only weeks before.
24 Western governments themselves have not always been so pristine. Until recently, Germany allowed the cost of bribes made abroad to be tax-deductible, while the UK government heavily lobbied the Czech government in 2000–1 to buy Gripen fighter jets from a British Aerospace-led consortium, in what was widely viewed as quite an unnecessary and unaffordable defence deal.
25 Comment by a multinational importer into Azerbaijan, based on his private conversations with customs officials.
26 Business Eastern Europe newsletter, 22 January 2001, The Economist Intelligence Unit, Vienna.
27 World Bank: Anti-corruption in Transition: a contribution to the policy debate, 30 Sept 2000, pp. 33–5.
28 Business Eastern Europe newsletter 31 March 1997, EIU, Vienna.
29 Bill Browder of Hermitage Capital has long headed a group of foreign investors lobbying for greater transparency and protection of minority shareholders in Russia. There are other campaigners elsewhere in the region. One, Raimondo Eggink, has campaigned specifically against French tyre maker Michelin. He accuses the firm of unfairly taking profits out of its Polish subsidiary through transfer pricing, and is quoted as saying 'I'm doing it for fun'. The Economist Survey of Banking in Central Europe 14 Sept 2002.
30 J. Hewko, ibid, p. 16.

Chapter 8

1 J. Bhagwati, 'In Defense of Globalization' (Oxford: Oxford University Press, 2004) p. 162.
2 G. Schopflin, 'Politics in Eastern Europe 1945–1992' (Oxford: Blackwell Publishers, 1993) pp. 284–5.
3 J. Hall, 'Civil Society, Theory, History and Comparison' (UK: Polity Press, 1995) p. 24.
4 Off-the-record story told at an Economist conference in Vienna.
5 One simple case of intervening to even out the relative balance of power of the players occurred when the inexperienced post-revolutionary governments of East-central Europe were looking to sell state enterprises to western investors. Financial assistance from US AID enabled the authorities to hire expensive top-flight financial advisers to match those retained by the prospective buyer.
6 International institutions were also moving with the times. James Wolfensohn, the president of the World Bank, began working closely with Bono, a famous rock star, on third-world debt relief, for example.

7 'Europe Enlarged: Understanding the Impact', The Economist Intelligence Unit 2003, p. 34.

8 Author meeting at the IMF offices, Sofia in 1998.

9 J. Hewko, 'Foreign direct investment: Does the Rule of Law Matter' Rule of Law series no. 26, April 2002, Carnegie Endowment for International Peace, p. 23.

10 G. Lodge 'The Corporate Key: Using Big Business to Fight Global Poverty', Foreign Affairs July/August 2002, vol. 81, no. 4, pp. 14–5.

11 'Unleashing Entrepreneurship: Making Business Work for the Poor' Report to the Secretary General of the United Nations, New York, 1 March 2004, pp. 29–30, 37.

12 V. Havel, Speech to the IMF Conference, Prague, 26 September 2000, www.vaclavhavel.cz.

Selected Bibliography

The vast majority of the research for this book has involved first-hand interviews with company executives, politicians, representatives of non-governmental organisations and journalists. However, I also relied heavily on The Economist Intelligence Unit's own databases and EIU publications that I have edited, including the weekly newsletter *Business Eastern Europe* and the quarterly *Business Operations Reports*. There are also a number of interesting research papers on foreign direct investment in Eastern Europe published by the World Bank, the IMF and other international organisations, a few of which I have listed below. The other publications listed, covering Eastern Europe, globalisation or international business more generally, represent a very small sample of available material.

Allen M. An IMF representative in Poland 1990–3 (IMF staff paper, vol. 48 special issue 2001).

Arnold J. *'Distribution and Retailing in Eastern Europe: supplying the new consumers'* (The Economist Intelligence Unit, Vienna 1998).

Aslund A. (ed.) *'Russia's Economic Transformation in the 1990s'* (London: Pinter Publishers, 1997).

Balcerowicz L. *'Polish Economic Reform'* Balcerowicz Polish Economic reform.

Balcerowicz L. *'Post-Communist Transition: Some Lessons'* (31st Wincott Lecture, 8 October 2001, The Institute of Economic Affairs).

Balcerowicz L. *'Socialism, Capitalism, Transformation'* (Budapest: Central European University Press, 1995).

Bednarski P. and Osinski J. *'Financial Sector Issues in Poland'* (National Bank of Poland, 2003).

Bevan A. and Estrin S. *'The Determinants of Foreign Direct Investment in Transition Economies'* (Centre For New and Emerging Markets, London Business School, Discussion paper no. 9, October 2000).

Bhagwati J. *'In Defense of Globalization'* (UK: Oxford University Press, 2004).

Buiter W. and Szegvari I. *'Capital Flight and Capital Outflows from Russia: Symptom Cause and Cure'* (EBRD Working paper no. 73, June 2002).

Campbell R. *'Soviet and post-Soviet telecommunications'* (Boulder CO: Westview Press, 1995).

Campos N. F. and Coricelli F. *'Growth in Transition: What We Know, What We Don't and Should'* (Discussion paper no. 3246, Centre for Economic Policy Research).

Campos N. F. and Kinoshita Y. *'Foreign Direct Investment as Technology Transferred: some panel evidence from the transition economies'* (William Davidson Working paper no. 438, January 2002).

CEE Bankwatch Network *'Mountains of Gold: Kumtor Gold Mine in Kyrgyz Republic'* (Budapest, May 2002).

Cottrell R., Franklin D., Palmer A. et al. *'Europe enlarged: Understanding the Impact'* (The Economist Intelligence Unit, London 2003).

Crowley S. and Ost D. (eds) *'Workers After Workers' States: Labour and Politics in Postcommunist Eastern Europe'* (US: Rowman & Littlefield Publishers, 2001).

Djankov S. and Hoekman B. *'Foreign investment and productivity growth in Czech Enterprises'* (The World Bank Economic Review, vol. 14, no. 1, 2000, pp. 49–64).

Freeland C. *'Sale of the Century: Russia's Wild Ride From Communism to Capitalism'* (New York: Crown Publishers, 2000).

Fries S. and Taci A. *'Banking Reform and Development in Transition Economies'* (EBRD Working paper no. 71, June 2002).

Garton Ash, T. *'The Polish Revolution'* (London: Granta Books, 1991).

Garton Ash, T. *'History of the Present: Essays, Sketches and Despatches from Europe in the 1990s'* (London: Penguin Books, 1999).

Goldman M. *'Slovakia Since Independence: A Struggle for Democracy'* (Westport: Praeger, 1999).

Gorg H. and Greenaway D. *'Much Ado About Nothing? Do domestic firms really benefit from foreign investment'* (Discussion paper no. 3485, International Trade, Centre for Economic Policy Research, August 2002).

Gropp R. and Kostial K. *'The Disappearing Tax Base: Is Foreign Direct Investment Eroding Corporate Income Taxes?'* (IMF Working paper WP/00/173, October 2000).

Hall J. (ed.) *'Civil Society, Theory, History and Comparison'* (UK: Polity Press, 1995).

Hellman J. S. *'Winners Take All: The Politics of Partial Reform in Postcommunist Transitions'*, World Politics 50.2 (Baltimore: Johns Hopkins University Press, 1998).

Hewko J. *'Foreign Direct Investment: Does the Rule of Law Matter?'* (Rule of Law series no. 26, April 2002, Carnegie Endowment for International Peace).

Holland D. and Pain N. *'The Diffusion of Innovations in Central and Eastern Europe: A study of the Determinants and Impact of Foreign Direct Investment'* (National Institute of Economic and Social Research, June 1998).

Hunya G. *'The Recent Impacts of Foreign Direct Investment on Growth and Restructuring in Central European Transition Economies'* (Vienna Institute for International Economic Studies, Paper no. 284, May 2002).

Innes A. *'Czechoslovakia: The Short Goodbye'* (New Haven: Yale University Press, 2001).

Johnson S., Kaufman D., MacMillan J., and Woodruff C., *'Why Do Firms Hide: bribes and unofficial activity under communism'* (EBRD Working paper no. 42, October 1999).

Kekic L. *'Foreign direct investment in Eastern Europe: Trends and Forecasts'* (East European Investment Prospects, The Economist Intelligence Unit, 2001).

King L. P. and Varadi B. *'Beyond Manichean economics: foreign direct investment and growth in the the transition from Socialism'* (Communist and Post-Communist Studies, no. 35, 2002, pp. 1–21).

Kirschbaum S. *'A History of Slovakia'* (New York: St. Martin's Griffen, 1995).

Krkoska L. *'Foreign Direct Investment Financing of Capital Formation in Central and Eastern Europe'* (EBRD Working paper no. 67, December 2001).

Lim E. G. *'Determinants of, and the Relation between, Foreign Direct Investment and Growth: A summary of the recent literature'* (IMF Working paper wp/01/175, November 2001).

Lodge G. C. *'The Corporate Key: Using Big Business to Fight Global Poverty'* (Foreign Affairs July/August 2002, vol. 81, no. 4).

Maksimenko P. A. and Adjubei Y. (eds) *'Foreign Investment in Russia and other Soviet Successor States'* (Basingstoke: Macmillan, 1996).

Maksimenko P. A. and Rojec M. (eds) *'Foreign Investment and Privatisation in Eastern Europe'* (Basingstoke: Palgrave, 2001).

Martin R. *'Central and Eastern Europe and the International Economy: The Limits to Globalisation'* (Europe-Asia Studies, vol. 50, no. 1, 1998).

McDermott G. A. *'Embedded Politics: Industrial Networks and Institutional Change in Post Communism'* (Michigan: University of Michigan Press, 2002).

Mellow C. *'Consumer Marketing in Russia: Beyond Nouveau Riche'* (The Economist Intelligence Unit, Vienna, 1997).

Mencinger J. *'Does Foreign Direct Investment Always Enhance Economic Growth?'* (KYKLOS vol. 56, 2003).

Mesa 10, Centre for Social and Economic Analysis, *'From Common To Private: 10 Years of Privatisation in Slovakia'* (Bratislava, 1999).

Micklethwait J. and Wooldridge A. *'A Future Perfect: the challenge and hidden promise of globalisation'* (London: Random House, 2001).

Mody A., Razin A. and Sadka E., *'The Role of Information in Driving FDI flows: Host Country Transparency, Source Country Specialisation'* (IMF Working paper 02/148, July 2003).

Moosa I. *'Foreign Direct Investment: Theory, Evidence and Practice'* (Basingstoke: Palgrave, 2002).

Pacek N. and Thorniley D. *'Emerging Markets'* (London: Profile Books, 2004).

Pissarides F. *'Is the lack of funds the main obstacle to growth?'* (EBRD Working paper 33, November 1998).

Reed Q. *'Political Corruption, Privatisation and Control in the Czech Republic: a Case Study of Problems in Multiple Transition'* A doctoral thesis (Oxford: Oriel College, 1996).

Remnick D. *'Lenin's Tomb: The Last Days of the Soviet Empire'* (New York: Vintage Books, 1994).

Rose R., White S. and McAllister I. *'How Russia votes'* (Chatham New Jersey: Chatham House Publishers, 1997).

Sachs J. *'Poland's Jump To The Market Economy'* (Lionel Robbins Lectures, Cambridge Mass.: The MIT Press, 1993).

Schopflin G. *'Politics in Eastern Europe 1945–1992'* (Oxford: Blackwell Publishers, 1993).

Shepherd R. *'Czechoslovakia: The Velvet Revolution and Beyond'* (London: Macmillan Press, 2000).

Skalnik Leff C. *'The Czech and Slovak Republics – Nation Versus State'* (Oxford: Westview Press, 1998).

Smarzynska B. *'Does foreign direct investment increase the productivity of domestic firms'* (World Bank Policy Research Working paper 2923, October 2002).

Smith A. and Ferencikova S. *'Inward Investment, regional transformation and uneven development in Eastern and Central Europe: enterprise case studies from Slovakia'* (European Urban and Regional Studies).

Stein E. *'Czecho/Slovakia: Ethnic Conflict, Constitutional Fissure, Negotiated Breakup'* (Ann Arbor, University of Michigan Press, 1997).

Stein J. (ed.) *'The Politics of National Minority Participation in Post-Communist Europe'* (New York: East-West Institute, 2000).

Stiglitz J. *'Globalisation and its Discontents'* (London: Allen Lane, 2002).

Svejnar J. *'The Czech Republic and Economic Transition in Eastern Europe'* (San Diego: Academic Press, 1995).

UNCTAD *'Transnational Corporations'* (December 2001, vol. 10, no. 3).

United Nations, Report to the Secretary General of the United Nations, *'Unleashing Entrepreneurship: Making Business Work for the Poor'* (New York, 1 March 2004).

UNECE *'Economic Growth and Foreign Direct Investment in the Transition Economies'* (Economic survey of Europe 2001, Paper no. 1).

UNECE *'Sustainable Growth in the ECE Region'*, Papers from the ECE Spring Seminar March, 2003.

United Nations Environmental Program *'Report on the Cyanide Spill at Baia Mare, Romania'* (UN Office for the Co-ordination of Humanitarian Affairs, June 2000).

Vinton L. *'Managing Human Resources in Eastern Europe'* (The Economist Intelligence Unit, Vienna 1999).

Vinton L. and Slay B. *'Poland to 2005: The Challenge of Europe'* (The Economist Intelligence Unit, Vienna 1997).

von Hirschhausen C. and Bitzer J. (eds) *'The Globalisation of Industry and Innovation in Eastern Europe: From Post Socialist Restructuring to International Competitiveness'* (UK: Edward Elgar Publishing, 2000).

White S., Batt J. and Lewis G. *'Developments in Central and East European Politics'* (Basingstoke: Palgrave Macmillan, 2003).

White S., Pravda A. and Gitelman Z. (eds) *'Developments in Russian Politics'* (Basingstoke: Palgrave, 2001).

White S. *'Russia's New Politics: The Management of Post-communist Society'* (Cambridge: Cambridge University Press, 2000).

World Bank Extractive Industries Review *'Striking A Better Balance'* (Washington DC, December 2003).

World Bank *'Anti-Corruption in Transition: A Contribution to the Policy Debate'* (Washington DC, September 2000).

World Bank *'Transition – The first ten years: Analysis and lessons for Eastern Europe and the former Soviet Union'* (Washington DC, 2002).

Index